REMARRIAGE
A Family Affair

REMARRIAGE
A Family Affair

Lillian Messinger

Foreword by Mel Roman

Plenum Press • New York and London

Library of Congress Cataloging in Publication Data

Messinger, Lillian.
  Remarriage, a family affair.

  Bibliography: p.
  Includes index.
  1. Remarriage—United States. 2. Divorce—United States. 3. Family—United States.
4. Remarriage—Canada. 5. Divorce—Canada. 6. Family—Canada. I. Title.
HQ1019.U6M47   1984   306.8'4   84-11671
ISBN 0-306-41770-7

FOREWORD

Families distanced and reorganized through divorce and those further reorganized through remarriage are still poorly understood and often incorrectly perceived. This book is a rich and useful distillation and exposition of the findings of divorce research and of the author's extensive clinical experience with remarrieds and their children. Although primarily written for remarried parents, it will be of value to those in the helping professions working with stepfamilies.

Last year in America, there were approximately one million divorces involving 1.3 million minor-aged children. Some 80% of those who divorce remarry. Of those remarrying, 50% divorce a second time. It is reasonable to say of these children and their parents that they constitute a population of risk for the development of emotional and somatic problems.

Whereas first divorces usually relate to spousal conflicts, second divorces often relate to parental conflicts exacerbated by the ambiguities of role relationships in the new family and the baggage of unresolved issues from the previous family.

A colleague of mine is fond of saying that one can make two mistakes in thinking about and in counseling stepfamilies: The first is to assume that they are just like any other family; the other is to assume they are not.

The structure and tasks of the stepfamily are unique. Stepfamilies must deal with loss and separation, trust, conflicts of loyalty and authority, and most importantly, with the challenge of

v

developing a new identity which may and often does include her children, his children and their children. No easy task.

Additionally, people often select each other in second marriages for conscious and unconscious reasons similar to those which governed their first marriages and thereby repeat old scenarios and tend to run into the same conflicts any couple would encounter.

In stepfamilies all of the issues of the new and old interact and amplify each other. What stepfamilies need and what this book offers is a psychological mapping of the processes and events needing attention and time. It does so with sensitivity and understanding and is rich in insights and illustrations. Mrs. Messinger has made a significant contribution to our appreciation of what some have called the new American extended family.

MEL ROMAN
Professor and Director of
Group and Family Studies
Department of Psychiatry
Albert Einstein College of Medicine

PREFACE

Glass in hand, Paula proposed a toast: "Evelyn dear—I hope your coming marriage will bring you and your family happiness and that this time round will be a great improvement on your other marriage. I hope Frank will be good and loving to your children." "I'm going to add my two cents," said Kate. "I think it's great that you're getting married and that you really like the guy, but—there's a but—keep your salary separate—hang on to your independence—it was hard to come by—don't lose it—I know whereof I talk." "I'll drink to that," added Paula. "That's sound advice."

Three women—good friends, drawn together by the pain and loneliness of the past few years—shared a history that they felt no one would really understand unless they too had lived through it—divorce, one marriage off and a new one on, as well as everything involved in building a new life with a new family.

Evelyn's response to her friends' good wishes and advice was slow in coming. Her fingers caressed the glass and thoughtfully she said, "You know, it's funny—I do care for Frank but I'm frightened—the idea of marriage scares me. Marriage makes me feel that I will once more turn my life over to someone else. I won't be in charge of my own life. I really don't want to become the traditional wife again that I was before—and I'm concerned that maybe that's what marriage is all about. I really love my job, I feel so much better about myself now than I did when I was married. Sometimes in the middle of my work day, I say, Evelyn, it's great, you're a capable adult—how come you didn't know that for so many years? I have grown up, I'm no longer the dependent child who always had to get permission from someone in my life. I'm an adult and I can make adult decisions. I think Frank understands what I'm saying when I tell him this— I'm not sure about myself, though.

"I've been brought up in a traditional kind of family. The first thing my mother said when I told her that Frank and I were going to be married, was 'Evelyn, that's wonderful, I'm so happy you won't have to work so hard—or maybe you won't work at all. You deserve to have life easier; it's been so hard for you.' What can I say? Of course it's been hard, but it's been challenging. I want the best of two worlds, to grow, to be challenged, to advance on the job—*and* to have Frank. I don't know if it can work that way; that's what frightens me. There is a part of me that loves doing things for Frank, preparing his meals, making family life attractive for him. But then I find resentment welling up inside of me—what am I doing this for?

"Is it because I'm a woman—do I always have to meet everybody else's needs? I ask myself, what about my needs? I get angry with Frank, but he's not asking me to be the busy 'little wife.' He appreciates my spirit of independence. My fight is with myself and the impulses that I've grown up with: that that's what woman, wife, and marriage are all about. I guess I'm just a mixed-up kid."

Evelyn's soliloquy was sobering. Her friends identified immediately with her feelings. They each had yearned for the comfort, the warmth, companionship, and intimacy that they had dreamed would be part of marriage. Each of the women had lived through the disappointment and pain of being uprooted from married life. Divorce had been like an amputation; a part of them was gone. In the beginning they had not known whether they could survive it. But they did and here they were two years later, with Kate about to be remarried, Evelyn once more considering marriage, and Paula with a live-in partner but most hesitant to legalize the bond.

The first months after the separation had been terrifying, but each in her own way had survived. They had gone from the early panic days to picking themselves up by their boot straps. The two years were not lost ones for them. Each of the women talked about how much better she felt about herself: more confident, more decisive, and really functioning at a high level.

They had been fortunate enough to find each other, to support each other on this survival trip. There was no playing the game of "let's pretend everything is fine" with each other. They talked about themselves and about each other. Trusting each other enough to accept criticism without feeling attacked, they were in a privileged position. Their own support group developed as an extension of the support group through which they had first met. Together they now understood better what had contributed to the downhill descent of their marriages and what their personal share had been in that. It had not happened overnight, neither the marriage breakdown, nor the recovery from it, nor the renewed striving to look to the future. Once life outside marriage began to settle into a daily family pattern, each of the women had taken a job. They became part of the labor force of men and women. It was good to be part of the outside world, no longer spending time and energy ruminating and dwelling on personal loss and failure. They now felt better able to deal with their children and to recognize how shattering the separation and family disorganization were in the children's lives. Having learned that they could survive, they could be whole people making independent decisions.

Family life was now taking on a different daily pattern. The disturbing dilemma was becoming, "Why upset the stability by marrying again and bringing a new adult into the family group?" They were plagued by concerns: If they should remarry, did they want to, or did they have the right to expect the children to accept and make room for another person in their family life, a man who would be husband to their mother, a husband who would behave in paternal ways even though he was not the children's father? He would sit in daddy's chair, sleep in daddy's bed, tell the children what they should and what they should not do. He might even not like the children! Would he think he had the right to make the new rules for the family, to order the children about or even to punish them? If so, the children might not like *him!*

Whenever these mothers got into the discussion of how a new husband would fit in with their family and its idiosyncracies and how the children would adapt to him and his idiosyncracies, they would express a mounting anxiety and indignation. What rights did he have or would he expect to have or would they want him to have with their children? How dare he order or scold or punish them? He's not their father! He wasn't in the labor room with them when they were born. He hadn't held, fed, diapered, and bathed them. He hadn't watched them grow up and take their first steps, hadn't thrilled at their first words. When they began on this route, the women would check each other. Stop! We're torturing ourselves, the past is over, we have to look to the future. They were caught between their need for adult, intimate attachment and their fear of bringing a new family crisis into their children's lives.

Evelyn's conflicts triggered off their own apprehensions about the risks involved in committing themselves to all the unknowns of a second marriage. It would be so easy if they could wipe out the memories of the past, forget the whole history of their first marriage, the excitement of their first love, the wonder of their first pregnancy and first baby. Marriage had been different for each of them, but for all of them there had been good times and bad times. There were still times that they felt so lonely that they hurt from the memories of days they had shared with a former partner. The emptiness and loneliness would crowd back into their consciousness. Memory plays funny tricks;

one cannot separate oneself from past memories. They are always there, tucked away in hidden crevices of the mind, the good and the bad together.

How typical are the feelings of Evelyn, Kate, and Paula? How many of the two million men and women who divorce annually identify with these emotions? Divorced people and single parents constitute a growing poulation. There are few of us who have not been touched closely in our personal, family, social, or professional lives by people whose marriage and family life have been disrupted through divorce. Divorce is no longer headline news. When we hear about yet another couple who are splitting up we tend to respond with "so what else is new?"

How many who have not experienced the disintegration of a marriage and the disrupting of family life really understand how it feels? How many times have we heard people at the point of separation vow "never again," whether they be the rejector or the rejected? Yet statistics report that four out of five divorced persons remarry three, four, or five years after their divorce. Thus, divorce and remarriage have become a prominent social pattern in the past two decades. Despite this growing population of remarrieds and legally reconstituted families, social and legal changes have not kept abreast of the differences between the remarriage family and the nuclear intact family. There is a lag between the problems relevant to the traditional family and to remarried families. We intend to address the latter problem here.

ACKNOWLEDGMENTS

I am grateful to Dr. S. J. J. Freeman, chief psychiatrist of the Social and Community Psychiatry Section at the Clarke Institute of Psychiatry for entrusting me with the freedom to research the stress factors involved in post-divorce marriages with children from the previous marriage. I extend deep thanks to the many couples who participated in the research and who opened their lives to me. I learned a great deal from them about the predictable problems that remarried people encounter. In the course of my pioneering work, I was fortunate to meet and to share perspectives with professionals throughout North America who were also faced with understanding the new population of divorced and remarried people. A special note of thanks to Linda Regan, sponsoring editor, whose support sustained me throughout the book.

A special vote of thanks is given to Fran Marks for her indispensable and diligent commitment in organizing and collating my material. And finally, my gratitude goes to my husband and children for their support and encouragement to pursue the task of writing this book.

CONTENTS

INTRODUCTION
A REPORT OF THE STUDY ON WHICH THIS BOOK IS BASED

Remarriage is on the increase following in the train of the rising divorce rate in North America. In the past decade, marriage counsellors and family therapists have been confronted with a different set of problems from people who have embarked on their second and even third marriages. In order to identify the particular qualities of the reconstituted family with its unique structure, a team of researchers and therapists at Clarke Institute of Psychiatry in Toronto began a research project in 1974. The goal was to identify the factors creating tensions among this newly constructed group for which society has not as yet established norms and guidelines. Since the early 1960s, the 1970s, and into the 1980s, there has been a growing acknowledgment that the institution of marriage and the family is in the process of rapid change.

We hope that this book will in some small way serve to alert both men and women to more effective ways of coping with the changing family patterns that have emerged within recent years. The questions we at Clarke Institute set out to explore in our survey dealt with how remarriage does or does not fit the ideal model which society has defined for the "normal family" of parents and their biological children. Reconstituted families have reported that there is little in the literature or the media with which they can identify. Couples and children have reported that television programs like "The Brady Bunch" and "Eight is Enough" fail to portray realistically the complexities of living in a family with a parent's partner who is not the child's parent.

In 1976 the National Centre for Health Statistics of Canada reported on the relationship between health and marital status:

> Generally, widowed, separated and divorced persons had higher rates of illness and disability than married or never married persons. Separated and divorced persons seem unusually vulnerable to acute conditions.

These studies of the stress involved for separated and divorced people led our researchers at Clarke Institute to consider how the stress for divorced people and their families can affect a parent who remarries. Our goal was to study the extent to which divorced people and their families have a higher propensity for physical and emotional illness as well as family unhappiness.

On the basis of this premise of increased vulnerability for divorced people and their families, our team set out to investigate the special nature of stress for divorced people who go into another marriage. To further our examination we drew up a questionnaire that considered many aspects of the transition from separation and divorce to remarriage. We posed questions on how couples dealt with the breakup of a marriage that had started out with the high hopes of "till death do us part." What does it mean to separate from a partner with whom one has shared many firsts, who has been parent to the children, shared family traditions in everyday life, and celebrated such special occasions as Christmas and birthdays? How does it feel for families to separate who have laughed together and cried together? What are the effects on people of such disruptions to their lives?

From our work with intact families, we know that each family builds its own history and rituals. Each family unit has a uniqueness that distinguishes it from other families. On the basis of our knowledge of family life, we questioned what happens to this sense of family identity when the family becomes fragmented. How does each of the members in the family cope with the disruption to the family patterns which have been built into his life? Both parents and the children raised from birth, cared for, protected, and nurtured have their roots in their family group. This is where they learn where they belong. We asked children from intact families, who belonged in their family? The reply was clear: "My mother, my father, my brothers and sisters." However, when children in a remarriage family were asked the same question, the response became less clear. The child often responded by asking: "Do you mean the people who live in my house, like my mother and her husband and his children, or do you mean my 'real' family?"

We asked ourselves, How does a couple get uncoupled? How are children affected whan a parent is absent from the daily family life and becomes a visitor by appointment? We wondered how the noncustodial parent fares when he is no longer a member of the family that has made up a major part of his daily life. We pondered the nature of the personal adjustments, the sexual adjustments, the social and the familial adjustments when a parent remarries. Who does the new partner become in the lives of the children? What are his rights and his responsibilities in this "instant family" that he acquires, a family that up to now has been a distinct unit with different membership? As a stepparent, what kind of parenting is expected from him since the children have a parent outside the home? And how does the children's absent parent feel when another adult is taking his place in his former family life, with his former wife and with his children? Does he, as their father, harbor resentment that they will call that man Daddy as well? Will that man living with the children be a better Daddy? Will he, their father, lose his children to that man? Are grandparents replaced by a different set of grandparents? How do children adapt in this day and age, among this new society of remarrieds, to having four potential parent-figures, eight grandparent figures, sibs, and stepsibs and half-sibs? Can society accept that remarriage can integrate all these people as well as the extended blood relations in a family? These and other questions were the basis for our study into the lives and concerns of remarried partners and their new families.

The book chronicles the life experiences of many of the people who generously volunteered to give us access to significant information concerning their private lives. This book about the "formerly married" who were divorced and are now "once again married" is written to promote insight into the world of remarrieds. It is aimed at developing guidelines and goals for couples who remarry and their families as well as for therapists. It is intended to help couples planning to remarry to anticipate some of the complexities in creating a sense of family for themselves and their children. The goal is a realistic sense of the feelings, confusion, and conflicts that people bring to a new, second-time-around family.

Our study began in a period when society was reeling from rapid social change and a range of experimentation with alternate personal and family life-styles that appeared to be shaking the very foundation of the institution of marriage. Statistics have conveyed, however, that the rate of remarriage has been running parallel to the rate of divorce. This indicates that although divorced people may reject their first marriage partner, they are not rejecting marriage itself nor a family life.

We learned from demographers Norton and Glick that "an estimated ¾ of women and ⅚ of the divorced men eventually remarry" (p. 9).[1] The same demographers projected that "four out of every ten marriages contracted by women born between 1945–49 would eventually end in divorce." That projection demands serious consideration about the nature of marriage, divorce, and subsequent remarriage.

It is common knowledge that the legislation which determines the divorce process had been lagging behind the actual reasons for divorce until the late 1960s. It had long been public knowledge that the existing grounds for divorce at that time were not consistent with reasons people wanted out of a marriage. Adultery, cruelty, or desertion, had continued to be the most frequent submission for being granted divorce. At long last, in 1967–8 in the United States and Canada, as well as in some of the European countries, divorce legislation was finally liberalized to include a "marriage breakdown" clause. The inclusion of this clause meant that after a stated period of time following separation when the couple no longer resided together, the legislation would accede that the marriage had indeed broken down and divorce would be granted. The length of separation time differs in different states in the United States and different provinces in Canada. In Ontario, a three-year period of separation is required before divorce can be legitimized, whereas in California and Nevada, divorce is granted soon after application.

Following the introduction of the breakdown clause in the divorce act, the major reason for filing for divorce changed from adultery to breakdown. An explosion of divorces came in the wake of the inclusion of the breakdown clause in the divorce act. Glick and Norton reported that between 1967 and 1972 the divorce rate increased close to 10% annually in the United States. In Canada, from 1961 to 1980, the number of divorced women rose by 56% and of divorced men by 52%.

From 1972 to the present time, there has been a leveling off in the rapid escalation of divorce. Yet, the report from the Department of Health, Education, and Welfare (HEW) indicated that divorces continue to increase annually. The 12-month period ending with July, 1980, showed over 3% increase in divorce for the comparable period ending in July, 1979. The galloping rise in divorce rates has slowed, but there is no indication that separation and divorce between partners will not continue. There is increasing social and legal acceptance that divorce is a reasonable alternative to an unhappy marriage. Psychologist Mary Jo Bane projects that by the end of the twentieth century only 56% of all marriages will remain intact.[2] That implies that nearly 50% of all first marriages in the United States will terminate. Canadian trends follow closely behind the American scene.

At the same time, it is reported that in every three marriages in the United States and in every five in Canada at least one of the partners is in a second marriage. Bane further reports that one out of every five children in the United States is living in a reconstituted family with a biological parent and the parent's spouse who is designated as a stepparent; Canadian statistics report that this is the family status for one out of seven.

A new society is being created. Guidelines are needed for learning how to cope with its diversity. I have quoted statistical reports about our changing world to convey that we are dealing with vast numbers. Behind the statistics are the people. They are our relatives, our neighbors, and our children's friends. They are an essential part of us and the world in which we live. Acceptance of the diversity of family life patterns and life-styles can enhance our capacity to accommodate individual differences and aid us in stripping away many of the biases and prejudices that are deeply woven into our social fabric. Stereotypic belief systems of what is defined as normal tend to contribute to conflict in accepting people with different customs and traditions.

In addition to the remarrieds and the professionals, this book is thus addressed to the general public, to those who live in intact families, to teachers and school systems, to doctors and lawyers, in short, to people who live and work with people.

For the purpose of our study of people who divorce and remarry, we recruited participants by an invitation issued throughout the media. The survey, which began in 1974, was among the early explorations of this rapidly growing family pattern. It received cooperation from the press, radio, and television. *Chatelaine* magazine, which is distributed across Canada, in a published interview with the author, elicited 200 respondents. *Maclean* magazine, the University of Toronto Bulletin (December, 1976), the *Toronto Star*, *Toronto Sun*, the Canadian Broadcasting Corporation and radio, and Canadian television networks all held interviews that publicized the project. This visibility resulted in couples responding to questionnaires and in many instances sending letters indicating their appreciation for a study "at long last" recognizing that the remarriage family is a unique kind of family group.

The target population in our study was addressed to remarried couples in which (1) at least one of the partners had experienced a previous divorce and (2) there were children from the previous marriage, either living in or visiting the remarriage household on a steady basis.

We cannot claim that the response represented a broad socioeconomic cross section, it was admittedly small and self-selected. The greatest value of our study was not the gathering of hard data but rather the discerning of a similarity of concerns that were plaguing the participants. This created a valuable source for study despite our awareness that in general people who volunteer to participate in a research project tend to be middle-class, knowledgeable, and more cooperative than those in a random sampling. The respondents were predominantly white Anglo-Saxons, representing a fairly wide range of occupations in education, social work, journalism, television production, and research. Most had completed high school and some had higher academic degrees. The ages ranged from 25 to 56, with the large majority in the 30 to 40 years age range. The significance of the age range was that the majority had children of minor age from the previous marriage. The median number of years for the first marriage was ten years before divorce. Since the research invited responses from couples in which at least one partner had been divorced, responses were forthcoming from couples in which one of the partners may have had a different previous marital status as well as different parental and custodial arrangements. The largest number of divorced people were married to other divorced persons. The next largest group consisted of marriages between divorced and previously single people. Divorced people who married widowed partners constituted the smallest group.

Each combination reflected a different set of dynamics. There were a variety of custodial arrangements. The largest number of the remarried women were sole custody parents. A few of the remarried fathers had sole custody. The rest of the men had visitation rights with their children, who lived with the former spouse. Only two of the couples had children by the remarriage. In the marriages between a divorced custodial parent and a previously single person, the single partner came into an instant family with instant parental responsibilities for the children. Many of the couples went into marriages at different stages of their life cycle, as well as their family cycle, in terms of age and marital and parental experience.

To supplement the questionnaires, we invited participants into personal interviews to bring flesh to the bare bones of written responses. The findings from both the questionnaires and the interviews were strikingly consistent and reflected clearly that people who remarry are generally poorly prepared for the special complexities of remarried family life. The discussions focused primarily on concerns with the children of the previous marriage. We also held seminars for the couples and for the children alone. These seminars illuminated the major problems of this new family unit.

This book describes what we have been privileged to learn from our "friends" who have remarried. We will, of course, disguise the names. The life situations will be a composite account of much that we learned and that the couple and their reconstituted families learned about themselves in the process of interviews and group and family sessions.

We will begin at the beginning when one or both partners make the decision to leave the marriage. We offer some guidelines, based on our research findings and clinical experience.

REFERENCES

[1] Norton, A. J., and Glick, P. C. "Marital Instability in America." In *Divorce and Separation*, edited by G. Levinger and O. C. Moles. New York: Basic Books, 1979.
[2] Bane, M. J. "Marital Disruption and the Lives of Children." In *Divorce and Separation*, edited by G. Levinger and O. C. Moles. New York: Basic Books, 1979.

CHAPTER 1

NO TYPICAL MARRIAGE, NO TYPICAL SEPARATION, NO TYPICAL DIVORCE

Given that two people have agreed to end their marriage, what can be done to ensure that they will do so in a constructive and co-operative manner, rather than destructively with lingering hostility?[1]

THE DECISION TO SEPARATE

Each life situation is different. It is not possible to refer to the typical marriage, the typical divorce, or the typical remarriage. Each marriage develops its own history. But there are enough commonalities of feelings and experiences to make it worthwhile to gain some perspective on how others face the rocky road from the decision to leave a marriage to begin living a new personal life. This new life might be as a separated parent with custody of the children or a noncustodial parent with visitation rights to the children, or frequently as a coparent sharing the care of children in separate homes.

When a marriage falters and deteriorates, home and family life lose their comfort. Tensions run high. There are frequently friction, disagreements, irritations and alienation. Negative feelings take over, sometimes for only one partner and sometimes for both until that final straw is reached that apparently makes the marriage intolerable. Arriving at the decision to terminate a marriage is most often a major life crisis. The moods become mercurial. Ambivalence runs rampant. To facilitate the actual move out of the marriage, the negative aspects of the relationship often reach an all-time high for all concerned. It seems as though most people must blot out any positive feelings and accelerate the hostile feelings before they can fully make the decision to separate. The more intimacy and personal involvement a couple has achieved during the marriage, the greater is the likelihood that hostile feelings will be pushed to the forefront before the decision to separate can be reinforced.

Marriages which achieve little cohesion are more easily broken. For the most part, when couples have been living together they see each other stripped of defenses with their frailties exposed. The dependence between married partners often carries a combination of opposing emotions. There is need, caring, protectiveness combined with resentment, lack of respect, and disdain. Marriage seems to bring out the best and the worst in couples. George Bach calls his book on warring couples *The Intimate Enemy*.[2] Couples can be bound to each other like parent and child are bound. Severing such bonds often leaves one or both partners with a feeling of rawness.

I have worked with hundreds of couples who have decided that they cannot live together any longer. The more this feeling builds up, the more intolerable the marriage becomes. Tensions mount, the emotions carry on a constant battle. The fight is building before it is even begun. The retorts are flying as soon as the husband enters the house. While he is driving home from work he is building up the dreaded anticipation of what will greet him when he walks in—he'll be ready. The script was written a long time ago, rehearsed and replayed with new ad libs added, each time more vindictive. The chemistry is explosive. Neither partner wants it, but neither knows how to stop it, to rewrite the script—to give different, new cues or to respond differently to the old ones.

Divorce is no longer headline news. If the present prognostications prove valid, roughly half the married couples in the United States who start out with celebrations and high hopes will end up in the divorce courts. The high divorce rates reflect the fact that marriages today are not necessarily permanent. There is an àlternative to continuing in an unhappy marriage—namely to get out of it, to separate and get divorced. Why, then, is it so difficult to arrive at the choice of freeing oneself from a state of unhappiness? What are the factors that make it so difficult to break marriage ties? Instead of a sense of relief and freedom from the stress of the marriage, after separation there is so frequently a feeling of profound loneliness and fear, a dismal sense of dislocation and disorganization.

Many divorced people report that before they finally became divorced there were separations and then reunions and then separations again, sometimes several times. Despite the discontents, divorce is seldom an easy route. Many divorced people, sometimes even after they are remarried, still find themselves dwelling on or reviewing how impossible it would have been for them to remain in the marriage. The sense of a marriage failure needs self-justification. Unless the issues that broke the marriage are clarified and especially when the emotional ties between the ex-spouses have been ambiguous, there is more likelihood than not that old emotions will keep coming to life. When the emotions from a past marriage have not been laid to rest, they can continue to affect a person's future adjustment during the period of divorce and after remarriage. Carrying unresolved feelings from the former marriage not only affect ex-spouse relationships but can profoundly affect the ability of the divorced couple to have any mutual agreement about how to bring up their children.

When remarried people discuss their previous marriages

they can become as vindictive and vicious in attacking the former partner as though the separation had just taken place. They are back into the old marital battle. To listen to some divorced people, one would believe they had never had a good day together in all the years of marriage. For some it seems important to wipe out any good memories: "He never understood" "He always criticized, belittled, and embarrassed me particularly in front of our friends" "I gave him the best years of my life and what did I get in return—aggravation" "I faked every orgasm" "I was Mr. Money Bags to her and got nothing in return" "She was always a cold fish" "He never understood that I had a right to sexual satisfaction." The *always* and *never* surface as though they described the totality of the marriage history.

At the time people threaten to leave a marriage, they may say they can't wait to get out, but when they do separate the fantasy of the joy of freedom from the marriage frequently turns into distress. The euphoria of not having to account to someone can lose its luster once one is out of the marital home. The dreams of freedom often then turn sour. Instead of freedom, there can be a loneliness and longing for the comfort and safety of home, for the assurance that someone cares enough to worry, that each must be accounted for. The oft-repeated "You could have called me. How did I know if you were still alive?" that had jarred before separation is frequently missed afterwards.

In his book *Marital Separation* Robert Weiss aptly refers to the dichotomy involved in struggling to make the decision to separate. He describes the emotion as "The erosion of love and the persistence of attachment." He continues, "Although love for one another has faded, oddly enough their sense of connection of being emotionally bound to the other may remain" (p. 37).[3]

Partners who have been contemplating separation continue frequently to remain together. They claim all kinds of reasons. They say that they stay together "for the sake of the children." Or one may say with patronizing disdain that the partner cannot manage without him: "She's so helpless, she doesn't know how to change a bulb or a fuse." This may be after years of a husband's fostering his wife's dependence, since it served his needs in their early years together. She may say, "He has ulcers, he doesn't know how to take care of himself." The result is that many couples fight, threaten to separate, and continue to use a variety of excuses for why they must remain together, "at least for now" or "until the children grow up." Obviously for such couples the marriage must have enough satisfaction and rewards, internal or external, for them not really to want to lose it.

Separations do not always end up in divorce. Sometimes after living apart from each other, partners experience such doubts and loneliness that they wonder whether they have made a terrible mistake; otherwise why would they be feeling so lost? The couple may reunite, which brings some relief. Home feels like home when they are together. Marriages that have gone through a separation experience and are reunited can be revitalized. Partners can find each other again. Attachments can once more be reactivated with renewed feelings. Reunions can be like a shot in the arm to the marriage. The separation may serve as a cooling off and reassessment period, or a shock treatment in confirming for the couple that they really do not want to lose the marriage. There can be renewed intensity, heightened sexual excitement, fresh promises, and new hopes.

The attachment and intimacy that two people achieve in marriage is like no other relationship. The feelings may change, but the sense of belonging remains. Weiss refers to the loss for each partner as "separation distress." I believe that couples who separate need the time and maybe professional help to sort out their feelings as well as their marriage problems. In Canada, the three-year marriage breakdown clause in divorce legislation supports the belief that during the separation period each partner needs time to work out whether he or she wants to move from separation to divorce. Despite some criticism waged against the requirement of a three-year waiting period, it is my belief that a time factor is necessary before a couple is capable of assessing whether the marriage should dissolve. There are many factors, nonetheless, that militate against the opportunity to sort out feelings. Internal dissatisfactions and external family pressures, social pressures, and the current legislative process may contribute to increasing the marital tensions inhibiting chances for reassessment and reengagement. Problems that arise in the inner emotional life can profoundly affect the discontented feelings regarding the marriage. Some people reach a point at which they feel an overriding desire to chuck it all, to change their whole life-style, to run away to the South Sea Isles and start over again.

One 52-year-old man, Tim, who had been married for 20 years, told me that he must be going through a midlife crisis. He said, "I feel there must be something more than this. I've been on the same job for 20 years, with the same woman for 20 years. I feel that I've become a robot, getting up at the same time every morning, doing everything that everybody expects from me. I don't really know what I would like to do if my life weren't so efficiently programmed for me. I am not particularly interested in the things that interest Elsie. I find I am not listening to half the things she's talking about. I turn off my hearing aid. I'm not there for her. I'm not there for me. I'm not bringing anything to her or to my job, or to me."

Through counseling, Tim and his wife came to the realization that his feelings of discontent were not with the marriage and that getting out of his marriage would not have relieved his dissatisfaction. As the couple described their long history of attachment to each other, it became apparent that for him leaving Elsie would mean a deep loss. He began to realize how much he had withdrawn into his own private world, alienating himself from Elsie. This had left her feeling rejected, and she in turn distanced herself from him. Tim had been "going along" with plans and decisions that Elsie made for them. She also felt he was always "accommodating" her. Whenever she would ask what he wanted to do, his reply invariably was "whatever you want." He had not participated actively in planning or initiating plans for a long time. He had been allowing his outward life to be programmed for him while he had been living his own internal life. The counseling of which this couple availed themselves helped them to sort out these feelings and to recognize that what had worked for their marriage at one stage had not been working for them in recent years; they were in danger of losing each other. By recognizing what the problems were, they were able to renew their interest in each other with a fresh charge to the marriage.

This is not an unusual situation. People deal with their discontents differently. Some people look to an extramarital sexual affair to awaken their emotions; others like Tim may project their discontents onto the partner or the children or the job. They may avoid facing up to their basic concerns by externalizing their problems.

Clarifying the marital problems may reactivate the marriage or it may help the partners to recognize and accept the fact that the marriage is no longer working for them. With Tim and Elsie, the opportunity to gain personal insights into their problems revitalized the relationship. The important thing is to understand the reason for the discontents. No ailment can be treated until it is diagnosed. Couples get lost in day-to-day grievances. It is helpful for them to have objective professional aid to get beyond the symptoms to the causes. Professional counseling can interpret interactional marital responses and help people to achieve clearer insights into the discontents and assess whether these can be rectified within the marriage. On the other hand, this counseling process can lead couples to the recognition and acceptance that the marriage is over and that the most productive route is to terminate it. Dissolution of a marriage is painful. However, couples who have clarified the sources of marital problems and arrived at the decision that the relationship does not and cannot work for them are then closer to accepting that they are well advised to separate. This can be a cleaner amputation than dragging unresolved and unclear problems into the future long after separation.

There is a growing realization that it is mentally healthier to get out of rather than remain in a destructive marriage. Divorce is the available means. It is imperative, however, to make sure that it is the marriage relationship that is at fault rather than self-dissatisfactions which are being projected onto the marriage. To be mistaken here can only add to the problems without alleviating them. It is the unresolved internal problems that can be reenacted in future relationships. Psychiatrist Edmund Bergler points out that one cannot marry out of one's neurosis (pp. 23–24).[4] This may be true for some marriages that are terminated without the partner's understanding the causes for his discontents, which will often be carried into other relationships. We may be able to leave a difficult situation, but, to borrow a cliché, we can't run away from ourselves.

There is little question that it is neither easy to get out of a marriage nor easy to get into another one. Evelyn, Paula, and Kate, the three women whom we met over lunch in our introduction, were participants in our study and members of a group seminar that was part of our research. All three, of course, had different views of their decisions to separate.[5]

Evelyn at 22 had just graduated from college. The future held infinite promise. She had a flair for writing and was deliberating between postgraduate studies in journalism or commercial art, which was her second love. As one of those fortunate people, she was not forced into an immediate decision concerning her future after college. Her loving parents, who were always supportive, had encouraged her to take the summer after graduation to rest and to decide which avenue held more interest for her. Always their little girl, she was told that whatever decision she made would be fine with them if it made her happy.

Evelyn decided to spend the summer as a camp counselor contemplating her future. There she would be able to do some freelance work in both writing and art. She was easily accepted as counselor at the camp she had attended as a child. It was there that she met Ted, the camp director. In charge, he knew what he wanted and how to achieve it. He was tall, handsome, and intelligent. Evelyn was bowled over by his attention. Over all the other counselors, he had selected her as his favorite. Though Evelyn had never been short of dates, most of them had been with students her own age. This was different. Ted was mature, confident, and seven years her senior. Moreover, he had an important position. Having worked in personnel management, he had accepted this position to develop a design to reduce staff turnover, which had in previous years disrupted summer programs. Evelyn was not quite sure what his methods were; all she knew was that they worked for her and for others. Ted seemed to bring an orderliness to the camp routine, and his planning made such good sense. The summer went quickly and Evelyn's plans for writing and drawing went by the board. All her attention and emotions were absorbed by this first love.

When Evelyn and Ted were married, Evelyn was 23 and Ted 30. He was well located in a growing corporation as personnel manager. Evelyn had spent the better part of the past year after camp making plans for a large wedding, the kind her mother had always dreamed of. Evelyn's plans had been to get settled into a residence after the wedding and then take some courses in journalism. Happy and in love, she felt she was getting everything she wanted: a mature and dependable husband. She had wanted his children, a home, and family life with Ted. She eventually got all that. What went sour? When had it all started to deteriorate? Where had she been when the seeds of discontent had begun to flourish? Now, after 12 years of marriage, they were full grown and ugly.

Lisa was born a year after Evelyn and Ted were married and Jan followed within two years. The strength that had originally attracted Evelyn to Ted seemed now to have turned into domination. His sense of orderliness and efficiency, that had been so

effective in making the camp run well and in bringing him recognition in his place of employment, had left Evelyn feeling that
there was no room for her to make personal choices, no room to
make independent decisions. Ted's decisions were final. For him
there was a right way and a wrong way. His way was the right
way. Evelyn felt controlled and dependent. When the children
had been infants and dependent on her, she had not noticed
how her life was being managed by Ted. Here she was, an adult,
a wife, a mother, but in a childlike role, dependent on Ted as she
had been dependent on her parents.

At the same time, she was ashamed of her unhappiness. This
was a good man, she told herself. He takes good care of all of us;
his judgment is wise and decisive. But why did he always leave
her feeling that her judgment was poor? She had begun to feel
stripped of self-confidence, uncertain of any decision she had to
make. It became a vicious circle. He would be critical and she
would then question her own logic; he would support his position with so much black and white logic that she would retreat.
The more often this happened, the less she was ready to risk herself in expressing any point of view. The realization grew slowly
that there was no room for her to grow in this marriage. She was
in danger of becoming a passive, unmotivated, and unstimulated
woman. It was hard to stand up to Ted, and she seemed to have
less and less energy to try. But as her discontent grew, Evelyn
knew that she had more potential than she was drawing on. She
couldn't go on this way.

Even when she tried to convey her feelings to Ted, he was
impatient with her "childish" complaints. The more successful
he became at his job, the more managerial he seemed to be at
home. When Evelyn told him she could not continue to accept
his demands for compliance with his wishes and that she felt she
was dying inside, Ted did not seem to hear her. She knew that
she must arrive at her own decision about this relationship and
this marriage. It became clear to her that Ted would continue to

be Ted and that if she could not live with his behavior and his expectation then the decision to terminate the marriage would have to be hers alone.

The final determination to separate was triggered by Ted's telling their 11-year-old daughter, Lisa, that she wasn't old enough to make any decisions for herself and that she must do as she was told without questioning the reasons. Ted gave Lisa no permission to develop or express her thoughts and feelings; he silenced her abruptly and she withdrew sullenly. Evelyn's indignation reached a boiling point. She identified with what her child was feeling. Both for herself and on behalf of her daugher, she said to Ted, "Damn it, I am not going to let you do this to our children too. I won't let you turn them into passive, ineffectual nincompoops who can't think for themselves." Evelyn then unleashed a tirade of stored-up angry feelings which ended with her telling Ted that she must get out of this marriage, that she felt stifled and suffocated and that she had long ago stopped caring for him. For her survival and for the children, she said, she must get out of the marriage.

When Ted finally realized that Evelyn was dead serious and that the marriage was over, in his systematic way, he began to organize plans for separation. He agreed that he would leave the home. Of course, he added, there must be no dramatic display. They were two intelligent people who would handle this separation in a mature adult fashion. Naturally the children, he said, would remain with Evelyn in the home. Knowing how limited his time was for personal matters, Ted would visit them whenever he chose. Evelyn offered to find an apartment for Ted and even to furnish it for him, to make the move as smooth as possible. Evelyn and Ted agreed that they would tell the children together. They also agreed that the children must not be damaged by the separation. Ted would assure his daughters that they would spend as much time with him as possible after he moved. This couple could have written the text about how parents should tell the children together and at the same time assure them that marital separation meant only separation between the couple, not between parent and the children.

The plans were good, but a major factor was overlooked. This disciplined factual format was too intellectualized. It left no room for emotions. It inhibited all the questions about the unknowns of life without father at home. The girls were frightened and felt alone, not knowing how they were all going to deal with a different kind of family life.

Once the decision to separate was made, Evelyn knew she must hold onto her determination not to sink back into the vacuum of this marriage. This would be her one big break from dependence. She had to make it to survive and to rescue her children so that they would have the opportunity to grow. At the same time she *was* frightened. So Evelyn embarked on her new life as a separated woman and as a separate parent. Because of their separation she would have to learn many new skills and redefine a personal role for herself different from that of being part of a married couple. She would have to make all the decisions about everything, including parenting and finances. In short, she had to reorganize her personal and family life with a different script. She could not live with Ted, but could she live without him?

Kate, Evelyn's luncheon companion, was divorced from a marriage that had traveled a course quite different from Evelyn's over its span of 12 years. Instead of a fun-loving girl, Kate had become an angry, resentful woman, fearful of ever making a commitment to another marriage.

Jim and Kate had been like two kids playing house for the first three years of their marriage. Having been high school sweethearts, they felt they were ready for marriage by the time they had finished school and were married when Kate was 19 and Jim 21. Though neither had learned marketable skills, both were bright and resourceful. Kate got a job with an advertising company and financed Jim through a real estate course. They both enjoyed their work and their recreational time together. After work, they met, played tennis and swam, and had fast-food dinners. They were a happy couple. But parents, social pressures, and the traditional expectations of a three-year marriage made them decide to have a child because it was the thing to do. Kate gave up her job, and after Scott was born her life changed completely. She was involved in the baby world of diapers and feeding and routine chores, while she watched Jim leave home bright and early in the morning to go out into the interesting adult world. Jim worked by appointment, morning or evening, and when he had evening appointments he would stay downtown to play tennis, swim, and have fast-food dinners. In Kate's perception, Jim's life was glamorous and hers was dull and boring. She was discontented and felt that Jim's life had not changed at all with the coming of their child, whereas hers began to be to service his needs and their son's. The fun of the marriage was replaced by resentment. She felt that having the child meant she had lost her youth. She wasn't ready for the responsibilities. She resented the fact that Jim would come home at the end of the day ready to play and have fun with the baby, while she, at the end of her day, was tired and needed adult stimulation. She resented Jim's boyish charm that had once drawn her to him. She felt dowdy and felt that her life was dowdy and that she had become a bitchy, complaining housewife. She and Jim were out of touch. They were living in different worlds, and she was not enjoying her world.

Before Scott was born, Kate's parents had extended a gift of a down payment on a house. The selection of the house was made by Kate's parents, who tended to be ambitious about material comforts they wanted for their daughter in keeping with the social milieu in which they moved. The house proved to be in excess of Jim's income, and he was having trouble meeting the payments. Kate and her parents felt that if Jim were only a competent, mature, ambitious family man, he would spend less time playing tennis and and more time working. They ganged up, heaping criticism on him, and he responded by withdrawing and refusing to discuss his financial situation with them. He felt personally inadequate in not being able to measure up to the financial demands made on him and to the standard of living of many of their friends. When Kate refused to accept the fact that they could not afford some household furnishings, Jim's response would be, "Stop worrying, we'll have everything we want. I just happen to be short now." It was when checks began to bounce and creditors were hounding them for payment that Kate became suspicious. She believed Jim was doing well because, she said, "he could sell anybody anything," and she wondered where his earnings were going. She was filled with suspicious ideas and became accusing and hostile. Jim dealt with this behavior by withdrawing and spending less and less time at home. This couple had become angry strangers to each other.

Kate was well fortified by her parents in her criticism of Jim. She had built up a backlog of resentment that neither she nor Jim had known how to deal with. Her perception of Jim's lack of responsibility was tied in with her perception of what a mature husband should be, modeled, no doubt, on her father, whose full commitment had been to his wife and daughter. The more attacking Kate became, the more secretive Jim was and the more inadequate he felt. His loss of self-confidence spilled over into his salesmanship, which began to suffer. But Kate did not know this, and Jim's battle with his self-image prevented him from discussing it. She was no longer a friend, he no longer trusted her reactions, and would not expose his weakness to her.

The breaking point came one day when Kate had just hung up the phone in despair—another unpaid bill—when Jim came in wearing his tennis shorts and swinging his racquet, ready to "play the game" that everything between them was great. Kate greeted him with "Did you pay the electric bill?" "Of course I did," said Jim. "How come the utility company just called to say it hasn't been paid and they threatened to turn off our electricity?" "Who knows? What are you doing, checking up on me again?" "Yes, why shouldn't I, what have you ever done to earn my trust? I can't depend on you, you know damn well you didn't pay that bill!" "So I didn't, big deal, so I'll pay it tomorrow." "It sure is a big deal. I'm sick of the promises of tomorrow. In fact, it's such a big deal, that I've had it. I'm finished. I can't stand anymore of the promises, the lies, the bounced checks, the creditors bugging me. I'm sick of your double talk. In fact I'm sick of you." Kate, feeling her anger mounting, knew that if she did not stop herself, she was going to say it. This time she had to be sure she meant it. She mustn't turn chicken. "I've had enough, I can't stand you, I can't stand me! I can't stand the way we live. I'm finished! Get out." There, she said it! Jim simply replied, "When?" "Now," shouted Kate. That was it—it was over! This wasn't the first time that Kate had been at the end of her tether. She felt so unhappy. She had threatened many times to end this marriage and hated the nagging shrew she had become. This time she knew she had to mean it. It had taken years to reach this point. She pointed out to him that she had shut her eyes and ears to so many things in the past. There was the time she had allowed herself to be sweet-talked out of her indignation when she learned that he had paid the mortgage by forging her name to a check, taking money out of an account her father had given her. She shouted that she could no longer keep deceiving herself about how much he was deceiving her. Finally she had reached the point of always feeling suspicious and distrustful, particularly since she never knew when he was lying. Never being able to believe him, she could not tolerate this way of life any longer and had to get out of the marriage. When Jim went upstairs, she asked herself, did he know she really meant it? Would he pack and leave, or would he come down with his hangdog expression and tell her how sorry he was and that he wanted to kiss and make up and do better? Would she get cold feet and once again cover up her upset as she had done so often? No, this time had to be the showdown. She had built up such a strong case against Jim and attributed so many of her discontents to him that she was convinced that if she wanted to retain the last vestige of self-respect she had to get out of this marriage.

Automatically, as her mind buzzed with conflict, she continued with routine jobs, her heart pounding. A part of her was warning that she was making a major decision. Was she prepared to carry this out and stick by it? While she washed the dishes and put them away, one ear was tuned to sounds upstairs. Then she realized that Scott, now nine years old, would soon be coming home. She would have to tell him. If only she could depend on Jim to share the responsibility of explaining it all to Scott. She conjured up the script: "Mommy and Daddy have not been happy together for some time. We have tried to settle our problems. We have tried to understand and to change the things that upset us about each other. But it hasn't worked. We are going to separate. Daddy is going to move out. You will see Daddy every weekend—or even more often. It's Mommy and Daddy who are going to separate, not Daddy and you; we both love you and will always be your parents." Tears began streaming down Kate's face as she reviewed this script and as she anticipated Scott's response. Both she and Jim would hold and comfort Scott; he would know how much both parents loved him. As Kate stood over the sink, crying quietly as this difficult drama unfolded itself in her mind, Jim came into the kitchen. He was carrying a suitcase. Looking sheepish, with an inappropriate smile, he said, "Well I guess this is it. Tell Scott I'll call him tomorrow," and he was gone. Twelve years of marriage and "this was it." Once more Kate would be left to carry the burden alone. Jim could not face the difficult job of telling Scott and he had walked out on this job as he had walked out on every situation that had been tough to deal with. Kate stood there, rooted to the spot. She had to decide how she could deal with it. Did she really have the courage to stay with the determination that this was the only course for her? The separation would have to become public information. She would start with her parents, then her friends. News like this travels quickly.

"Where's Dad?" asked Scott, bursting into the kitchen. "He promised he would come and watch the ball game and he wasn't there." Scott stopped short. He looked at his mother and knew something was wrong. "Mom and Dad have decided to separate." Kate had started on her script. She had rehearsed this moment for years now. The telling made it real. The words took on an unretractable reality that was the first step in changing their family life.

This is frequently the way in which many couples arrive at the final decision that the marriage is over. One parent must leave the family home. The actual decision to separate may be triggered by some inconsequential disagreement. It is the tip of the volcano that has been smouldering for years with periodic eruptions, until, like Vesuvius, the top blows off. As many people who terminate a marriage know, the final decision is terrifying. As with Kate, even though she had told Jim to go, his going, bag in hand, symbolized such finality. She was overcome with her sense of aloneness. She would be another separated woman, a single parent. Her marital breakup would be added to the divorce statistics.

Carrying out the decision to separate is never sudden, never easy. It is usually, as with Kate, preceded by a buildup of months or years of unhappiness, reconciliation, compromise, excuses, protection, and concealment of marital dissatisfactions. Kate had gone through all this many times. And yet looking at Jim, she had often felt waves of warmth. A part of her continued to care for Jim in spite of their problems. She would tell herself, "He's kind and gentle. In his own way he really loves Scott and me. There is certainly nothing mean about him. His worst crime is that he doesn't want to grow up. Is that enough of a reason to break up a marriage?"

The decision to separate is difficult enough when both partners reach the realization that the marriage is over. It is much

more difficult when one partner is opposed to it or has built a
life around the marriage and has not been aware of, or has
denied or has refused to hear, the spouse's discontent. Paula,
Evelyn and Kate's friend, did not initiate her separation. She felt
unprepared when Jack told her he had been involved with
another woman for some time and that he was leaving her and
the marriage. Paula had always loved Jack, an intense, unpredictable man who had remained an enigma to her over the eight
years of their marriage. These years had roller-coastered from
hills to valleys, with no plateaux. Jack could be loving and tender
or violent and harsh. He was alternately strong and fragile.
Involved with his own pain, he said he had to get out of the
marriage since he could no longer continue his life of duplicity;
the guilt tortured him and made him feel "dirty." Since he was
unhappy, Paula comforted him as she always did when he hurt.
He first responded to her comfort, then pushed her away.
"You're making it harder for me. Why can't you get angry? Why
don't you tell me to get out—I've been a rotter. You just make
me feel guiltier. Sharon sure wouldn't let anyone treat her like
this. She would fight. She knows how to fight anger with anger.
You're like a punching bag. You deflate when I strike out. It
makes me furious. I can't deal with it." Paula's response was simple: "Jack, I love you. When you're upset, I want to comfort you.
I don't want you to leave, but I won't hold you back." Jack's sense
of shame was mixed with intense frustration and ambivalence.
He did not want to hurt this gentle woman; he genuinely cared
for her and their two children, but his emotional turmoil pro-
vided no relief for him with Paula.

Sharon, who had been in his life for the past two years, was
a highly volatile woman who excited, challenged, and frightened him. Her passion and intensity matched his. Marrying her
would be like walking into a lion's den. Like him she was
involved with her own needs. They were both hurting so many
people with their self-indulgence. They had both agreed that
their love for each other was the primary drive in their lives. It

came before their marriage and their children. They both agreed to leave their families and live together. The chemistry that exploded when they were together alternated between wild orgiastic bouts and violent physical battles. Jack was no longer in control of his emotions; they were carrying him. He was involved to the point where his marriage had become inconsequential.

For Paula, life had revolved around Jack and his needs. With all his unpredictablity, she had never thought that life without him could be better. There had been no time or process to help prepare for his moving out. The ending was abrupt. Jack simply left. The blow was harder for Paula than it would have been if Jack had died, and at least if he had died that would have been final. But this was a voluntary choice for Jack to leave her and their family for another woman, and this devastated her. She could not believe this was happening and yet Jack had packed his clothes, his books, and everything and was gone. He simply moved out of her life. How could she ever trust another man, another marriage? Her love and attachment had given her no preparation for building any sense of personal, single-life autonomy. For months she made no attempt to adjust to the reality that Jack was no longer with her, that she was separated, or that Jack was with another woman living a different life.

There are other situations in which one partner initiates the separation. After a period of separation, he or she wants to renege on the decision but finds that the marriage door has been locked and he or she cannot get back in. The rejected partner, still hostile and offended, is not willing to be reunited. This was the case of Christine and David. They had lived the "good" life for twenty years and had two "wonderful" children and a "beautiful" home. They were members of a private golf and tennis club and participated in an active social life. In short, they conveyed the picture of the ideal marriage. They had moved along all the traditional life cycle stages. Their marriage was the "made in heaven" marriage that parents wish for their children. Theirs was a union between two families, compatible in social, economic, religious, and educational terms. Sounds good? It could have been if only Christine and David had been aware of the distance that had grown between them as well as the need to do something about recharging their marriage, to release them from their mutual state of boredom.

For a long time they had each formed friendships outside the marriage that were more stimulating than anything they brought to each other. Together they had become "old hat." They didn't bother sharing their real interests or feelings with each other. These they discussed with their friends outside the home. Though they were also involved as a couple in social situations, they would come home and feel emptiness between them. David was a successful businessman, who was interested in his work and respected at it. Christine felt that her life was aimless, though she felt guilty for her discontent, since she had so much to be thankful for. Finally deciding she must get something with which to occupy herself, she became a schoolteacher after many years away from her profession. Once she had applied for and received a teaching assignment, she found the work fascinating and rewarding; a new world thus opened for her. The staff, friendly and cooperative, included her in their group, and Christine came to life. She was now with people whose lives had purpose and dedication. Having lunch with staff, she eagerly listened, learned, and participated. Her newly found sense of challenge, interest, and stimulation was infectious. Everyone was attracted to her.

This was a heady time for Christine. A chemical reaction was sparked between her and the school psychologist. The vibrations between the two awakened her senses. It seemed like a love match, and Christine was available. Her perspectives were becoming distorted. Nothing, not her husband, her children, or her home, was now important to her. She was ready to forfeit everything and everyone to hold onto this precious new experience. For these wonderful stolen moments together, her logic and loyalty went by the board. Despite the outrage of her family, her parents, and her friends, Christine moved out of her home, and rented a small apartment. The plan was that she and Tony would use this as their interim rendezvous until he was able to leave his wife and his two daughters. But Tony was finding it hard to leave his family and begged her patience. He insisted that he needed the right time to tell his family. But the time never seemed to be right and Christine was constantly left alone. They were spending less time together now than they had when they were having brief encounters at school.

The realization for Christine was that only her life had changed radically and only she had given up so much. Since Tony had remained at home, his life had barely changed. The guilt he felt about having an affair was increased by the guilt of Christine's plight and his own realization that he could not and would not leave his family. When he finally told Christine that he couldn't do that to his family, the effect on both of them was sobering. It drew Tony closer to the family he had almost given up. And Christine felt lost. She became overcome with loneliness for her family and former life. Unfortunately for her, her family was not ready to take her back. They had been deeply hurt. Her husband's sensibilities were offended because Christine had broken his trust. She had disrupted his life and that of his children. She had upset the respectability of the family. Since she had made her choice, he refused to see her. He could say only that she had made her bed and could lie in it. As far as he was concerned, the sooner she started divorce proceedings the better. Unrelenting, he was supported in his indignation by family and friends. He was consoled, included in social gatherings, and sought out. He had social sanction. On the other hand, Christine had social disapproval and rejection. She felt frightened and alone.

This couple, like many others, had drifted apart over the years and were virtually strangers to each other. They became prone to seek their satisfactions outside the marriage. They lost interest in each other; the emotional chemistry and intellectual compatibility had died. The stimulation of outside activities that brought interest to their lives accentuated the bleakness that overcame them when they were together. Married couples who can grow through new experiences and new social relationships can develop as individuals and enrich the marriage. It is when the partners grow apart from each other as they expand their horizons that they lose each other.

It has been apparent to me that when there are two people living in the intimacy of a dead marriage it is healthier to bury it than to continue to live together. However, there are many couples who deal with conflict and anger and with continued threats to end the marriage. Sometimes they get the ball rolling toward divorce and don't know how to stop it. As with Christine and David, there are many couples who divorce and then live with deep regrets about having terminated the marriage because of angry, spiteful, or resentful feelings. Divorce is a serious lifetime decision and the reasons for it must be well understood. Too many divorced people continue the "if only I had done this or that differently" monologue. Their continuing grief for the former relationship makes it difficult for them to get on with their lives and make a commitment to another relationship.

Evelyn, Kate and Paula, the three women whose separations I have described, all began their marriages at a point in their lives when the mates they had selected had been compatible with their emotional stage. Evelyn looked to a husband as someone who could protect and care for her. Kate had a playmate who could share the freedom of her youthful activities, and Paula responded to her need to be needed and to be the good girl meeting her partner's every wish. Their marriages had all had good, loving periods. The problem with these three marriages, as with many marriages that become unhappy, was that people's needs are not static. In the marriages described, the couples had not kept each other in touch with their changing needs. Their personal growth had brought a distance and estrangement between the partners. But the couples had each shared a history of caring for each other, parenting children, having a deep attachment that is not easily left behind with the physical separation. Some couples who marry may never form the attachment bond. In some marriages the value systems, goals, the emotional temperaments may prove to be incompatible from the outset. It is as though the partners were talking unrelated languages. Such separations may free the couples with less of the pain and animosity when the unhappiness between the couple is identified.

On the basis of our study and clinical experience with remarried couples, we are impressed by the extent to which many divorced people carry unresolved, hostile, conflictive feelings, and unresolved emotional turmoil into another marriage. These emotional ties to a former spouse can interfere with the future relationships as well as relationships between the ex-spouses as parents in caring for the children of that previous marriage.

There are some suggested guidelines that couples would do well to consider in the transition between their marriage breakdown and the reorganization of their lives prior to a new marriage. The couples must first clarify what their marital problems are and why they can no longer live together. Once they are certain that they can no longer remain married, immediate plans must be discussed for the care of the children. In order to be able to make these plans with the children's interests at heart, the couple must untangle their marital emotional difficulties from their children's welfare. The next step requires that each of the partners consider what is involved for both of them in separation. Telling the children about the separation and involving them in family planning is another wise step prior to the physical separation. Emotional problems and practical living problems develop when family life is disrupted. The emotional problems have a major impact on how practical problems will be decided. Severe tensions between the partners are bound to influence custody arrangements and financial settlements. The children become easy targets for their parents' animosity. When decisions about children and money matters become confused, they are the most powerful weapons with which the couple can fight. For the sake of the children's welfare and family reorganization, the couple must first verify their feelings toward each other.

Before the separation takes place, professional help may be very productive to ensure that it will be effected as constructively as possible in regard to partners and children. Disruption of family life requires many decisions and many changes that need immediate attention. These tasks come at a time when the ability to arrive at decisions is usually least effective. Some people report confusion and panic. Social and professional support can be valuable at this time. This is usually when the couples seek legal counsel. Feeling—and being—vulnerable, they experience an urgency to learn their legal rights. These legal rights concern custody and visitation of the children as well as the division of financial assets. The resolution of these issues is often colored by emotional prejudices which in turn can influence the eventual legal recommendations. In most parts of North America, the adversary system continues to prevail. This means that each separating partner selects his separate legal counsel, whose job it is to work for the "best interests" of the client. When finances and "best interests" of the client, as well as the client's views of "best interests" of the children become enmeshed in the legal system, children too often become pawns in the legal maneuvers. Partners hurl threats over each other's head: "You can't see the children unless you are ready to pay me what I ask for." Or the reverse: "You don't get a penny unless I can see the kids when I want to." The children become incidental weapons for angry mud-slinging as the legal battle mounts and the bargaining reaches points of rigid contention. The legal process becomes a win–lose battle, tending to further raise the hostile feelings between the spouses. The anticipation that there will be a battle and opposition to a mutually satisfactory agreement is frequently fostered by the divorce lawyers and further exacerbates animosity.

Since parents for the most part do love their children and do not want their marital plight to damage the children's lives, plans for the children's future that are satisfactory to both parents are best arrived at before legal counsel is sought. Some of the wisest people, whose judgment may always have been sound and dependable, have frequently reported that they surprised even themselves with some of the malice they demonstrated at court proceedings. Upset feelings that may have been dormant for years emerge and manifest themselves in hitting below the belt. Parents frequently begin to vie for children's loyalty—turning to the children to take sides against the other parent. Couples may involve their own parents, family, and friends in some of the grievances they hold. When partners involve people who are close to them, they are forming their own adversary camps, which makes the reorganization of the two parts of the family more difficult. It means that there will be losses beyond those between the marital pair. The couple must recognize how important it is for them to separate their marital problems from their continued rights as parents, as well as the rights to retain significant relationships with in-laws and the children's rights to their grandparents, relatives, and friends.

Anthropologist Paul Bohannan is quoted as saying: "My ex-wife will always be my son's mother and my ex-wife's mother will always be his grandmother."[6] The separation surely does not necessitate a break from significant relations like grandparents, in-laws, other family, and friends who have been involved in relationships with both partners. It should not mean having to choose a side and viewing the other side as the enemy camp. Reorganizing the family life could be made so much easier if the separation did not impose a loss of so much that had been part of the marriage, family, and social life that two people have built and shared together over the years.

Another step that can ease the transition from married life to separate life is for the married couple to begin by *preparing* for single life in practical ways. Couples who have lived a part of their lives in the close and intimate relationship of a marriage develop a dependency on each other in many ways. They fall into an everyday pattern of dividing the labor and responsibilities. Each partner achieves competence in some areas and remains dependent in others. This means that, once separated, each must learn some new skills to be independent. Separating partners are faced with so many changes and decisions at the same time that they can find it useful to sort out specific, individual plans in a setting removed from the turmoil of the home. Independent decision-making can help strengthen each one's confidence in the ability to manage separately. A number of women panic at taking responsibility for some of the practical aspects of their daily lives that they have not dealt with, such as paying bills and arranging finances. Many of them have known nothing about the state of the family's finances. The more frequently I hear perfectly competent women say they feel helpless and frightened about everyday life management, the more convinced I am that the intact first-marriage relationship requires partners to share responsibilities in family and home management on a peer basis rather than as a senior–junior partnership. The service component that women have accepted as their job with the children and home life has left men equally dependent in daily family living areas which makes separation unnecessarily difficult for men. Frequently after separation, men have said that they had not realized that they had really lived on the periphery of the family rather than as an integral part of it. Their personal needs have been taken care of for them. They have frequently had a minimum of direct one-to-one intimacy with their children. Wives, too, often become the mediators between fathers and children in the ways that men are too frequently the mediators between women and financial management. This is particularly true for the protective wife and the protective husband in the intact family. It restricts the growth and independence of each partner in daily life, not to mention in the event of separation or bereavement. The syndrome "Daddy is tired, don't bother him" or "I don't want to worry the little woman" does a great disservice to both men and women.

Separation tasks can have damaging repercussions when they are not dealt with prior to the actual separation. The reality that the children of separating parents experience a major disorganization to their lives is well established. Children are the children of both parents. Their parents' separation affects them profoundly. Since their lives and their future are deeply affected, they must, with all certainty, be told in advance about their parents' decision to separate and they must be involved in future plans for their family life with each parent.

Amid the turbulence of the separation, it can be very difficult for the family to communicate effectively. It may be highly productive for the whole family to have the opportunity to meet in an objective, professional setting that can offer protection for free expression of thoughts and feelings. Family sessions enable all members of the family to grasp the reality that the couple has reached the decision that the marriage is over. There is little doubt that by this time the tensions have been felt throughout the household. The pervasive atmosphere in the household may be icy cold or explosively violent.

Upset feelings explode in all directions. They are not only confined to the couple. The children become easy targets, unhappy victims of unhappy parents. Each parent may vie for the child's loyalty, bringing the child into the middle of the marital battle with such volatile remarks as: "Your father, he has lived like a bachelor since we were married. Don't let him sweet-talk you. What's he ever done for you?" or "Your mother, the only thing that has ever mattered to her are her friends. You'd think the telephone was attached to her ear." These statements convey negative, hostile, angry feelings that children do not want to hear. Children have so often said that they wish their parents would leave them out of their fights. They feel like a yo-yo tossed back and forth between the emotions of each parent. They do not want to have to choose sides and turn against one parent.

Family sessions in a counselor's office can be very productive. Because the turmoil of separation can make communication very difficult, children can become extremely frightened. They are dependent people who need both parents. They worry about who will care for them. Who will take care of their mother? Who will take care of their daddy? Where will he live? The children have to know what the plans are for the impending future, how life is to go on for all of them. The counselor's role in family sessions must focus on specific plans for how the family life will be reorganized once the parents separate. A counselor can help the family to deal with the practical planning while helping to control the emotional issues of the marital conflicts.

The semantics that adults use frequently do not have meaning for a child. To say, "We are going to separate" may mean for a day, a week, a month. *Divorce* is an adult term. The implications of the finality of divorce must be conveyed. Some parents with the best intentions to protect their children may say: "Mommy and Daddy are having trouble together, and Daddy has to be alone to think things over." They have been unhappy at the thought of poor daddy, alone, thinking things over. As one depressed ten-year-old boy said "I waited a week, a month. I was sure that he had had enough time to think things over. I didn't know that separation could be so awful." Children are a vital, palpitating part of their parent's separation. Since they are involved in the marital fighting, they must also be involved in the plans for the future. Parents who care for their children do not want the loss of the marriage to mean the loss of a parent for the children. The children must be assured of this. They must be helped to understand that even though the parents are going to live separately and that family life will be different, the children will have two family homes, each with one of their parents. The counselor's role is to help the parents clarify these plans for the children while orchestrating the sessions to prevent the parents from getting back into the marital battle or competing for the children's loyalty. This is a painful time for both adults and children; everybody is hurt and frightened. It is wise for everyone to recognize that the pain is not individual, the separation is not casual, and the decision has not been arrived at lightly. Parents who tend to intellectualize the facts without venting their hurt feelings create a destructive atmosphere that encourages denial and secrecy. On the other hand, parents who tend to fight viciously and openly can leave the children frightened and threatened, thinking that if their parents have fallen out of love with each other, then there is nothing to prevent the parents from falling out of love with them. The opportunity to express feelings with the solace of being comforted as well as offering comfort can reduce the sense of being alone and fearful in this life crisis.

During the preseparation period, working on these tasks can reduce the stress involved when the actual physical separation takes place which divides the family into two parts. Before the separation the stress can be reduced, although probably not eliminated; there will be pain.

There is little question that the height of crisis for separating partners is at the time that one parent packs the bags and leaves the family home. This crisis is handled in many different ways. Sometimes, the tensions are so high that one partner will simply leave home suddenly. There will be no telling the children that the parents are separating, which may seem to a child like sheer abandonment. A child may interpret this as "How could he leave me when he said he loves me?" It may feel more like a personal rejection than a marital separation. Furthermore, if one partner leaves the marriage and the home and the other partner is left to tell the children that daddy (or mommy) is gone, the telling is frequently one-sided, colored by the upset feelings of the resident parent. This, too, can reinforce the feelings that not only has the parent left the marriage but that he or she has left the family as well.

Our experience with separating couples indicates strongly that for the sake of future adjustment both partners should share the telling with the children. If the parents find they are too upset to handle this together, we have found that a family counseling session can ease the difficulty considerably. The general reasons for the separation and divorce that are discussed with the children should be accompanied with plans for the immediate future of the family life and the assurance that both parents will remain in the children's lives, albeit under different living arrangements. The ideal situation is to be able to convey that the children will have two homes, each one with a parent.

The plaintive cry from many children is "Why didn't they tell me?" Parents tend to project their buildup of marital discontent and preparation for separation onto the children. Parents have frequently said that with all the palpable tension, hostility, and coldness between the parents, they had believed the children would be well prepared for and even relieved by the separation. Children have said they were not prepared and that they had learned to live with a particular family life style which included fighting and threats to separate. They had simply seen this atmosphere as characteristic of their parents and their family, but they had never realized that their parents could separate forever. They had taken their family life for granted with both parents living together.

To summarize: Preparatory steps for a separation can be helpful in reducing some of the anxiety over what is to come. The guidelines described above specify, first, that the married couple clarify their reasons for deciding to separate. Once they have decided that separation is the best solution to their problems, then they must acknowledge that in order to separate they have to plan for their separate lives and for their children's lives. This planning can best be achieved if the partners are capable of separating their marital feelings from their legal rights and responsibilities as parents. Children do not belong to one parent alone. The axiom that marriages may not be permanent but parenting is forever must underlie the struggle to arrive at joint decisi. that are mutually acceptable. These decisions come at a time when the couple is having trouble feeling agreeable about anything at all. Objective professional help can be useful at this time. For couples who are living together unhappily and saying, "I can't live with him (or her) but can I live without him (or her)," each partner may benefit from the opportunity to sort out the immediate plans for the future through counseling. It will help for the family as a whole to be involved in participating in planning for the future. This helps the children to recognize that the family life will continue for them with each parent. With preparation, children will perceive their family as headed not for disintegration but for reorganization. Children need the protection of being reassured that they will not be neglected and abandoned like Hansel and Gretel. They want to know where their father will live when he leaves the family home and who will take care of him. They want to be told how their mother will manage when their father is living someplace else and whether they will be able to see him. They also need to be reassured that the separation is not because of them nor any fault of theirs, nor is the separation from them. In short, children need to understand the specific immediate plans for the family reorganization. One of the threatening aspects for children is that adult relationships may be temporary; if their parents have fallen out of love with each other, what is to prevent the parents from falling out of love with them too? This thought certainly can destroy a child's sense of trust in the dependability of a relationship. To prevent such distrust in the children, a great deal of reassurance is needed from both parents. Parents must always bear in mind that marriages may terminate but parenting is permanent. Therefore, these planning sessions may require firm control to keep the focus away from the marital battle and onto practical terms. The job of marriage reconciliation is now finished. The job at

hand at the family session is to open up the discussion so that
everyone may participate in how the family will reorganize.

Family life will be different after the separation. Our next
chapter covers the early steps in reorganizing the family unit
when parents separate.

REFERENCES

[1]Kressel, K., and Deutsch, M. "Society for the Psychological Study of Social
Issues." In *Divorce and Separation*, edited by G. Levinger and O. C. Moles. New
York: Basic Books, 1979, p. 1.
[2]Bach, G. R., and Wyden, P. *The Intimate Enemy.* New York: William Morrow,
1969.
[3]Weiss, R. S. *Marital Separation.* New York: Basic Books, 1975.
[4]Bergler, E. *The Basic Neurosis.* New York: Grune & Stratton, 1949.
[5]Their names are fictitious, as are all the names in the case studies throughout
this book.
[6]Norman, M. "The New Extended Family: Divorce Reshapes the American
Household." *The New York Times Magazine,* November 23, 1980.

CHAPTER 2

SEPARATION
BREAKING UP IS HARD TO DO

Marriage has been described as a rhythmic epic—hedged between love and hate, between power struggle and traditional dependence.

ANONYMOUS

Once a married couple separate, family life is disrupted. The membership of the family remains the same but no longer in an intact unit. This, in turn, changes the daily patterns of each member of the family. One of the major problems that must be faced is reorganizing family life to create a minimum of loss for the children, nonresident parent, grandparents, and other relatives. A continuity between parent and children and between in-laws and children is difficult to maintain, since the divorce system is predominantly adversarial and tends to turn people against one another. These legal and social attitudes create prejudices that make ongoing relations hard to continue after separation. Moreover, there is still an unfortunate stigma associated with divorce. Society continues to view the intact family with parents and children living together as the normal standard. Normality, however, is largely dictated by a particular culture, and with a million divorces currently taking place annually there must be guidelines for acknowledging different standards of normality for the separated parents and children, if we are to keep abreast of the social reality of our culture. Living in two homes, maternal and paternal, has become the normal family life for a growing number of children. Demographer R. C. Glick estimates that by 1990 one out of every three children will experience parental divorce before reaching the age of 18, and each parent will live in a separate home.[1] Surely one-third of the population of children cannot grow up feeling they are viewed as deviant from the norm. Consideration must then be given to how family life can be reorganized in the least stressful way after separation. It has been well demonstrated, after all, that when people are under stress the pressures become aggravated in other areas of life to the point at which some people can leave their jobs, city, or country. Joint membership in organizations and clubs, church affiliation, plans for burial grounds, insurance policies, wills—all are affected and changed when a marriage breaks down. The early period, right after separation, brings about many changes and is usually the most stressful. In addition to emotional upheaval, there are legal arrangements, housing, economic questions, division of responsibilities to be reorganized. Whereas it is difficult to reach the decision to separate, once the separation has taken place it is difficult to adapt to a different life.

When a couple has reached the decision to terminate a marriage, negative feelings have escalated until they can no longer tolerate living together. Once they are separated, however, ambivalent feelings tend to soar. People admit to a mixed bag of feelings that run the gamut from anger, rejection, and hostility to emptiness, sorrow, and loneliness. A separation is thus easier to handle for many when they keep the conflictual aspects in the foreground of their minds rather than allowing themselves to dwell on the good times and the good feelings that they have experienced together. And memories can create disturbing, confusing, and nagging doubts about the wisdon of having terminated the marriage and disrupted the family. Logically, one might anticipate that separating from an unhappy marriage would bring only relief; instead, people confess to feelings of despair and panic. There are few people who do not feel that separation has been a major crisis in their lives, making them feel dislocated and throwing them into a state of imbalance. The taken-for-granted rhythm of every day has been broken, the familiar patterns of life disrupted. Separation is no temporary holiday from routine; it involves permanent change at a time when' emotions are in a state of turmoil. It can be difficult to think clearly and make sound decisions. It takes time to get off the old tracks and begin to establish new directions. People often find themselves caught at a crossroad.

Some people cope with crisis by running back to the partner, or back to parents, or back to a familiar life they have known, good or bad. Other people use crisis to challenge themselves to move in new directions, to try to expand their horizons, to experiment with new experiences in their efforts to reach for a new lease on life. People grapple in many different ways with their sense of loss or sense of release from the confines of an unhappy marriage that is now over. As one woman said, "I went crazy, I didn't know myself. I did things that weren't me. I stood outside of myself and watched me in amazement. A part of me was defiant. I told myself I was free to do anything. Another part of me was filled with guilt and shame. I didn't like me or anything that I was doing and I felt lonely." A man who had just separated related his sense of dislocation. Having enjoyed an extramarital affair prior to his separation, he felt separation would be easy since he had someone to whom he could turn. But he did not even want to see her or anyone else once he was separated. He said he felt bruised and vulnerable and wanted to be alone. He wondered about many of the separated men he knew who boasted about their freedom to have one-night stands; how could they have the inclination, not to mention the capability?

There is little doubt that the life crisis of a marriage separation is a shock to the emotions. The accustomed life-style is disrupted. There is temporary falling apart from the familiar world of what is known into a dark abyss of the unknown. This can be a time of regression or a time of growth, but it is always a period of struggle; a struggle that has been described as having dynamics similar to bereavement. The loss of a partner, the loss of being part of a couple is a period of grieving. Holmes and Rahe in their study of life-event stress state that separation is found to be second in stress only to the death of a partner.

There are some factors in marital separation that may be even more difficult to cope with than they would be in the case of the death of a partner. In separation, the partner is alive. Separation from marriage is a voluntary decision made by one or both partners, whereas death is involuntary. Death of a spouse meets with a sympathetic response, whereas separation is viewed as a failure to fulfill the promise of a permanent bond. It is threatening to the institution of marriage. Death terminates the marriage contract; separation is an imperfect act of finality between living ex-partners who have voluntarily left the life and love they had shared with their children. Their history of being a family together remains with them. The emotional aspects of the marital ties outlive the legal dissolution. Death is the involuntary and final end to the marriage, separation the voluntary termination of a deteriorated marriage. The parents are still bound to each other through mutual love of their children.

The height of crisis is the period right after separation when the structure of personal, family, and social life is disrupted for both partners, more so than the legalizing of the divorce. It takes time to redefine one's personal identity from the "we" of the couple to the "I" of the separate person. Couples often report that they are plunged into an identity crisis. As a couple, partners are a psychological and social unit. Once separated, many people convey that they are confused about how they should behave to each other, how they should move from the intimacy of marriage to the impersonal detachment of separation. People are bewildered by the intensity of the emotions they feel for each other. The couple relationship is like no other in terms of intimacy. How, then, does one behave, act, and feel toward a person with whom one has shared such intimacy and with whom one has been family?

That which was shared will live on in each of them; even when the love bond has eroded, the ties persist. The patterns of interaction that couples develop together are not easily changed. They become as automatic as walking. Responses can be viewed as a chain reaction. One partner says something which triggers a familiar response which in turn gets a predictable reply. The couple is stuck with one script. They know what to expect from each other and what is expected from them. When the end of a marriage has been filled with bickering, criticism, and one-upmanship, this usually is the way people continue to behave toward each other in their early days of separation. They have not yet developed a new script. A number of separated women have discussed their confusion about visits their husbands make to see the children. As one woman said, she experienced a sense of excitement and anticipation about her husband's coming into their home. Though she rehearsed that she would deal with him in a casual and friendly manner, they were back into their old battle a few minutes after her husband arrived. He was criticizing, she was reacting. Another woman talked about her confusion when her husband came into the house, unannounced, went to the fridge, helped himself to food, went up to the bathroom, shaved—in short, carried on as though he were still living at home. She wondered, did he have that right? Did she want him to have the right? One man discussed his conflict about dealing with his visits to the children. He said he just couldn't ring the bell to his own home. He had retained the house key. To him giving that up symbolized a level of emotional separation for which he wasn't ready. Although he had initiated the separation since there was someone else in his life, and although he did not want to go back to the marriage, he found that he still needed to hold onto it in some way. It felt too final to take all his clothes out of the house. Moreover, he was always leaving something there. The house still felt like home to him and his apartment did not. He also reported that he rehearsed his behavior before visiting. He would be polite and distant; "after all," he would think, "she means nothing to me now." He would be polite and distant. But when he saw her, he didn't feel distant. There was a rush of warmth, the knowledge of her body, her smell, the memory of how she felt—all bombarding his senses; and yet when they started talking the hostility flowed back. Angry feelings were easier to deal with than the deceptive sense of warmth and the comfort of familiarity.

Negative emotions are as strong a force to keep people tied to each other as are feelings of love. Though hostile feelings are totally different, they keep the partners actively involved in each other's life. As long as these intense responses remain, the partner is not free to make a full commitment to another relationship.

The period immediately following the departure of one parent is the time of highest stress for each member of the family. There are numerous changes in personal and family life that must be faced immediately. Many people have said that despite preseparation preparation, they felt immobilized when this disruption became a reality. It is nearly impossible to foresee how the separation will affect the personal life of every member of the family. Important decisions must be made at a time when people feel least able to make decisions. Frequently people turn to family members, friends, clergy, lawyers, doctors, or mental health counselors to order their lives and relieve them of the burden of having to face issues.

These were some of the disturbing emotions that Evelyn reported (the reader will remember Evelyn, Kate, and Paula from our introduction and Chapter 1). She said she had not anticipated that once Ted had finally accepted that the marriage was over and that she really wanted him to leave her and the family home, she would be thrown into an intense crisis once he finally packed his bags and left. She felt she should have experienced only relief. Instead, she felt uprooted.

The plan to separate was certainly not an impulsive act; it had been germinating in her for the past few years. Yet once it was accomplished, she felt frozen! She wasn't sure where to begin, what to do first. As she sat on her bed that first day, wondering what steps to take, the phone rang. It was her mother. "How are you dear?" It was good to hear her mother's kindly voice. "I'm fine, Mother," said Evelyn, "how's Dad?" Her mother inquired about the children and then about Ted. Evelyn responded "Ted's fine. Mother, there is something I have to tell you." "What is it, dear?" "Mother, Ted and I have separated. Ted has moved out." There was a deadly silence at the other end. "Mother, are you there?" "Yes dear, I'll come right over," was her mother's reply. "Or maybe, Evelyn, it might be better for you and the children to come here. You will spend a few days here, to give us all time to decide how we should handle this." "Yes, Mother," said Evelyn. Suddenly she was the good little girl again, letting her mother tell her what to do! Her first impulse was to tell the girls to get ready to go. It might relieve the immediate tension she was feeling. But she stopped herself; she knew that this would be the simple thing to do but that if she succumbed to this impulse she would be allowing her parents to take over her life and once more make her their little girl. That could so easily happen and it would be comforting, but despite her despair, Evelyn realized that she would be defeating her own purpose. She must sort things out alone and decide what she needed to do to get started with her new life. Evelyn knew she must fight the urge to allow herself to be lulled back into the child's role by her well-meaning and protective parents. She must not permit herself the comfort of a return to mother's milk from which she might find it hard to wean herself. Evelyn was fully aware that her parents were lonely and that she and the children could give them back the parental role in which they had been happy. But she found the strength to assure herself that the separation was her problem, that she alone must make decisions. She could not satisfy her parents' needs by turning her life over to them.

She telephoned her mother, telling her that she needed a few days to sort things out. Her mother said she understood and then she added, "Let me take the children off your hands for a few days." When Evelyn declined, her mother assured her that all she wanted was to be able to help in any way and that she and dad were always there for her. Then her mother asked her, "Whose fault is it, dear? Is there anyone else? Do you think that Ted will change his mind and come home?" Evelyn replied wearily, "Mother, the decision to separate is mine. It's no one's fault and there is no one else. I have known for a long time that the marriage is no good for me. It is destroying me. I'm a nonperson with Ted." Evelyn knew it would be hard for her mother to understand how a marriage that could offer so much protection could not be good for her daughter. And her mother had not heard her; she was asking, "Have you told the children, Evelyn? Don't tell anyone just yet. You may change your mind and this is no one's business." "Yes, Mother," said the child part of Evelyn.

Evelyn's experience of telling her mother and receiving her mother's response to a separation is one that frequently occurs. The comforting support of parents and friends is, of course, very helpful. It can also be seductive and hard to resist. The opportunity to get some relief from the immediate tension is tempting. Social support from family and friends means that there are people who care about what is happening and want to offer their help. However, it is wise for separated people to be alerted to how to use help. Support can be nutritional, but it can also nurture dependency and foster weakness rather than offer strength when strength is most needed. The help that people can receive from counselors can be more productive for some people than that of family or friends, who cannot be objective and usually carry a bias to their own family member.

If Evelyn had followed her impulse to go to her parents' home, it might have defeated the goal that had helped her decide to leave the marriage. It would no doubt have served her parents' need to parent her, but she might then have had difficulty in disengaging herself from them. If she had permitted her first steps in reorganizing her life to be to move into her parents' home and become their little girl again and then move out to achieve her search for independence, she would have once more experienced loss and disorganization. Evelyn's determination to reject her mother's invitation was her first major step toward recognizing that she must draw on her own strengths.

There are a number of other pitfalls that can complicate the early stages of separation for some people. These complications tend to make readjustment and remarriage more difficult. For example, if Evelyn had succumbed to her mother's desire to shelter her daughters from the pain of the moment, her mother might have tried to protect Evelyn by taking care of the girls and entertaining and distracting them. This would have kept them away from Evelyn at a time when the separation was not only a crisis in her daughter's life but in her grandchildren's lives as well. Now was the time they would need one another, since the need for support and comfort between parent and children is essential at this time. Children must be helped to understand what is happening in their parents' lives and how it will affect family life. They must be involved in plans that are being made for reorganizing the family after separation.

The alternative to this kind of involvement is frequently seen in children of divorce who become socially withdrawn and depressed. If Evelyn's mother had advised the children not to tell anyone about their parents' separation, the message conveyed would have been that something terrible and shameful was happening in their family which must be kept secret. This can leave children burdened by a family secret that no one must know about. It preoccupies their thoughts, and if they cannot talk about the feelings that are uppermost in their minds, they are likely to withdraw from contact with their friends and isolate themselves. In efforts to cover up the family problem, parents frequently present two faces, one to the outside world and one at home. After all, "it's not necessary to air our dirty linen in public," is a frequently heard comment. So children are sent off to school, where they spend many hours of the day and many days of the week. But children are not as skilled as adults in the games of "cover up" and "carrying on as usual," and they display their upset and depression in different ways. Children can be aggressive or withdrawn and sullen. They are preoccupied with their internal upset and their classroom concentration can suffer. When parents restrict children from talking about family problems and the teachers in the classroom do not know what is happening in the child's life, the teacher may see only the symptomatic behavior of a child's not applying himself or herself, being belligerent or antisocial, or not concentrating or participating in classroom or social activities. The teacher may deal only with the behavioral manifestations at a time when understanding and social support could be so valuable. This kind of support from school, friends, and family can help to reduce the sense of aloneness during a family crisis.

In Evelyn's situation, her parents could have been significantly and productively helpful if they had understood more about Evelyn's reasons for leaving Ted and how the breakup of the family affected the girls. Grandparents can be an important support system. Their love and comfort can be a wonderful balm for wounds. But they can alienate the family if they introduce their own personal prejudices and judgments when the family is trying to come to grips with their own feelings and their own decisions. For instance, Evelyn's mother might have wished that Evelyn would come to her senses and return to the marriage and may have thus conveyed to the children that if it were not for their mother the family would not have to be going through this crisis. This would put a tremendous burden on Evelyn's role with the children, which could result in their feeling very hostile to her and sorry for their father. It could also foster the fantasy that surely their mother would smarten up and return to their father. This fantasy, which many children carry, sometimes for years, that their parents will reunite usually arises from not being helped to understand the reasons behind the separation and impending divorce. As long as this hope remains with the child, it becomes a major factor in resisting and resenting any intruder who would marry the parent and block the parents' reunion. As one child said sadly, "Now that my father has married, my mother will say, if he can do that, she'll do it too and then I'll lose both my parents." The dream of parental reunion is shattered when a parent remarries. A death wish fantasy may develop toward the new partner, or efforts may be made to sabotage the marriage with the hope that parents will then come back together.

The first few weeks after the separation, Evelyn went through a struggle of self-doubt, ambivalence, and loneliness. She felt she must sort things out and resist letting her parents influence her efforts to do so. She frequently had to fight against an impulse to get Ted's views on her plans. After all, she had always discussed everything with Ted. She kept telling herself that she must learn how to cope with this transition in her life alone. It was not that Evelyn had no friends, but she knew she had to develop her own resources. Her friends were ready and eager to advise her. But the most well-meaning advice usually has an overlay of the advisor's personal experience and personal bias. The end result could be conflicting ideas which end up confusing the questioner. Evelyn, aware that she had a tendency to rely on others to make decisions for her, did not want to fall into that trap now. Consequently, she deprived herself of the immediate comfort of support in order to build her own independent skills.

Now that she was alone, the house felt big and empty, the bed cold. A part of her knew that it wasn't Ted, the person, she was missing, but rather being part of a couple. The familiarity of all the daily routines, such as having her husband beside her when she awoke in the morning and when she went to bed at night, was gone. She missed shopping to prepare his favorite meals, setting his place at the table. Time began to lose its usual rhythm. The day no longer ended with Ted's coming home from work (she had to remind herself that she used to anticipate his coming home with dread because she felt her freedom was restricted when he was there). She missed the daily pattern of Ted's toilet habits, the smell of his shaving lotion in the bathroom, all the intimacies that couples live with, take for granted, and are not consciously aware of. All were absent now, reminding her that Ted was gone, that she was alone and would have to get used to it.

When she reviewed these lonely feelings, she wondered whether she wanted Ted back. Despite her loneliness in this new life, she knew her loneliness was not for Ted. Yet at night she found herself clutching the pillow where Ted had slept for so many years. She knew that she had not embraced Ted that way for a long time. In fact, she had withdrawn from his sexual advances. Sexual intercourse had felt like another form of control that Ted had imposed on her. Her body was the one thing she had felt that she could own. Even when she had submitted to sexual intercourse, Evelyn had withheld her sexual response. He couldn't order her to respond. As Evelyn lay in bed embracing Ted's pillow, she knew that she didn't want him there. Her loneliness was not for his comfort. What she was missing was being with a person, having a person with whom she shared the familiarity that is part of a couple relationship. The sociologist Robert Weiss in his book on marital separation refers to this feeling as "separation distress without an object" (p. 43).[2]

The first five to six months after separation were suprisingly difficult for Evelyn. When Ted called and she heard his voice it confirmed her feelings that she did not want him back in her life. He was not the object of her "separation distress." She avoided discussing her concerns or problems in adjusting, not wanting to hear his businesslike voice on the other end of the line organizing her next moves. She dreaded his patronizing way of conveying that he felt she needed help in making decisions. Ted had no comprehension of her level of anxiety in being able to handle her life and proving to herself that she could stand on her own two feet. The fear of whether one is going to be able to cope independently in the early stages of separation is fairly universal. Evelyn, like many other newly separated people, had to test her own resources for coping.

People manage in different ways during this period. There are many changes with which separated partners are confronted—changes in personal life, changes in ways of relating to a partner with whom you have spent intimate years. Separated people not only have to cope with their own personal feelings but have to deal with the feelings of family and friends about the separation. When the story of Evelyn's separation became public information, she found that even with her closest friends there was an embarrassment, a discomfort about how to respond to their reactions. Some friends extended congratulations saying, "That's great, Evelyn. You look as though you've got a new lease on life." Others offered condolences saying, "I'm sorry, Evelyn. If there's anything I can do, let me know. You look beat." These are common responses to news of a separation. There are no rules. It is not the same as the death of a friend's partner, when there is a ritualistic kind of sympathetic response. Friends attend the funeral and share the grieving period. In the case of separation, however, there are no guidelines on how to respond.

Several years ago *Mad Magazine* printed an article in which invitations were devised to be issued on the occasion of the unwedding ceremony. Invitations from the parents of "the soon-to-be-ex-Bride" proudly announced the divorce of "the beautiful, intelligent and sweet daughter" from "that foul-mouthed irresponsible sadistic, no-damn good megalomaniac son-in-law. Reception following the ceremony." Whereas the parents of "the soon-to-be-ex-Groom" invited their relatives and friends to their son's divorce from their daughter-in-law whom we "will not lower ourselves to describe."[3]

Despite the increase in divorce, marital separation has no institutional public form. For a separated person, social standing and social relationships change drastically. Friends may ally themselves with one partner and drop contact with the other. Or the separating persons may both be left out of social contacts because some friends do not want to discriminate against one or the other. To some people the fact that friends have broken off the marriage ties can feel like a threat to their own marriage relationship. It may be too close for comfort. Husbands may offer their sexual services. Some separated women may be seductive with their friends' husbands, chiefly to confirm their own sexual attractiveness. Frequently, invitations that may have previously been forthcoming are no longer issued. It is still a society of couples and a single woman may be a source of embarrassment, although a single man may be an asset. Well-meaning friends may extend invitations to separated women—to match them up with a separated man, as though, as in Noah's Ark, social relationships must come in couples.

Evelyn spent a good deal of time in the first year of separation reviewing what had gone wrong in her marriage and why she had decided to terminate it. Taking stock of the history of the years spent with Ted gave Evelyn a better understanding of herself, who she had been when she first married, and how her needs had changed during the marriage. She understood better how she had dealt with her growing discontent. Understanding Ted more now, she knew that he was not a bad man but that his idea of being a man and a good husband required having the power to control his family. The more he had controlled, she subsequently realized, the more she had withdrawn, which created more frustration for Ted and more need for him to exert control. A vicious cycle had taken place, with Ted aggressive and dominating and Evelyn passive-aggressive through withdrawal.

By ruminating on her marriage history, Evelyn gained an understanding of how she needed to change her pattern of response to domination. Her pursuit of self-awareness helped her to relate differently to her parents and to her friends and later aided her in selecting a man for her future marriage. Reviewing the history and problems that lead to the termination of a marriage is a valuable aid in putting a marriage to rest and being able to move on to future relationships. Separated people must understand their own share in what went wrong with the marriage.

It is often easier to attribute the problems of a marriage to the partner than to find one's own flaws. This was the way Kate dealt with the early stages of her separation from Jim. She could focus only on Jim's inadequacies, his lack of responsibility, and his deceptions. Her family and friends fortified her in this approach. Bringing them all into her adversarial camp with her side of the stories about Jim and their marriage, Kate had no awareness of how she had behaved throughout the marriage. She believed that her bitterness and sharp tongue were only reactions to Jim's behavior. She did not consider the possibility that she and Jim had been reacting to each other in destructive ways. The more she talked about him, the more sympathy she received for being a martyr. This response from her supporters heightened her hostile feelings and added to her justification for ending the marriage. She was so busy misusing her energies in a hate campaign that she remained locked into the battles of the past and had trouble getting on with reorganizing her life.

Kate's family and friends united with her to confirm how wise she was to move Jim out of her life. The "fault," the failure of the marriage, was attributed to Jim. Since no one questioned any share that Kate might have had in the faulty interaction of the couple, there was no attempt to involve Jim in plans for the separation. He was thus ousted from the family life and from his son's life. Kate had built up a backlog of resentment against him. She was blaming him for her life, which she found unstimulating and confining. She did not enjoy the housewife role and resented Scott for tying her down. She had not been ready for such commitment. She glorified the early years of the marriage and felt that Jim was still enjoying them without her. In her mind she imagined that her parents had given her a beautiful home, without realizing that the downpayment had involved Jim in a struggle to meet the payments on it. Nor did she understand that Jim was attempting to measure up to a standard of living that was not in keeping with his earnings. Failure to achieve this standard would have been considered a blow to his sense of adequacy, in Kate's eyes as well as in his. But these people kept their feelings to themselves and did not share them, thereby fostering mutual resentment, distance, and antagonism. This type of separation is not unusual when people leave a marriage in this manner. They most often do not gain any true insight into the role each played in the dissolution of the relationship. Kate's outbursts, filled with accusations, were not focused on particular issues. There was no beginning, no end, and no resolution to fights. Jim, who could not deal with anger, retreated. However, the more he withdrew the more strenuously Kate attacked. Interpreting his passivity as indifference, she concluded that his capacity for emotional involvement and commitment was limited. She had become a shrew and he was frightened by her violence. Rather than risk being honest with her, he deceived her in regard to issues that were upsetting to him, and he became increasingly deceptive. It was easier for him to lie to her than to face up to her attacks. But neither of them understood how each had contributed to the pattern of interaction that did not work for them and their marriage.

Kate's concerns after Jim left the home focused on her legal rights. She wasn't going to let him get away with anything. She was going to make him pay for her years of unhappiness and for carrying single-handedly all the home responsibilities. This was the attitude she brought into the lawyer's office. In discussion with her lawyer, she conveyed her reasons for wanting out of the marriage. The lawyer, a friend of Kate's father—who had in the past discussed Jim with him—supported her decision. He told Kate that he understood that Jim was a "taker" and that she deserved better. He assured her he would investigate Jim's income and get as much financial support for her as possible, even if it meant bringing Jim into court. Furthermore, he told her to leave all the arrangements to him and not to discuss anything with Jim. On leaving his office, Kate felt righteous in her conviction that she "had been done wrong." From the lawyer's office, she visited her parents' home to bring them up to date. Their response was similar to the lawyer's. They supported her and agreed that Jim was not trustworthy, that they had even known this for a long time. "Good riddance to him," was their response. Kate's parents and her lawyer formed an adversarial camp against Jim. There was no consideration given to Scott's feelings about the loss of his father.

Scott loved his father, but with all the disparaging attitudes that surrounded him, he did not feel free to convey his sadness, regrets, or sense of loss and loneliness. He heard only one parent's views and those were that his father was not worthy of his mother nor her family. Overhearing Kate's complaints to her parents and friends, he learned that Jim was neither dependable nor trustworthy as a husband and had not been a good father. The attacks on Jim were loud and clear. It was apparent to Scott that he had better ally himself with his mother or she might reject him too as unworthy. Jim's place in the family seemed easily covered over. Kate and her parents were now in control, and only Scott seemed to miss his father. Feeling lonely and abandoned, he did not know that his father had been warned by his mother and her lawyer not to contact his son until the child had learned to live in a one-parent family, and incidentally until Jim had discharged his financial responsibilities. This little boy felt lost in a home surrounded by adults who were busy talking to one another while no one was talking to him or recognizing that he was hurt, confused, and neglected. Jim did not contest the divorce, the custody arrangements, or the financial obligations. On all scores he acquiesced. This was easier for him than fighting Kate.

This type of separation is not unusual. The influence of the legal counsel, together with the adversarial stance of the family, can create a "fault" divorce situation. Jim was painted as the villain, Kate the innocent victim. Jim was therefore excluded from any decision-making in the separation agreement.

Divorce counseling or mediation might have been productive with both parents to involve them in arriving at some mutual decision about future arrangements. Instead, Jim was ordered to make childcare payments and told how and when he could see his son. Scott was left feeling that his father did not love him, which left him depressed and rejected. When marriages are terminated with one parent left out of the arrangements, the child can feel that he has been abandoned and that the divorce is not just between his parents but from him as well. When a parent is lost from family life, without the child's understanding the reasons, it can damage the child's trust in risking emotional commitment and intimacy in any future relationships. There was no finality for Scott, no closure for family life with his father; consequently, his sense of loss lived on.

In the way that Kate externalized the blame for the failure of the marriage onto Jim, some people tend to internalize the blame and see their marriage breakup as a result of their personal inadequacies. They are often heard to say, "I don't know what happened, I didn't know he or she was unhappy. How did I fail?" This was what Paula felt. Self-recriminations were all turned inward.

Paula had met Kate and Evelyn in the Remarriage Seminars, and the three women had formed a friendship. Different as they were, and different as their marriages and separations had been, they offered one another support and normal perspectives to some of their fears of remarriage. When Jack, Paula's husband, left her, she was devastated. Completely unprepared, she later said she had thought that she had had a good marriage and had no idea that Jack was unhappy. She blamed herself for being so obtuse and insensitive that she hadn't realized that the man she loved wasn't in love with her. Left in a state of shock, her emotions froze. From day to day she believed Jack would surely come home and they would take up their life together again. She kept telling herself that it was all a mistake, and that Jack would tell her that. He couldn't possibly be finished with their marriage. But Jack did not return.

Paula went through a period of depression; her sense of self-worth deteriorated. She could see only her own inability to keep the marriage. Making no attempt to come to grips with the reality that the marriage was over, she tried to carry on the daily routines as though Jack would be coming home any moment. When the phone rang, she jumped. The song "Let it be him" kept running through her mind. Shopping for Jack's favorite food, she would fantasize how pleased he would be when he came home to have his special meals—no one else could possibly know so well what pleased him. Dressed for dinner, she set Jack's place at the table. When the children asked if Daddy was coming home for dinner, Paula would say, "He may." She not only lived with denial for herself but allowed the children to live with the fantasy that their daddy would be coming home at any time. The family was in a holding pattern.

Gwen, their six-year-old child, who began watching Paula closely, was frightened by the dreamlike quality in which her mother appeared to be living. There was no doubt that Paula was in a daze. Paula looked back at this period as a nightmare from which she kept expecting to waken. Three weeks after Jack left home, Gwen jostled her into reality by asking timidly, "Mommy, where is Daddy eating and sleeping? Is he dead, Mommy?" Then Paula knew that she must pull herself together or she would be creating serious damage for her children. She had to tell the children that their father would not be coming home to live anymore, that he had moved out. Fighting her sense of numbness, she knew that she had to face reality for herself and for the sake of the children. In her state of crisis and shock, she had not been in touch with what Jack's absence meant to them. She had been so deeply involved with her own emotions that her ability to nurture the children had been minimal. Even getting out of bed in the morning was a burdensome task. She would pull the covers over her head and curl up fetal style to shut out the reality of the world.

Paula knew she had to begin to rally, to come out of the cocoon into which she had withdrawn. Looking at her children as though for the first time, she thought, "They are beautiful and tender and sensitive." She told herself that she mustn't damage them. Then anger began to emerge. "How can he leave his children whom he says he loves?" The anger energized her. Paula determined that she must pull herself together and learn to live without Jack. Though she had lost her husband, she must realize that the children had lost their father. In the state of turmoil that Paula had been in, she had given them little in understanding and attention. She now began to emerge from the state of crisis and to plan for a different kind of life for the family.

Paula's state of imbalance and turmoil is not unusual when a marriage terminates, particularly without advance preparation. It is important for people who experience this kind of disruption in their lives to know that the emotions of panic they may experience are not unique to them. It does not necessarily mean they are experiencing psychiatric or pathological disorder. Professional help can be very supportive in this difficult period of family disorganization. It is useful for people who are living through the stress of a life crisis to know that it is natural and normal to feel somewhat derailed. The crisis of separation is a shock to the nervous system no matter how good or bad the marriage. Unquestionably, breakdown in a marriage changes life radically. For partners who make a mutual decision to separate, it is less stressful than when only one partner arrives at this decision and then informs the unprepared mate. Ending a marriage with a unilateral decision, as Jack did, can throw the unprepared partner and the children into a state of imbalance. Separation is a major life crisis and requires preparation for future family plans.

Marriages end. There is pain and adjustment when the family is divided, but it should not be necessary for their whole world to crumble around them. Parents who plan to leave a marriage have a grave responsibility to each other and to their children to prevent unnecessary turmoil. The decision to separate cannot be unilateral. There are transitional stages that must be respected from the time the plan to separate is made to the time of preparing the members of the family to accept the decision. Incorporating the knowledge that the family will be divided takes time for everyone. Children cannot be expected to be told the night before the separation and to accept it easily. They must recognize that their parents have had a struggle to reach the decision. Since everyone's life—including the children's—will change, all the family members should know how the changes will be dealt with. The ways these stages are handled are closely related to how each member of the family will be able to cope with the separation and later with a parent's remarriage.

REFERENCES

[1]Glick, P. C., and Norton, A. J. "Frequency, Duration and Probability of Marriage and Divorce." *Journal of Marriage and the Family*, 1971 33, 307–317.
[2]Weiss, R. S. *Marital Separation*. New York: Basic Books, 1975.
[3]Doud, E. "Unwedding of the Future." *Mad Magazine*, June 1976.

CHAPTER 3

GOING IT ALONE

A TIME OF STRESS

Students of crisis report that being thrown into a crisis situation may result in beneficial effects. It may lead to a more adequate or higher level of functioning, although, on the other hand, it may result in a lower level of functioning and a lower level of mental health.

Marital separation is just such a crisis in the life of the family. The peak point of the crisis is at the time when the actual physical separation is taken. Former habits must now be changed.

No matter how unhappy the marriage may have been and how often the couples have threatened to leave each other, once they actually separate and one partner moves out, this is the public declaration that the marriage is over. The accustomed pattern of life changes in this crisis as it does in other life event crises. The members of the family are thrown into a state of disequilibrium. The separated partners must make immediate important major decisions about where to live, legal matters of childcare and custody, visitation rights, financial arrangements, and division of property and possessions accrued in the life the marriage. All these decisions are fraught with tension at a time when emotional stress is at a peak. Even the most decisive people, whose skills in making decisions and solving problems have always been effective, report that during this period of separation they feel inadequate, helpless, and ineffectual. Some people describe physical symptoms. They have trouble breathing, they tend to sigh deeply, their eating and sleeping patterns are disturbed. They report a sense of physical exhaustion.

Studies report that the acute stages of a crisis are of short term. They are characterized by tensions that rise to a peak, subside, then peak again. The stress does not signify that the members are sick; it is an appropriate response to the time of crisis. The ability to cope with the crisis productively can improve one's mental health and leave one with more self-confidence. As the crisis phase subsides, people begin to regain some balance, but there are ups and downs in mood fluctuations for many months to come, frequently for as long as a year. For people with family and friends, there is comfort and support to help them through the difficult days. For separated persons without this network of support, groups like Parents Without Partners and Single Parent groups are now available in most communities. These groups can offer valuable sources of friendship, shared experiences, and normal perspectives.

Once the crisis period begins to abate, people tend to move through transitional stages in accepting and adapting to different lives out of marriage. People are different and the circumstances in their separation are different. There is no one way of coping. Some people become dependent and take regressive steps and make maladaptive adjustments to their life situation. Others report impulsiveness, on-the-spot decisions that are reactive to feelings of the moment, while still others complain about feeling stuck in a morass of indecisiveness. Some people, on the other hand, are able to use the crisis as a turning point toward growth that is productive and enhances their feelings of confidence about themselves. They begin to understand that they can handle their lives independent of the marriage and become more self-reliant in restructuring their lives. However, this does not happen overnight.

Studies report that it takes one to two years or longer for most people to get on with their personal and interpersonal lives comfortably. In the process of adjusting, people experience fairly universal stages. These stages are similar to adjustment in other major life event stress, like the death of a spouse. Elisabeth Kübler-Ross in *On Death and Dying* lists grief responses to the death of a spouse that range from shock and denial to anger, bargaining, depression, and finally acceptance (pp. 34–99).[1] Crisis is a state of temporary disequilibrium.

Robert Weiss describes experiences of shock and denial immediately following separation.[2] He reports that during this period some people tend to retain their preseparation routine and pattern of life as though nothing had happened. Robert Garfield, a psychiatrist, describes the separation process as it moves from a "relationship loss" to a "period of mourning" to a "healing process" (pp. 4–14).[3] The transition phases are described as being literally *in transit* whether it be adjustment following the loss of a partner through death or through marital separation.

Holmes and Rahe,[4] in their social Readjustment Rating Scales of Life Events, rated divorce the highest stress second only to death of a spouse. In separation adjustment, moods tend to fluctuate between despair and euphoria. The individual's perception of self, and how he or she believes others are viewing the marriage break-up, is affected. There is a loss of the continuity of personal identity; now that one is no longer a wife or a husband, the sense of self must be redefined. The stability of familiar anchors, physical and social, like home, in-law relations, former associations and activities, all become skewed. In a crisis period former coping skills may not work. This is a normal, not a pathological response to crisis. Most people in a crisis event experience a state of shock and numbness: the "frozen" feelings. Thinking is frequently somewhat disoriented, and when realization strikes home that the marriage is really over, other emotions pour in. The usual course of feelings ranges from anxiety to depression to guilt and anger. There is a general sense of mourning for what was and what could have been. As people begin to live with the reality of the loss of the marriage, they tend to move back and forth between denial and acceptance. Depression and anger characteristically dominate feelings. Anger is a natural part of the grieving process. It must be dealt with or it will keep cropping up in situations and with people where it can be destructive. Anger can be projected onto the children, or family, or friends, or business associates, and if it is not dealt with it can affect future relationships. It is difficult to form new attachments until the old emotions are finished.

Paul Bohannan, an anthropologist, in his book *Divorce and After* describes six "stations" involved in divorce. These range from emotional divorce to legal divorce to economic divorce to coparental divorce to community divorce, and finally to psychic divorce (pp. 34–62).[5] In varying degrees and with a range of different problems for different persons, these stations describe the usual route that people take in the separation–divorce process.

We have described the crisis period following separation as either maladaptive and regressive or growth-enhancing. Now we will look at ways in which separated partners and their families begin the tasks of restructuring life into separate-parent households. Since the family home is usually with the mother, we will first consider the mother-headed household and then the noncustodial household with a father who has been granted "visitation access" to his children.

The separated and divorced family is frequently referred to as the "broken" or "fractured" family. This view of the family in divorce conveys a picture of a pathological family with only one parent. Unless a parent has opted out of the family life, the divorced family has not disintegrated. It has, rather, reorganized. Most frequently, whatever the custody arrangements, there are still two parents who in some ways are both parenting their children. Restructured families with parents living in separate households have not yet achieved social normality in the family life cycle, despite the large numbers of binuclear families with two parents in two homes. Separated families continue to be considered deviant. Moreover, the finger is pointed at children of divorce as being at higher risk for displaying delinquent behavior. Children are, in fact, overrepresented in treatment centers. This may, in part, grow out of their feeling that they are viewed as different from other children and other families. However, consideration must also be given to disturbing events that led to the parental separation. The preseparation family tensions can certainly play havoc with children's emotions and behavior. The behavior of parents prior to and after the separation affect the children, as does the later relationship between the ex-spouses and the ways they are able to work out their coparenting arrangements. These factors all deeply influence the behavior of children of divorce. We do not have to stretch our imagination to project ourselves into the life of a family that once was intact but is now divided into two parts. Whatever the couple have shared they must now learn to live with differently, whether it be children, home, furniture, car, dog, or cat. Everything that was "theirs" now becomes "his" or "hers." Emotions get mixed up in decisions about the possessions. As one woman said, "How can he expect me to take care of the children, have a home for them, while he insists that I give him the beds, the chesterfield, the desk, and the books?" while the man retorted "I've got to live too. I need a home, I worked hard for everything you think is yours." One home and its belongings, one income split between two households. Two people who have loved each other and shared their lives find it hard to believe there can be so much hostile and punitive behavior between them.

When partners separate, each keeps rehashing and reviewing the events that led to the split. Weiss[2] refers to this as taking inventory. I am always impressed with the different perceptions of "his" marriage and "her" marriage, two different pictures of one union, each partner struggling with the dissatisfactions that he or she had felt in the marriage. The retrospective examinations are filled with many "maybes" and "if onlys." The more frequently I hear the "if only" reports, often tinged with deep regrets, the more convinced I am that separating couples must get beyond the day-to-day conflicts that are symptoms of the discontent and get down to the underlying problems.

In the book *The Intimate Enemy* George Bach and Peter Wyden (p. 76)[6] aver that many marriages that flounder or break down could be saved if people learned the art of fighting "fair," that is, learn to discern the origins of the fights and then learn to negotiate their differences. This course of identifying the true problems that have led to the breakup of a marriage and then coming to agreement about the terms of separation can lead the partners toward understanding the ways in which they have used destructive emotions with each other. To finish a marriage with this kind of understanding and resolution can reduce hostile tensions. It is than more likely that coparenting will be more compatible and future relations more amicable.

When couples separate so much is happening at the same time. While the partners are grieving over the loss of the marriage, they are also required to adjust to a different style family life, and at the same time they are involved in working out their parenting roles and responsibilities. Since there is no easy solution to dividing children equally, like some property, mothers usually are made the primary caretakers. Women who are sole custodial parents then have the responsibility of reorganizing not only their personal life but the life of the separate parent household. Naturally coping devices are different. Some women can move through this transitional phase effectively. Others find that their energy is consumed by the struggle of making personal adjustments and they frequently have little energy left for nurturing their children. At the time that the children most need parental support, it may be at the lowest level. It can be difficult to meet children's dependency when your own is hungry for fulfillment.

There are some custodial mothers who may need to compensate for the failure of the marriage and strengthen their enfeebled feelings of self-worth by making their full emotional investment in their children and trying to be "super moms."

Then there are some mothers who lose confidence in their ability to carry all the parenting responsibilities alone. They feel frightened and inadequate. They often report they are inconsistent with their children. They throw out orders, criticisms, and judgments depending on their moods and then back down because they do not have the energy to persist or deal with the forthcoming resistance. Mothers ofter admit that they feel guilty at unfairly unloading their pent-up emotions onto the children. A cycle of responses can be engenderd. The children are also upset and respond negatively to their mother's emotional behavior, and everbody is then over-reactive, hurting one another at a time when each needs the other most. Researchers have recently reported that boys have a more difficult time adjusting to their parents' divorce than do girls. Wallerstein and Kelly (p.165fn)[7] cite Mavis Hetherington's data showing sons to be more vulnerable than daughters. Wallerstein and Kelly report further that boys manifest increased aggression and need for attention and also take a longer time to settle into the reorganized family life than girls do. Mothers say that difficulties with sons add to their agitation and resentment about the separation. They feel they are not able to give their sons the discipline that fathers can give, and they also feel their sons are not so ready to accept ground rules from mothers. Many mothers have reported their feeling that men get off scot-free in the matter of responsibilities, and yet the same women do not want to forego their custodial status. It becomes a Catch-22 situation.

Another stress factor, a major difficulty for the custodial mother, is the financial situation. The same income that had supported one household is now supporting two. When mothers are the parents providing a home for the children, they resent the fact that the noncustodial father has only himself to care for. Many women feel that the childcare allowances, if forthcoming at all, are not adequate to provide for the children's needs. Here, too, the extent to which emotional resolution has been achieved by the separated partners often affects the willingness of the men to continue to provide the childcare monies. Many fathers who withhold payments or make sporadic contributions are usually expressing their hostile, punitive feelings not toward the children but toward the children's mother. A *Newsweek* article (January 10, 1983) reported that the custodial mother's income was reduced by 73% by the end of the first year after separation.[8] Women who have primarily been the homemakers, not the moneymakers, are often thrown into a panic and say "How am I going to be able to provide for my children?" The panic is justified since only one-third of divorced women receive regular child support payments from their husbands and many women do not receive any support by the end of the first year of separation. Does this mean that fathers do not love their children or that they are irresponsible? Or is it yet another acknowledgment that the legal process governing separation and divorce needs reform in the light of the recognized negative effect of its present adversarial nature? Money, custody, and visitation access are the chief weapons when the marital battle continues after separation and divorce. Losing custody of a child leaves many men feeling they are less of a father, and they may refuse to make payments to a former wife who is solely responsible for rearing the children. This can result in severe financial distress for sole-custody mothers, particularly if they have not been kept informed about income and money management by their husbands. Many women report that they do not even know the amount of the family income or where and when bills are paid. Many wives have not had any independent source of income or even a bank account. After separation women who are so woefully uninformed about practical financial issues are at a severe disadvantage. This financial dependence is frequently accompanied by emotional dependence and a marital history of accountability. It is difficult to feel like an independent adult capable of making decisions and running a household when one does not have any money.

Despite the financial pressures, many homemakers are not equipped with skills for entering the labor market. They may have gone from the dependency of the parental home right into marriage. Most women who work after marriage still remain at home during the child-rearing years or work only on a part-time basis. Even the increasing number of married women who are permanently in the labor market for the most part have not been the chief wage earners. This all means that in addition to the stress involved in reorganizing family life after separation women face the necessity of *achieving* financially independent status. They must now redefine their roles. They become responsible for carrying out two jobs, one as homemaker, the other as at least partial breadwinner. Alimony, when paid, is usually for a limited time to allow women a brief period to learn some working skills. These are some of the major hardships for the sole custodial mother.

Catherine Napolitane and Victoria Pellegrino in *Living and Loving After Divorce* relay the comments of one woman after divorce who said she was left "reeling from all the changes I had to make in my life and all the problems I had to confront. I was scared; I was lonely; and I had to take care of two children all by myself. I had little money, no job and I was bitter about the fact that my husband had told me he was in love with another woman"(p. 13).[9] Whether or not there is another woman involved, this is the frightened cry I have heard from many women. The extent of the emotional upheaval and the financial anxiety are largely determined by how dependable the financial situation is; this in turn depends on how much a woman can learn about financial management. When the divorcing spouses are both determined that their children must not suffer from financial uncertainties, the stress of separation and reorganization will be considerably reduced.

Most women must work after separation, whether or not they had worked before. This has proved to be a benefit for many women in adapting to a different personal life. The essential factor is that in order to reorganize and stabilize family life the custodial parent must have a dependable income, whether it is through consistent childcare allowances or by supplementation from self-employment.

The ages of the children and the community facilities are other determining factors in work programs. If the children are young, daycare arrangements must be made for them. Women with young children have described the hectic pace involved in screening the inadequate supply of daycare facilities and then taking the children to babysitting arrangements before work, picking them up at the end of the working day, and then starting the housekeeping and childcare responsibilities, preparing meals, bathing the children, putting them to bed. There is frequently no respite, no time for oneself, little time for recreational or social life. The mother who carries the sole custody of her children is therefore left with financial pressures and an overload of tasks. There is no one with whom to share responsibilities. The day of a divorced woman can feel like joyless drudgery. This frequently increases her anger at the husband whom she perceives as scot-free and having only himself to worry about.

However, the "scot-free" noncustodial father tells a different story, a tale of loneliness and dislocation from his familiar world. As a result of having lost his home and family life, he feels less of a father when he sees his children infrequently. He reports that he becomes confused about how to be a father while he is a visitor with his own children. A study[10] with men who were interviewed six to twelve months after divorce reported that 60% of the respondents described loneliness as their major emotional problem. Marriage leads to an attachment that remains long after even the most unsatisfactory marriage is legally ended. Anger is generated by both separating partners when they are not able to work out their differences and share the responsibilities for their children. One study reported that divorced men have a higher rate of psychiatric admissions than do divorced women. The authors add that "more than seven percent of males with disrupted marriages are hospitalized annually because of psychiatric condition."[10] This study of divorced men also reported a higher vulnerability to accidents and alcoholism. Whereas women, in spite of all the financial and child care pressures, retain the familiar structure of their family lives with children, men have only their daytime structure but no family home life at the end of the day. The result is that the sole custody mother has too much family responsibility and the noncustodial father is bereft of family tasks and family identity. The separated women and the children of divorced parents have received more attention than the divorced noncustodial father, who has suffered the loss of family and parental identity.

Women have more difficulty getting back into the mainstream of social life then do men, who are popularly received as being readily free and accessible for dating. However, men say that they tend to get involved in a flurry of social activities as a way of resolving their loneliness and identity problems.

For both separated men and women, disruption to marriage is described as a "stressor of the first magnitude." The National Center for Health Statistics reports that important links have been established between marital disruption and death rates. Suicide, homicide, and disease mortality are all higher for persons who experience the stress of marriage breakdown.

Sole custody mothers sometimes forfeit the parental executive functions; the generational parent–child boundaries can become blurred. A child may take on parenting roles and responsibilities for the younger children or may develop a sibling relationship with the mother; or there can be a role reversal between mother and child, with the child taking care of and protecting the mother. Some mothers become so overinvolved with their children that both they and the children are inhibited in pursuing peer relationships.

When the custody disposition is sole custody to mother and the father is displaced from custodial rights, each parent tends to see the other in a preferred position. The woman can feel overwhelmed by her family and financial pressures, whereas the man is resentful that his basic parental role has been taken away from him and that the only ties permitted him are visiting and the obligation of financial support. With the adversarial procedure and the hostility and resentment fostered by it everybody loses. It appears that much of the loss could be reduced by changing the custodial system, which in turn would ease the burden of overload for mothers and role loss for fathers. In that event the couple, though separated, could still both remain parents and share the parental responsibilities.

Studies of coparenting patterns indicate that fathers who remain actively involved with their children are known to be more dependable in maintaining both the fathering role and financial responsibilities. There continue to be divided attitudes in the legal and mental health fields about different coparenting relationships for divorced persons. The opinion shared by some professionals is that couples would not have divorced in the first place if they had been able to agree on anything and that conflictual marital attitudes would carry over into their agreement on decisions about their children's lives. When friendship or reasonably amicable feelings continue between divorced partners, some people tend to be suspicious, presumably wondering why the couple had to divorce in the first place. There is little acknowledgment that two people may not be able to retain emotional compatibility in the intimacy of married life but can still, so long as they live apart, sustain a friendship.

Divorce signifies the legal end to the marriage. Each partner must then redefine the unmarried relationship and the new parental role. What once constituted an intact family still has the same people in it, the same two biological parents and their children. But the geography is different, and all relationships will inevitably change. To make rules to assure separateness and independence for the ex-partners and security and comfort for the children will require maturity, patience, and much careful thought.

Some of the couples whom I counseled while they were in the process of separation vowed that they did not want to get caught up in the contentious court scenes with all the mud-slinging. Unfortunately, once the legal process gets under way, angry, punitive and competitive feelings too often emerge. Men often complain that they feel it is unfair to have to take responsibility for a woman who is no longer their wife. One man, who moved out of the home he had worked hard to provide, said, "Why should I continue to support you in the style to which you have become accustomed?" His wife retorted, "I made the house into a home for you and our children. I helped you to arrive at where you are. You made the money, but without me the money wouldn't have made a home and our children." Recently, one woman whose husband had left her for another partner was overheard saying, "Every successful man owes his success to his first wife, and his second wife to his success." She added, "I made my husband feel good and strong about himself and now he thinks he's too good for me." Each partner is fighting for his or her own survival and no longer trusts that his or her rights will be acknowledged.

It takes time to deal with the crisis of separation, to reorganize personal life and family and social relationships. Many separated people report that it takes the better part of two years to be finished with the former marital attachment and ready to begin anew.

In the process of separation people report that they become fair game for advice mongers—everyone seems to have the right answers for how they should reorganize their lives. This is not to gainsay the comfort of family and friendly support. But it can be confusing to be surrounded by differing and often conflicting points of view, many of which reflect other people's personal struggles. If people are to stabilize their own lives, they must themselves find the directions each wants his or her life to take.

One woman recently reported that her parents urged her to move in with them, whereas a friend who had lived through her own divorce struggle warned, "Don't do it, you'll get trapped there. They'll turn you into their little girl and think they have a right to tell you what to do. They'll take your children away and they will become their parents." Another friend urged her to "get out of the house, sell it, get rid of all the associations with the marriage, and start a new life." Others advised her "to move out of town, to put all the upsets about the marriage and the divorce behind her for her and for the children." It was all so confusing. She knew the advice came from people who cared about her and sympathized with her pain, and yet she also knew that she had to work out her own plans.

The soundest route during this turbulent period is, if at all possible, not to make major decisions and changes until emotions simmer down and judgment becomes more stable. It is also wise, when possible, to reduce the number of external changes to a minimum while in the process of adjusting to the disruptions in the intact family life. As much of a sense of continuity as possible should be retained in regard to the family, friends, and familiar places such as home, neighborhood, schools, and so forth. It takes time for each of the separated partners to adjust to the new unmarried identity. Once people begin to feel self-reliant and make independent decisions, they begin to build a stronger sense of identity and feeling of wholeness. This gives a sense of freedom which after an unhappy marriage can prove to be a liberating force.

Loneliness is perhaps the most debilitating emotion that separated people feel. It can be difficult, particularly for women, to get back into the social stream. Despite the progress of the liberated woman, most women continue to be less assertive than men in taking the initiative in establishing male–female relationships. There may be brief sexual encounters, but women report that they feel apprehensive about making any emotional commitment when they are recovering from a former marriage. The initial sexual experiences many women have after separation are reported to arise out of the need to confirm their sexuality and desirability, particularly when the marriage has ended with partners withdrawing from each other sexually and perhaps denying that the sexual satisfactions within the marriage have ever been fulfilling. A recent study of women after separation showed that four out of five women had sexual relations shortly after separation and most involved themselves with casual sexual activity with more than one man. The same study reported that the most important factor after separation which leads both men and women back toward a positive self-concept, is the establishment of a satisfying heterosexual relationship (p. 195).[10]

This chapter has dealt with the crisis period following separation and the pain and struggle required to restructure personal and family life. This struggle and the long period of time required to stabilize life are neither unusual nor pathological. There are, however, external forces that complicate the process and increase the pain. The next chapter will discuss legal changes that may be able to reduce the overload of tasks for women and the sense of loss involved for men.

REFERENCES

[1] Kübler-Ross, E. *On Death and Dying*. New York: Mcmillan, 1969.
[2] Weiss, R. S. *Marital Separation*. New York: Basic Books, 1975.
[3] Garfield, R. "Mourning and Its Resolution for Spouses in Marital Separation." In *Therapy with Remarriage Families*, edited by L. Messinger. Rockville, Maryland: Aspen Publications, 1982.
[4] Holmes, T. H., and Rahe, R. H. "The Social Readjustment Rating Scale" *Journal of Psychosomatic Research*, 1967, *11*, 213–218.
[5] Bohannan, P. "The Six Stations of Divorce." In *Divorce and After*, edited by P. Bohannan. New York: Doubleday, 1968.

[6]Bach, G. R., and Wyden, P. *The Intimate Enemy.* New York: William Morrow, 1969.

[7]Wallerstein, J., and Kelly, J. B. *Surviving the Break Up.* New York: Basic Books, 1980.

[8]"Divorce American Style." *Newsweek,* CI:2, 42–48, January 10, 1983.

[9]Napolitane, C., and Pellegrino, V. *Living and Loving After Divorce.* New York: Rawson Assoc. 1977.

[10]Bloom, B. L., White, S. W., and Osher, S. J. "Marital Disruption as a Stressful Life Event." In *Divorce and Separation,* edited by G. Levinger and O. C. Moles. New York: Basic Books, 1979, p. 187.

CHAPTER 4

SEPARATION AND THE CUSTODY DILEMMA

All litigations evoke intense feelings of animosity, revenge, and retribution. But none of them in their most aggravated form can equal the sheer unadulterated venom of a matrimonial contest.

LOUIS NIZER, *My Life in Court*[1]

Divorce is an accepted solution to an unhappy marriage. However, inherent in the solution is the controversial and painful dilemma of what to do about the children: who will have custody and how can both parents remain actively involved in their children's lives? After all, whose children are they anyhow? From a legal standpoint, the "best interests" of the child have generally been the basis for establishing custody arrangements, but there are few guidelines to determine how these interests can best be served. The decisions are influenced by the extent of the agreement between the divorcing parents, as well as society's attitudes about who is the parent better suited to serve the child's best interests. In addition, legislative decisions are largely based on the adversarial system which determines that one parent is more fit than the other. Parents, society, and law have not been able to arrive at any consensus as to how the "best interests" of

71

the child can be served when parents divorce. And this issue continues to be the overriding problem.

There are many factors that affect custody decisions and no one ruling fits all parents or all children, but there are alternatives to which parents and the law should give greater consideration.

There is enough evidence to demonstrate that children and their parents do not want to lose one another. If this is true, the present legal insistence on sole custody or no custody appears restrictive and unrealistic. It establishes a conflict of interests. The custody principle refers to the legal rights, privileges, and responsibilities a parent has for the minor-age child. "Sole" custody, which in 90% of divorce cases is currently awarded to the mother, gives her the sole legal rights and responsibilities for her child to the exclusion of the father. This arrangement has inherent in it the fact that the father is removed from retaining legal rights and responsibilities for his child. He is thus assigned to a noncustodial status with visitation access and with the obligations to pay child support. It is in this area of noncustody with visitation access that there is the greatest emotional difficulty for fathers and their children.

Divorce will always be a devastating experience, but it need not be a completely destructive one. Breaking off family ties can be hazardous to mental health. Meyer Elkin of the Association of Conciliation Courts comments:

> Throughout the centuries, the law has been concerned with the strengthening and preservation of family life. But when families sought divorce, this concern was shed and replaced by punitive attitudes and practises despite the fact that families are forever. Social concern for the family should not be selective. Concern for families should apply to all families, not just those who are defined as intact. (pp. 85–86)[2]

Up to the end of the nineteenth century, fathers maintained custody of their children and mothers were considered dependent chattel. In the twentieth century numerous social and economic changes (not the least of these was the influence of psychoanalytic theory and a new understanding of the mother–child bond) led to a reversal of this practice, and the mother became, almost invariably, the sole custodian. Historically, custody dispositions have meant that the child was placed in the sole care of one parent. A large body of opinion continues to support this belief that children need the continuity of one parent and cannot be divided between both parents. However, the losses involved in removing a parent from a child's life because of divorce are proving to be abominably destructive.

Options to sole and noncustody are meeting with increasing approval, and a variety of different custodial arrangements are being considered by some parents. The legal definitions for such options are not as yet standard, and custody arrangements are referred to in different terms and executed in diverse ways. In the final analysis, the effectiveness of any custody arrangements rests with the parents and their attitudes toward each other.

The responsibilities given to a custodial parent deal primarily with health care, education, religion, and vocational training; that is, matters of physical, intellectual, and spiritual care along with those covering protection, security, and safety. Custody has usually been considered to be synonymous with residential accommodation. However, when both parents participate in decision making for the children regarding major events in the children's lives, this is legally referred to in a variety of ways which include joint, divided, alternating, shared, split, and co-custody. When parents agree that they will both remain active in making decisions for the best interests of the child, it does not necessarily mean that the children will spend equal living time with each parent. This misguided assumption is probably the one that creates the most disapproval for joint custody or coparenting arrangements.

Whatever arrangements are made for the physical, emotional, and social care of the children depend on what is appropriate for a particular family. The parental attitude with which the decisions for childcare are arrived at and how they are carried out is more significant than the court's determination. When the marital battle continues after the divorce, the children are likely to be caught in the middle of punitive and competing forces.

Since divorce is the legal death of a marriage, the family unit is disorganized. This should not, however, result in the death of the family, but rather in its reorganization. The parents are no longer a married couple living together, but they are still the children's parents. Divorce does not create a single parent, but rather separated parents. Hence, the *single-parent family* is a misnomer. It is tied in with the sole custody disposition. The household contains a single parent, but the parent–child–family membership is not changed. The separated parents in the maternal and the paternal homes form subsystems of the former unit of an intact family. The expressions *sole custody* and *single parenthood* negate the reality that children of divorce continue to have two parents.

Parents have the responsibility to keep their marital feelings out of the parental relationships. When they are capable of doing this, there is more likelihood that they will be able to allow each other to remain as parents in the children's lives without imposing their personal prejudices on the children. Once this is achieved, life will be easier for everyone in the event that one or both parents remarry. The new partner(s) would then be able to carve out a role that would not compete or undermine the natural parent's role. Consequently all members—parents, stepparents, and kinfolk, biological and step—would be family to the children.

How can an amicable custody agreement be achieved between divorcing partners, and how will a new partner in a marriage feel about their mates' continued relationship with his or her former spouse? Is this a realistic and practical proposal? Maybe not for some people who are divorcing and maybe not for some other people who are remarrying, but for many people it could work, if necessary with professional help.

The concept of ex-spouses planning to continue to share the parenting of their children is relatively new. It requires clear role definitions for permanent coparent relationship. It enforces the reality that the remarriage has ongoing ties to the first marriage that must be acknowledged by the second marriage partners if it is to work.

During the stressful period of separating, the first traditional step that couples take is to seek legal counsel in order to learn what rights and responsibilities each should have. Married couples have shared important parts of their lives; they may have acquired homes and such assets as a summer cottage, cars, boats, and other material goods in addition to the children they have borne and raised together. Each turns to a legal counsel for protection against losing his or her share in what was acquired during the marriage. The job of a legal counsel is to advise the client about his or her legal rights. Some people report that in selecting a counsel they are advised to get a "tough" lawyer who will fight the battle for them. This advice is inherent in the prevailing adversary system which pits husband and wife against each other. When partners are separating and their tensions are at a peak, their judgment is frequently distorted. They are confronted with some of the most important decisions that will affect them and their children, as well as a division of financial assets. They turn to their lawyers for help. Each brings the story of the failure of the marriage to the lawyer. Each lawyer hears only the one-sided version. Since the lawyer's job is to defend his client, he assures his client that he will do everything to protect his or her interests, and that he does. A growing number of people agree that the adversarial system operates against the spirit of mutual agreement which in turn affects the chances for cooperation between parents in deciding together about plans for their children.

The prevailing adversary system can blur the issues in considering what constitutes the child's best interest, since issues concerning custody become mixed up with those concerning finances. Once litigation gets started, hostilities often tend to snowball. I must add that all divorce lawyers are not out to "get" their client's spouse, but they do have an inevitable bias in favor of their client. For the most part, a lawyer's training is not geared to the subtle emotional needs of a client, which are turbulent at the time of divorce.

Thus, the two major decisions that must be made at this time are: how the children will be cared for and by whom, and how to divide the finances, including income and savings, the matrimonial home, and other assets acquired throughout the life of the marriage.

Certainly family law is in the process of change, including the rights of the partners in the dissolution of a marriage. Moreover, what constitutes the best interest of the child is now being reassessed. There are still, however, a number of punitive components in the divorce procedure. Emotional situations tend to become exacerbated through the proceedings of traditional family law. Too often, decisions are recommended and enforced for people when they are suffering in a state of crisis. There is, to date, no formal encouragement or support for separating people who have shared a life together to make decisions together for the custody and care of their children. Elkin reports that "law and psychology have not touched similar bases in their common concern for humanity and the resolution of human problems" (p. 83).[2] Yet a growing number of family lawyers and therapists have emerged who believe that the two professions should join forces in a cooperative effort to help couples work through custody decisions. The increased incidence of kidnapping or child snatching by a noncustodial parent has reached alarming and damaging proportions. It would be interesting to know the motives behind this action. Is it because the noncustodial parent refuses to lose the child or because, as is commonly assumed, he or she is out to punish the former spouse? For whatever the reason, a parent's snatching the child from his assigned custodial parent demonstrates that the parent's need rather than the child's best interests is obviously of foremost consideration.

A dichotomy of views about the child's best interests prevail. On one extreme are Goldstein, Freud, and Solnit, who, in their book *Beyond the Best Interests of the Child*[3] contend that the psychological continuity of one parent in the life of the child serves the child's best interests. They further advance the position that since couples who divorce are not amicable enough to share parenting, the child would be caught in the middle of their conflicts. They recommend sole custody with the custodial parent having complete and exclusive control over the care and protection of the child. The noncustodial parent "should have no legally enforceable right to visit the child and the custodial parent should have the right to decide whether it is desirable for the child to have such visits" (p. 88).[2] This has the obvious potential of meaning that the parent with custody can determine whether or not the child should visit with his noncustodial parent, a decision which could be based on personal and punitive feelings. The opposing view, expressed by Roman and Haddad in *The Disposable Parent*,[4] strongly favors joint custody based on the father's increasingly equal role to the mother's in family life. Their research on divorced parents who share the responsibilities of bringing up their children demonstrates that when the child's needs are considered paramount, the parents learn how to separate their marital conflicts from their parental responsibilities.

Both these recommendations raise questions about whether there can be definitive rules that will suit every couple who divorce. When one parent opts out of the family life, it is self-evident that the other parent must assume sole custody. Joint custody may be best suited to a couple who through mutual agreement can arrive at a decision for both to remain actively involved in their children's lives and therefore can plan to make the necessary arrangements. There is little question that custody arrangements cannot follow one set of practices for everyone, but separating couples have the right to know that there are various options for custody, what these options are, and what their implications are for each parent. Parents should be aware of the potential damage to the child and to a noncustodial parent in sole custody arrangements in which the child and one parent are kept apart and turned into "visitors" in each other's lives. Roman and Haddad quoted a father as saying, "I don't want to be a week-end father. I love my children. I want to continue to be a part of their lives. They want to be with me and I am in a position to provide for them. I would like a half-time arrangement"(pp. 7–8).[4]

Too frequently both parents and the legal profession have unquestioningly accepted that the mother is the better parent, and decisions for custody favor her and are formalized through court procedure. Roman and Haddad say that the current social philosophy is "A man is a man and a woman is a mother." This traditional practice has not taken into account changing sex roles and family life-styles that prevail in the 1980s. Current child custody decisions reflect the social and legal practices of a former period in history. Because of the prevailing emphasis on the significance of the nurturing mother–child bond for the child's health, growth, and development, this view remains incorporated in the family court system awarding sole custody of the child to the mother. However, there is a growing body of parents, family lawyers, and behavioral scientists who believe that sole custody is not always suited to modern family needs. In the past, when sex roles and the division of responsibility between the sexes were clearly defined, women remained in the home full time, caring for their children and the household duties, while fathers were in the labor market providing for the families' material needs. In those days sole custody had some rationale. But generally in today's world this division of labor is blurred. Sixty-five percent of married women are working full or part-time, and men are sharing the primary care of children and household tasks.

Today's husbands are attending prenatal courses and donning sterile gowns to be active participants in the labor room during the birth of a child. Other than actual childbearing, society encourages husbands to take an active part in childcare. These practices are based on the premise that the father–child bond is essential to the healthy development of the child. And men are proving that it is not necessary to have a uterus to assume childcare responsibilities effectively. Men can also nurture and tend their children. Many fathers are contesting sole custody and refusing to be separated from their children. And many women are no longer accepting that the mother's role is synonymous with parenting. Fathers are parents too! Some mothers are voluntarily turning the custodial responsibilities over to the father while they accept visitation access. This may be because the mother believes that the father is better able to care for the children, emotionally or financially, or because the woman feels the need to explore and develop her own resources independently. For whatever reasons, whether sole custody is with one parent or the other, this creates the loss of one parent in the child's life. It is an interesting fact that the social attitude continues to prevail that the mother is expected to be the custodial parent and that there is a social stigma on the mother who voluntarily gives up the custody of her child. At the same time, the father who has custody of his child is given high praise. People exclaim how wonderful the father is in "mothering" his child. When fathers contest sole custody, they must prove the mother to be unfit, whereas mothers, unless proven unfit, traditionally are accepted as the custodial parent. This reflects the extent to which our intellectual attitudes to changing sex roles and our emotional responses lack congruence. We must begin to integrate the parenting concept with primary childcare for both parents.

In my clinical work with separating couples, I am left with

the conviction that when both parents wish to remain actively involved in their children's lives there should not be a contest between them as to which is the better parent. This is confirmed by Roman and Haddad, who report: "Our research and clinical experience affirmed what other researchers have documented; those children who fared best after divorce were those who were free to develop loving and full relationships with both parents" (p. 18).[4] Sole custody, whether it be awarded exclusively to mother or to father, is a loss to everyone. Social and legal agencies as well as other institutions which have influence and jurisdiction over the family, must overcome sex-role prejudices and stereotypes. No one type of custodial disposition can serve every couple's needs. There is a difference between what may be considered an ideal solution and what must be accepted as a realistic and workable arrangement. Every effort should be made for couples to be encouraged to separate their marital differences from their parental responsibilities and to discuss together, and if necessary with professional help, plans for the care of the children. Parents who can arrive at a mutually satisfactory agreement about custodial plans are much more likely to uphold these plans and be less divisive in allowing the other parent to remain in the children's lives.

The recent emergence of mediation or conciliation services has developed out of the recognition that separating parents benefit from help in arriving at what constitutes the best interests of their child. Conciliation services now have branches throughout both the United States and Canada. An organization called Family Services is most frequently able to direct couples to such services that are not readily known. The concept of divorce mediation is based on the idea that the best interests of the child are served by parents who succeed in developing a viable, cooperative relationship. Warring parents, unable to cope with the emotional divorce, make it more difficult for their children to cope with the divorce.

Divorce mediation or conciliation, a relatively new process, was first started in California. It is being recognized increasingly by family lawyers and mental health professionals in arriving at a divorce agreement. The Los Angeles Conciliation Court has served as a model for the conciliation or mediation service movement in the United States and in Canada. This service, which is being offered to spouses who are in the process of dissolving their marriage, is not a legal or judicial service, though it is frequently an adjunct of the court system. It is rather a way of arriving at marital agreement about issues that revolve primarily around child custody, visitation, maintenance, and division of financial assets. The service is offered to partners who are no longer interested in reconciliation—that is, in "saving" their marriage—but in conciliation, which is an approach to help couples traveling the rocky road to divorce work out some mutually agreed-upon decisions. The goal is to help couples work out the separation issues. One of the objectives that this divorce service is achieving is a closer understanding and working relationship between the helping professionals and family lawyers. The two professions, each with its own speciality, act as the mediators in helping the separating couple arrive at decisions that are mutually acceptable to both of them. The purpose of mediation is to help the partners avoid adversarial encounters when making decisions during separation. Divorce mediation focuses on both the legal rights and the emotional components involved in separation before legalizing any decisions.

Partners who are separating tend to use the same tactics for arriving at decisions as they did in their marriage conflicts. It is difficult for them to deal with each other differently. For this reason, mediators can intervene when the decisions begin to reflect the couples' emotional conflicts. Separating partners are frequently suspicious and distrustful of each other. The impartiality of the mediators, representing the interests of both partners, can be a stabilizing influence. Each partner needs the reassurance that he or she will get a fair deal. Divorce involves practical matters. Each partner has a right to know about family income, property rights, liabilities, and current expenses. After the partners have negotiated the arrangements through the mediation process, the court then becomes the tool for legalizing, not imposing, separation and divorce contracts.

Minor children must have legal guardianship for physical and emotional protection. There are a number of custodial alternatives that can be agreed on, only one of which includes sole custody. In recent years an increasing number of fathers are assuming sole custody, or coparenting or joint custody arrangements. Paternal sole custody is awarded when fathers win a contested custody battle, or when mothers voluntarily choose to withdraw from sole custody responsibility, or when both parents agree that in the interests of the child the father will be a more competent parent. In a 1983 news story in the *Sarasota Suncoast Today*, it was reported that there are 600,000 divorced fathers in the United States who have sole custody of their children. This is an increase of 7% to 10% in the past few years.[5] There are also split-custody arrangements whereby each parent assumes the custody for one or more children and visitation rights are exchanged between the parents. Coparenting or joint custody refers to arrangements by which both parents share the rights and responsibilities for raising their children after divorce. Each of these different custodial arrangements has supporters and opponents. No one arrangement suits every couple's needs or interests. However, there does appear to be increasing support by the law and by parents of the idea that in many cases both parents should remain in the children's lives.

The definition of the term *joint custody* is still unclear. It remains a social rather than legal concept in states where it is not yet legalized. Some form of joint custody is currently encouraged in 27 states; however, despite legislative attempts to encourage joint custody, 90% of court decisions still award sole custody to the mother. The state laws vary widely. Some states accept the parents' agreement to have joint custody, whereas some judges recommend joint custody before considering an alternative arrangement. The courts in several states, Delaware, Nevada, and Pennsylvania, for instance, require parents to attend mediation services and to prepare a written proposal for custody. The proposal, which then requires court sanction, sets forth an agreement on financial matters, the parents' living locale, education, health care, and religious training, as well as arrangements for holidays. For the most part, when parents arrive at an agreement about having joint custody, the courts accept the parental decisions. Research in the United States and Canada reports that when separating couples agree on custody and finances following mediation over three-quarters abide by the decision. The problems arise when courts impose joint custody even when the parents have not agreed on this arrangement and although their differences appear irreconcilable.[6]

A considerable amount of confusion persists about joint custody regarding how both parents, when separated, can have equal rights and responsibilities for their children. A common misconception is that equal sharing means strictly that the child lives with each parent for equal periods of time. Some parents have tried this arrangement. For some parents and maybe for some children it may work. There is not a long enough history to know how well children can adapt to this kind of living arrangement. Equal living time, I believe, has been given too much publicity and in certain respects has been equated with joint custody. The central idea of joint custody, however, is that both parents share in the decisions and planning for children, and both retain significant influence over the children's growth and development. It does not mean that a child must live equal lengths of time with each parent.

Many separated parents learn that they can adapt to a different family life in ways that can include the children in their lives with a minimum of discontinuity for parents and children. This can make it easier for everyone to adjust to the inevitable disruption of separation. Whenever it is feasible, many couples have been establishing their living quarters close to each other. This can reduce environmental changes for the children and provide them with the comfort of having both parents' homes easily accessible and available. Nevertheless, this can only work if the ex-partners recognize that they (1) both have rights as parents and (2) no longer have rights as ex-partners to intrude on each other's lives. Their continued connection to each other is through their mutual interest and concern about their children. Parents who have arrived at this acceptance are presently engaging in a variety of parental arrangements. Shared parenting patterns are in the infancy stages as yet, with various kinds of arrangements working better for some couples than others.

One father said that he resented the term *visitation*, since he did not want to be a visitor in his children's lives, seeing them by appointment. Other fathers have shared this feeling. Many fathers have demonstrated that "visitation access" tends to turn into entertaining the child on visits, planning a busy program of activities rather than offering guidance and influence. It is a contrived rather than a natural parental, father–child relationship. It can become uncomfortable, painful, and sometimes burdensome. Noncustodial fathers worry about their legal status with their children. One father questioned what would happen to his parental rights in the event of his ex-wife's remarriage or in the event of her death. What claims would he have, as a noncustodial parent, on his children? Another father complained of the problems in maintaining a relationship with his children. He wanted to be able to attend parents' night at school, to see report cards, to be informed of the child's progress in school, and to hear about the child's physical progress. However, he reported that neither the school nor the doctor would keep him posted without the permission of the custodial mother. These complaints reflect that society views the status of a noncustodial parent as that of nonparent. It indicates that our social institutions add to the distance between a noncustodial parent and the child.

When Evelyn and Ted separated, there was no conflict about custody. They agreed that the children would live with their mother and be cared for by her. Evelyn agreed with Ted that the girls should not lose him and that he would have flexible visiting arrangement with them. Evelyn also agreed that she would consult Ted about plans for the children's future. The preseparation arrangements were, to all intents and purposes, an ideal coparenting agreement. However, when Evelyn and Ted sought legal counsel, their divorce lawyers picked their agreement apart. The couple were caught in the adversarial system which promoted hostility and controversy between them. Evelyn, who had wanted out of the marriage, had explained to Ted that she did not want to put any obstacles in the way of the divorce. Evelyn's lawyer took exception to some of Ted's lawyer's proposals regarding financial arrangements. Ted's lawyer had drawn up a financial statement that would have given Ted the right to have an accounting of expenditures from the support monies he had agreed to pay. The rationale was that Ted did not trust Evelyn's ability to handle finances. Ted's lawyer advised him that he could keep control of the finances by paying the household bills himself. We observe here that the lawyers each became involved in the decision-making process which created friction between Evelyn and Ted, which was later resolved through divorce mediation.

The other issue that became contentious was the poorly defined matter of visiting access. The couple learned about divorce mediation, and through this process with a mental health consultant and a legal consultant both Ted and Evelyn recognized the future pitfalls in the proposals presented by Ted's lawyer. Divorce mediation, in which both later participated, pointed out that the financial arrangements would keep Evelyn tied in a dependent role with Ted. It virtually negated Evelyn's independent rights to her share of the family finances. As a marriage partner, Evelyn's contribution as homemaker and mother had given Ted the benefits of being a parent and having family life. Ted's legal proposal reflected that his support to the family was dependent on his judgment of what the family needed rather than on the concept of the marriage contract as an equal partnership. This reflected the traditional attitude that the income belonged to the person who earned the money and as such was Ted's to give or withhold. Had Evelyn agreed, this would have left her with an unpredictable financial future dependent on Ted's rules. Her future adjustment to a different life and later to a remarriage could have been restricted by Ted's interventions. Furthermore, the custody recommendation was that Ted would have "flexible access." Such availability could have meant that Evelyn's home would have to have an open door to Ted, which would have restricted Evelyn's right to her personal life. In the event of remarriage, the new marriage would have had difficulty achieving its own identity. The boundary lines for Evelyn's separated home had to be defined, as did the lines of parental authority between Ted and Evelyn and between Ted and their daughters. These are some of the areas in which mediation finally helped this couple to consider and arrive at agreements and thus made it possible for them to establish a friendly parenting relationship following their divorce.

Kate, Evelyn's friend, made separation arrangements which had different dynamics and different potential consequences from those of Evelyn and Ted. Jim, Kate's husband, did not contest any part of the separation contract drawn up by Kate and her lawyer. Jim was not informed of his visiting rights with Scott nor did he seek his own legal counsel for some months following the separation. Both Jim and Scott could have been spared the depression that both experienced in losing each other had Jim participated with Kate in mediation services.

Kate proceeded on the commonly held assumption that it was up to her alone, as sole custody parent, to make the rules to allow or disallow Scott to be with his noncustodial father. Kate's lawyer had advised her to keep Jim away from Scott until the child had become accustomed to living without his father. Kate and her parents did not protect the child from their discussions when they berated Jim or the kind of person he was. Three months after the separation, Kate gave Jim permission to spend the afternoon with Scott. Since the child returned from the visit ill with an upset stomach, vomiting, and diarrhea, Kate concluded that Jim had given him food that had upset him and that therefore he did not know how to take care of the child. She subsequently decided that she would not subject Scott to spending time with his father. As sole custodial parent, Kate had the legal right to withhold visiting between Jim and his son unless Jim contested this.

The prerogative that sole custody parents have to refuse visitation access is being contested by many fathers. Jane and William Noble in *The Custody Trap* state, "Custody means control. It means ownership, power and authority" (p. 69).[7] This certainly deprives the noncustodial parent—usually the father—of his parenting rights. A number of fathers have reported that the more infrequently they see their children, the less they feel like a parent.

Paula's situation was different again from Evelyn's and Kate's. When Jack left home, no separation agreement had been drawn up. Jack had chosen his priority and that was that he only wanted to be with Sharon. Nothing else had meaning for him at that time. However, after a few months of the ups and downs of this turbulent love affair, Jack began to experience a deep, overwhelming sense of longing for his children. He needed them so desperately that he felt he could not function without them. He sought legal counsel and pressed for joint custody. When his lawyer told him he didn't have a leg to stand on, Jack changed lawyers. He said he refused to be a noncustodial parent having his children "visit" with him. He wanted the children to be part of his regular daily life and be with him in the daytime and at night. He threatened Paula that if she did not agree to joint custody, with the children spending half their time with him he would take the children away where she could never find them. Paula refused to agree to the joint custody disposition on the basis that Jack's emotional stability was not to be depended on. This couple needed help.

Jack's lawyer prepared the case to contest Paula's sole custody. Jack's motive was based on his own need for the children, not necessarily on what was in the children's best interest. The fight, which proceeded in court, resulted in Jack's being vindictive and hostile toward Paula in their subsequent relationship. This left Paula feeling threatened and frightened. Tensions were created between them that strongly influenced the coparenting arrangements that they finally agreed on. Both these parents loved their children and each had the potential to make an essential contribution to the children's lives. The divorce mediation process could have spared this couple much grief.

The separation arrangements of the three couples were fraught with the complications and confusions of many separations. There were factors implicit in the three situations that could have benefitted all three couples through mediation counseling. Emotionally charged and outdated legal rulings prevailed, bringing about severe turmoil for everyone. Evelyn, Kate, and Paula were among the 90% of mothers who are awarded sole custody of the children.

My experience has shown that divorced parents are now dealing with the custody of their children in a variety of arrangements with few guidelines. Some plans are more successful than others. To illustrate, let us review Mary and Bill's separation. Mary is a sole custodial mother, with two children, six and eight years of age. She has been having a financial struggle maintaining the family. Receiving irregular support payments from Bill, she has made arrangements for her children in a daycare center while she works. Her life revolves around a very busy schedule of taking care of the children and the house and doing her job. Her day is full of rushing, stress, and anxiety. With little time for herself, she feels bitter about having all of the burdens fall on her, which has made her short-tempered and irritable. Thus, her children are both receiving treatment for emotional problems. The eight-year-old has constant nightmares. His disturbed sleep makes the day a tired period for both him and his mother. Mary, in turn, is impatient with him, which makes him whiny and unhappy. Her daughter is also demanding and clingy.

This has all become too much for Mary. There just doesn't seem to be any relief. The children's father calls them occasionally and he spends every other Sunday with them, presenting the typical "Sunday Father" picture. There are the zoos, movies, and ball games, bags of popcorn and quick-order suppers. The few hours in which he tries to pretend "aren't we having fun together" have become a chore for everyone. The children then come home exhausted and cranky.

In reviewing some of the problems that this family is experiencing, it is clear that sole custody is not working for any of them. This is a rather typical picture of postseparation problems. When this family lived together there was poor division of childcare responsibilities. Mary carried most of the responsibility, which left her feeling overtaxed and with little fun in her life. Accepting that this was typical of marriage, she made no effort to change the situation. Both she and Bill had grown up with the stereotypic model of marriage with the wife caring for the children and the husband being the financial provider. Bill's recreational activity was being out with the boys and having a few beers, whereas Mary had no recreation away from the children. This couple might have responded to an educational process. They really did not understand the essence of the marital relationship. Hence they ended up with a bleak, loveless marriage. Bill did not know his children and did not know how to be a parent to them before or after the divorce. After being separated for close to a year, his payments began to fall away. His use of visitation time became irregular. No one was happy with the final arrangements. Different custodial arrangements with coparenting may not ever have turned Bill into a coparent since he had never shared the job before. But the dangers in such situations are that they tend to be cyclical. Mary and Bill's children, who are experiencing little emotional nurturing, will in turn probably have little to give their children. They feel empty, deprived, lonely, and anxious. The parents and the children might have benefitted from enrichment and social support programs prior to the divorce. Their first step in the separation process might have been a mediation process to impress both parents with the serious impact on the children. As it was, Mary's overburdened life left the children feeling that they were burdensome. Bill's life could have taken on more meaning, if he had been alerted to his significance in his children's lives and if he had learned how to be a parent.

Some fathers have reported that during the marriage they had assumed little parental responsibility and really did not know their own children. It was only after separation, the fathers reported, that with direct contact with the children they developed a closeness in which they felt more paternal love and commitment.

I believe that there are some important lessons for the intact family to learn from couples who divorce. One is that there should be a more equitable distribution of responsibilities and relationships with children within the intact family. Many women tend to complain about feeling overtaxed with childcare jobs and household chores. They say they feel exploited and that they take care of everyone's needs and no one takes care of theirs. A frequent cry I hear from wives is, "When is it going to be my turn?" This is often one of the causes for the deterioration of the marriage. Men, on the other hand, have said they feel that they are kept on the outside of the family unit. They feel that there is a closed bond between the mother and the children as though they were her children alone. There may be, in fact, many secret messages or confidences from which the father is excluded. Furthermore, fathers have reported their feeling that children learn how to manipulate their fathers rather than how to have a direct one-to-one relationship.

I believe parents should be encouraged to assume coparenting within the intact family. This would ensure more family unity and improved marital relations. In the event of divorce, both parents would be equipped to share the care of their children.

This was illustrated in another marriage that terminated. Rose and Milton had two children, sons of ten and twelve years. One day Rose had packed her bags and left home without warning or preparation. She simply left. Milton was left alone with the children and the home. Though he liked the boys, he had always taken them and his home life for granted. He had had no active part in being a father or a family man. Things just happened. The children were just there and the routine of life just went on—until Rose left.

Milton then began to view his sons and the running of the home quite differently. Only then did he realize how little he had participated in what went into maintaining the daily pattern of life. It was then that Milton became available to his sons and they turned to him for advice in a way they had never done before. He felt better about himself as a parent than he ever had. There was a feeling of cooperation that Milton and the boys established together. The boys, nevertheless, missed Rose and yearned for her.

Prior to her leaving home, Rose had experienced a great deal of resentment and ennui at the emptiness of her personal life. She wanted out. Her leaving the family resulted in a crisis for everyone. Yet Rose soon knew that she did not want to lose her sons, and Milton knew just as well that he would not give them up. They both also came to the realization that their marriage was over. At this time, they were advised about the benefits of consulting a divorce mediator. As a result of the consultation, they agreed that they would work out a plan to ensure that neither of them would lose the children. Rose found an apartment close to Milton's home. They worked out plans for the children to be with Milton one week and with Rose the next. This way the children remained in the same school and in the same neighborhood. They also agreed to be flexible regarding time so that neither parent would be restricted from pursuing independent interests. Both parental homes were available to the children. Both homes were home to them. The marriage between Rose and Milton was finished, but the children did not lose either parent, nor did either parent lose the children.

I do not want to convey that everyone slipped easily into their different life styles with two parental homes. However, with the arrangements Rose and Milton made, they reduced the number of losses for themselves and for their children. And the children were left knowing that both parents loved and wanted them. It is unfortunate that it took a separation before Milton began to know his sons. He and they had lost some valuable years together. A positive factor in this new life-style for Rose was that the boredom she had felt before was relieved now that she had the time to pursue a personal life in addition to carrying on as a mother and a homemaker. For Milton, life was enriched for him as a parent; he felt he had proved himself able to care for and love his children and win their love. His ability to express his love opened up a whole new dimension in his capacity for intimacy.

Too frequently, couples get stuck in a rut of discontent. They do nothing to change the pattern of their lives. Mothers often do the marriage and family relationship a great disservice by assuming that children and home duties are their responsibility alone. This may have been the symbol of the "good wife" and "good mother" at one time. However, it no longer works for many couples in today's society and it results in losses for everyone. In the way that business people take stock of what works successfully and discard work patterns or merchandise that are not productive, so marriage patterns should be reassessed periodically. For early detection of problems, there are such things as clinics for "well babies"; marriages could benefit from similar checkups. If a pattern of interaction is not working well, it could be modified or changed if caught in the early stages.

Separation, family disruption, and divorce are never easy to withstand and there is no one solution. But for couples who are ready to explore ways of reducing the stress, separation and divorce can be planned with a minimal amount of pain and loss.

Jean and Murray, whom I counseled, exemplify how mediation can be helpful. This couple realized that they had been growing apart for some time. They each had their own interests and their own friends. Because of their differences, they irritated and criticized each other to the point at which they began dreading the time they had to spend together. They had two children, girls of six and eight, whom both parents loved dearly. They avoided facing the emptiness of their marriage because they could not tolerate the thought of hurting the children. They went through a process of marital counseling to identify what had happened to the marriage and whether it could be rectified. After several months of counseling when both partners, I believe, gave the marriage their best efforts, they came to the conclusion that they had grown so far apart and were so cold to each other that they could not tolerate sharing the intimacy of one bedroom. When the children became suspicious about the parents' separate bedrooms and asked "Mommy, are you and Daddy going to get a divorce?" the couple knew that they could no longer put off the decision to separate.

After the reconciliation counseling had proved not to be helpful in repairing the marriage, we started on a conciliation program to help this couple work out the transitional steps to their separation. A first task dealt with the parents' searching for separate residences. They both felt a great deal of pain over how their plans would affect the girls. Both parents had shared the many responsibilities of bringing up the children and both had good relationships with the girls. Neither wanted to lose the children or become a weekend parent in the children's lives. Though they had differences, they knew and respected each other's sense of dedication, acknowledging that they were both good parents. The pain was profound.

Because of their mutual respect for each other's love for the children, they wanted to learn about alternative custody arrangements and the advantages and disadvantages in each. In exploring the possibility of joint custody they wanted to understand exactly what it meant and how it could work without fragmenting the children's sense of well-being. They both agreed that for them it would work best if the children had one primary home with their mother since Murray's business took him out of town frequently. Next came the exercise of each drawing up a schedule for weekly living arrangements for the children. They brought this schedule to counseling sessions to discuss. On some aspects they agreed and on others they did not. The children attended a private school that was not in the neighborhood, to which their father had driven them daily. They agreed that he would continue to do that and that Jean would pick them up after school.

On Fridays the father would call for them and take them to his home. The first plan that Murray presented was that the children would spend the weekend with him and he would then take them to school on Monday morning. Jean's objection to this was that she would have only structured time, that is, time when there were rules for getting up and being dressed on time, doing homework, and getting to bed early—during the school week, whereas their father would have all the recreational free time. They struggled over how to overcome this without too many shifts for the children. The final agreement was that the recreational weekend time would be split between Jean and Murray. However, when Jean had an evening activity, if Murray was available, he agreed that he would spend the evening with the girls and get them ready for bed. They also agreed to try three weekday weeks with the mother and a full week with the father so that the father could have structured school time as well as recreational weekends. They were both aware that there would be trial and error and that the important factor was that they should discuss and cooperate about what they felt was working and what was not.

The financial arrangements needed to be ironed out. Jean, therefore, drew up an expense account and Murray listed his assets, and they discussed with me, as mediator, the changes that were indicated in their day-to-day life. The agreement was that Jean would remain in the home while Murray would find living quarters very near so that his home would be easily available to his daughters. Although he felt he was probably overextending himself in terms of taking on a heavy financial load, he said that he recognized that it was important for the girls not to have to make the additional adjustment to a different community while they were adjusting to two new homes and to their parents' separation. His plan was to get accommodations that would be on a par with his wife's so that the children would have an attractive home with him as well as with their mother. Jean said it sounded reasonable but she indicated that she felt uncertain as to whether she could depend on his maintaining this arrangement.

It was at this time that it seemed wise for them to engage legal services to make their agreement formal regarding custody commitments and financial matters. This was also to cover how Jean and the children would be supported and how she, once separated, would gain a sense of financial independence from her former husband. They discussed what financial expenses were to be covered. In addition to daily living costs, rents, and school fees, there was the question of medical, dental, and optical expenses. There were also the matters of insurance, the family estate, and wills. Questions were raised about the possibility of future changes in each of their lives, for instance, having new partners and how this would affect the financial status of each of the ex-spouses.

The agreement between Jean and Murray, was that during the legal process they would consult a mediator again if they met up with dissension to prevent hostility from building. They drew up statements of agreement about holidays, events like family gatherings, and school meetings, and they informed the school that both parents were equally responsible for the children and were to be notified of progress or problems. They also agreed that both of them were to be kept informed of medical progress or difficulties. All these issues were raised by the mediation counselor as possible sources of contention, factors that have proved to be pitfalls in other separations. The partners were encouraged to list any other concerns they had, to try to project how their life situation would change, and to try to foresee how they might deal with these changes.

They did their homework and arrived at each session with their own agenda for what they wanted to bring up for discussion. It was not all smooth sailing, however. There were many areas in which they had differences. The greatest value of this mediation process was that this couple discussed these concerns openly with the mediator, whose purpose was to keep them on track. They were not permitted to get back into marital conflicts. The process was not geared to reconciliation, therapy, or an analytical process. The subject on hand was to accept the fact of the separation before each partner got involved with his divorce lawyers and the adversary system which dealt with the division of financial assets. Through this route this couple would make their own decisions and then be in the position of having reached mutual agreement about the custody and financial arrangements. They both felt more comfortable and more respectful of each other because they were dealing with their feelings about the separation and the children in ways that left them ready to tell rather than to ask the lawyers about their custody arrangements. As counselor, I advised the couple to shape up their plans for separation, for living arrangements, and for provisions for the children before telling the children about the plans for separation. They could then give the children specific plans for living arrangements with each of the parents. This would help reduce the children's anxiety about what would happen to them. They also considered that a child's sense of timing was different from that of an adult. They wanted to tell the children after they had selected a home for Murray. Then he could take them to see it and they would know that their father's home was selected with them in mind for living with him part of the time.

The parents' voluntary contract in planning was as thoughtful of the best interests of the children as possible. Once they had decided to terminate the marriage, they were determined to work together for the children's protection. Now the question is, what will happen if and when either parent becomes involved with another partner? What will happen to the amicable planning between them in the event of remarriage. Is it reasonable to assume that in the event of remarriage these parents can maintain the kind of exchange in which Murray would pick up the children each morning for school and phone them to say good night each night? Will this permit the ex-partners to effect an emotional divorce or are their plans going to keep them tied closely to each other? It will require time to know the answer to these questions. At present, they have achieved areas of agreement and respect for each other regarding the love each feels for the children. This appears to make it unlikely that they will act in a way that would be prejudicial or competitive to prevent the children from having both parents in their lives.

Before parents arrive at their decision for child custody, they are well advised to consider alternative arrangements that are available for custody. Mediation counseling is geared to help both the emotional and legal components in planning. The ideal mediation service is a team of a behavioral therapist and a divorce lawyer, though mediation is neither therapy nor the practice of law. Both the therapist and the lawyer have special skills to inform the couple of their rights, to monitor emotional recommendations in the decision-making process, and to inform the couple about pitfalls and possible damage to the children from such emotional decisions and quarrels about rights.

In a mediation process, the counselors do not get into the past marriage history of the couple or allow them to renew accusations or recriminations. Again, this is a process of conciliation, not reconciliation. The contract should be clear. If during the course of the mediation it should become apparent that the couple have begun to have some doubts about separation, the counselor should identify this. Once the possibility is identified, they should all agree to focus in upcoming sessions on reconciliation and recontract for reconciliation service. There is little question that divorce lawyers who are attracted to mediation are a breed who, in general, do not accept the adversary system with its win–lose decisions for custody. They recognize that there are alternate custodial judgments which could be arrived at. Moreover, when both parents can be helped to agree on an arrangement, it is less damaging as well as less expensive than a battle and court decision for a contested custody case. A great advantage in conciliation or mediation is that both partners are equally represented by the same counselors with the goal of arriving at a fair deal for each of them. The arrangements that the couple are assisted to consider can then be brought to court, which then merely serves as a tool to legalize, not impose, separation contracts.

A recent *Time* report[8] of a custodial resolution in Michigan noted that a judge awarded three adolescent boys, ages fifteen, thirteen, and eleven, custody of their parent's house, while the mother and father alternate month-long visits. The boys remain in the home, and their parents move in and out and pay for the children and home expenses. The mother is quoted as saying she considers the judge's settlement "a good third option for people getting a divorce. This way no one loses." The children were all happy about the decision. One of the boys is reported to have said: "When my dad told me about it, I couldn't believe it, I thought my ma would get us. I'm glad one of the parents wasn't left out." The father was pleased because the children did not have to change schools or friends and they can visit the nonresident parent at will, since the other residence is a few doors away. The judge stated that he felt the decision was "natural" because both parents testified that the other was a good parent and that the children loved them both. The judge recognized that the dispute was between the couple as a marital pair, not as parents. This is not a typical legal disposition. However, it illustrates that the legal system is in the process of changing its views about having alternative custodial judgments.

There is little doubt that divorce contracts are becoming increasingly complex both in terms of custody and finances. Agreement on both issues at one stage of life may not be suited to a future stage as in remarriages, and a new agreement may have to be negotiated. The most productive route for such renegotiation appears again to be mediation services, so that each person need not seek separate counsel and get involved in the adversarial process.

Without doubt, there are major changes in everyone's pattern of life after divorce. The parents may each move in very different directions in reorganizing their lives and be highly critical about the life-style of the former spouse. These differences may make both of them very hesitant to expose their child to different interests and perhaps even different value systems when one or both parents remarry—possibly to different economic and even religious practices. It is easy to understand some of the difficulties a parents may have if he or she disapproves of the former partner's present life or the direction in which he or she is moving. However, from what is known to date, children appear to have the capacity to adapt to different life styles more easily than to the loss of a parent. Chief Justice Warren E. Burger in an article in *Family Mediation* (March/April, 1982) writes that lawyers and their clients, trained in the adversary system are "too combative and too concerned about winning rather than settling disputes."[9] Sanford J. Berger, in the same newsletter, writes that the courts in the United States have "been humane enough to outlaw cock fights, dog fights and bull fights and yet we do nothing about the barbarism of divorce fighting. We abhor police beating confessions out of alleged criminals, and yet we cheer and encourage lawyers to emotionally beat up and abuse two innocent people and their children because their marriage has foundered."[10]

Determining the custody of children of divorce is extremely complicated for both the parents and the law. When custody is determined by law, the decisions are frequently based on the bias of a particular judge. The law does try to protect children, but how the priorities for protection are selected rests with legal judgments of individuals. The distribution of financial assets is increasingly complex. When both partners have worked in a marriage and contributed to the support of the family, most frequently the husband's earnings have exceeded the wife's. Equitable distribution is difficult to arrive at. In many divorces, women have supported a husband through school to equip him for some skilled positions. Following divorce, the dilemma has been to determine to what extent, in this case, the wife has a right to her husband's subsequent earnings. Furthermore, a recent development has been that the question of alimony has come under dispute. For women who have not been working, this is a great hardship. Thus, there frequently is a ruling that the woman be supported while she is learning some skills for employment. In a report in *Newsweek* on divorce, Lenore Weltzman, a sociologist, is quoted as stating that women's incomes were reduced by 73% in the first year after marriage and that sole custody mothers and their children predominantly live below the poverty line and are in the majority of recipients of social welfare.[11]

In the United States and Canada, the resolution of custody problems that will best serve everyone's interests is in transition. There are those people who continue to support sole custody and are highly skeptical of shared parenting as a viable alternative. Even within the legal system there are opposing views. This may be illustrated by a recent proceeding in the Supreme Court of

Ontario wherein a few judges overruled one judge's recommendation to award joint custody for a child of divorcing parents,
commenting that they had "healthy cynicism" about divorcing
parents sharing the parental responsibilities. Judge Boland had
stated that "granting even the most liberal access does not confer
the right to participate in the upbringing of the child."[12] She
added that "the traditional award of custody to the mother and
access to the father is the cause of many of the problems and
most of the tensions between parents and children and between
the parents themselves." And her point in her recommendation
was: "It would seem logical to begin with a presumption in favor
of joint custody, as children who fare best after a divorce are
those free to develop full and loving relationships with both parents." The other justices condemned the Boland order as "mis-
directed" and agreed with each other that joint custody "is inher-
ently a bad thing." Still another justice responded by saying that
the judges who had opposed joint custody were setting back a
concept "that was becoming very viable and useful as a tool in
resolving difficult custody disputes." This judicial controversy
over custody continues to prevail throughout the United States
and Canada.

Even though it is easier to get a divorce today, the difficulties
for the legal system and the splitting parents are, if anything,
even greater. The rate of divorce is escalating so rapidly that the
law has not been able to catch-up with alternative ways of dealing with custody and financial decisions. More research with follow-up study is highly indicative into what works and what does
not work for all concerned. A researcher in Los angeles reported
that couples who share custody of their children are only half as
likely to return to the courts as those of whom only one parent
has custody.[11] The factors influencing this finding may be that
the divorce resolution which the particular sampling of couples
agreed on reflected a population who were able to work out any
differences without resorting to court appearances. There is little
doubt that when couples agree to the disposition of the custody

and can respect each other's rights, there is less likelihood that there will be difficulties about divided parental authority. But, to take the shared custody agreement one step further, consideration must be given to how shared custody between ex-spouses affects the 75% of divorced persons who later remarry. This question will be considered in a later chapter.

How does a father become a nonparent? Noncustody removes the legal rights to guardianship of a child from his parent. But what happens to the emotional parental ties, bonds, and feelings of a man who has fathered a child and watched a son or daughter grow from the first days of infancy. Can these feelings be legally excised? And should they be? The sole custody determination has inherent in it the concept that one parent is more competent to be a parent than the other parent and that the child belongs more to one parent than the other. This may be true in the case of the parent, who after separation leaves his or her family and shows no interest in retaining communication or even a relationship. Dependent children need guardianship and protection and of course if one parent withdraws the other parent must assume total responsibility. If both parents desert, society assumes the legal guardianship under the legal jurisdiction of *parens patriae*. But this occurs only in a small percentage of marital separations. For the most part, society has acted as though after separation children belong primarily to mothers.

This concept of sole custody for the mother continues to receive legal sanction and social support, despite the changing patterns of family life and the reality that a growing number of fathers are involved with their children and the home, while an overwhelming number of women are joining the labor market and are no longer occupied full time with the family and home responsibilities. And yet, as indicated previously, in 90% of divorces mothers continue to be awarded sole custody and fathers are granted visitation access with obligations to make child-support payments. This custody arrangement divests fathers of their legal right to participate in major decision-making for the child's life. On the other hand, mothers have full rights, privileges, and obligations for the care and well-being of their child, to the exclusion of the father's rights. The end result of sole custody is that mothers become overtaxed and children and fathers suffer a deep sense of loss for each other and feelings of abandonment. Everyone loses and no one wins with this custody resolution. The father's plight in becoming a nonparent has been overlooked until recently. Public notice has been given only to those fathers who failed to maintain relationships with their children and fathers who dropped their financial obligations or payments. There are punitive measures taken to make the scot-free father and ex-spouse meet his obligations. However, having worked with these supposedly scot-free fathers, both in my involvement with them in research and in my clinical encounters, I can say that for the most part fathers do not carry themselves with a scot-free abandon. Others studies of fathers who have been shut out of their parental role have substantiated my observation.

When a couple separates, it is typically the man who leaves the family home. His life changes radically. He no longer is a husband and loses his family life and the daily parenting of his children. He also frequently loses his relationships with his in-laws and the social support of friends. Many men have thus expressed their feelings about going through an identity crisis, since they must redefine their whole life. The women, burdened as there are with total care of the children, financial hardship, and new kinds of responsibilities, frequently receive more support and more social sanction for holding the family together.

Whether the man initiates the separation or not, men report profound upheaval in their lives when a marriage breaks up. Separated men have been shown in studies to have a higher rate of alcoholism, suicide, accident proneness, and mortality than do separated women. How a family is restructured after separation in relation to finances and custody largely affects everyone's ability to adjust to the disorganization of the family unit.

Fathers with limited access to their children complain that they feel shut out of their children's lives and devalued as parents. One father recently reported that his infrequent visits with his children are so contrived and filled with tension that he is mystified by his continued drive to persist in wanting to see them. He questions whether they would not all be more comfortable withdrawing from one another. Another father reported that he felt that his children were visiting him out of a sense of duty and that the visits seemed to have become a chore for everyone. And still another father stated that neither he nor the children knew how to use their time together comfortably. They all seemed to be trying hard, to feel and perform with parent–child feelings in unfamiliar circumstances and unfamiliar settings. It is hard to feel like a father when you see your children every other weekend and Wednesdays for dinner and to try and catch up with what has happened in their lives in the interim period. One father said he found himself asking a list of routine questions. They cover school, any happenings, how are things at home, and so on, and for the most part the children respond with monosyllabic answers that do not create a sense of parent–child warmth and intimacy. On a weekend or a holiday it takes time before they feel comfortable together, and then by the time some comfort is achieved it is separation time again.

Surely there must be ways for fathers and their children who care for each other and do not want to lose one another to be able to have more significant and flexible availability of time together so that they are not just visitors in each other's lives. However, if the father's visitation access has been infrequent and contrived and if the mother remarries and the father's parental relationship is unclear, her partner's role as a stepparent is even more ambiguous. If this hypothesis is valid, it means that for involvement in and commitment to future relationships, both for the biological parent and the stepparent, the continuity of clearly defined and accepted roles for both parents in sustained parenting must precede any future remarriage which involves step relations. The remarriage contract will then clearly convey the reality that the remarriage not only involves the couple but retains permanent ties to the former marriage through the children.

Erik Erikson in *Childhood and Society*[13] states that the key to knowing one's identity is that there must be continuity between past and future. This continuity is relevant to family ties. Despite the discontinuity of a marriage and the family as an intact unit, the ability for parents and children to be able to retain the continuity of their roots as a family appears a prerequisite for defining identity for each of them.

Because the noncustodial role is a painful and unnatural parent–child relationship, fathers have frequently withdrawn from it. They need support in knowing how to remain a father in different circumstances. If both parents can be helped to recognize the importance of working out some mutual parenting arrangements and to avoid using the children to continue their battle, both parents can remain custodial parents. The problem does not appear to be whether, for the most part, both parents want to remain in their children's lives, but rather whether both parents will allow each other to remain actively and flexibly part of their children's lives. The parents may be more ready to keep their marital strife apart from the parent–child relationship when the legal system involved in the divorce proceedings looks more favorably on shared parental responsibilities, rather than insisting upon sole custody or noncustody arrangements.

Legal changes always lag behind social change. A great deal of the stress for parents in divorce could be reduced if divorce did not mean that a parent and child have lost each other. Some fathers fight for their right not to lose their child by contesting sole custody to the mother. They fight, therefore, to gain sole custody for the father. To win a sole custody battle requires that the father must overcome the cultural bias that only mothers can nurture a child. To do this, he must take the "fault" route by discrediting the wife. This can have serious implications for all concerned. Many fathers have reported that they were not ready to perjure themselves nor were they ready to subject themselves or their wives to scathing attacks by the lawyers to prove that either father or mother was not competent to care for the children (as illustrated in the film *Kramer vs. Kramer*).

In the past few years, since more fathers have been raising their children alone, studies report that there is no difference in the children's development when they are raised by sole mothers or by sole fathers and that sole fathers face the same problems that sole mothers face, which are primarily loneliness and little time for self or for social and recreational activities.[5]

Though sole custody fathers are reported to feel comfortable in this nontraditional role for which their early socialization probably did not prepare them, the social and legal bias remains that mothers are awarded custody for minor children. Culturally, mothers have been brought up to believe that they have a maternal instinct. As mentioned earlier, a stigma attaches to women who lose or give up custody and assume the visitation role. A large number of the fathers who are the custodial parent retain custody when the mother has died, deserted, or is physically or emotionally unfit to carry on the parenting job. In recent years, a small number of women have felt that their personal and emotional needs make it difficult for them to be able to assume sole responsibility. They may feel that their husbands have more to offer the children on a full-time basis. They do not want to lose their children and are ready to accept visitation rights; or they feel that for their children's sake and for their own shared custody is more beneficial.

My experience with sole custody fathers indicates that they are as devoted, as committed, as concerned, and as impatient as mothers. They parent the children in very much the same ways as mothers do and tend to run into the same kinds of pitfalls. Some fathers form an intense, interdependent, nuclear, closed-family system that makes the entry of a new partner in remarriage difficult.

A case in point is Bill, who in his desire to compensate for the loss of his wife and his child's mother formed a close alliance with his son, Matt. Devoting all his free time to this child, he promised to spend his future with him. Making all their plans together, they decided to go traveling, hiking, camping, and skiing. They enjoyed each other's company and created an atmosphere of exclusivity to the relationship. Bill, who had been deeply upset by his ex-spouse's desertion two years ago, really had thought he would never marry again. However, he did meet and fall in love with Sylvia when Matt was twelve years old. Matt could not believe that his father would "do that to him." He refused to acknowledge the reality of the woman, or of the relationship, or his father's feelings for her, or his father's right to marry. Nor would he listen to reason. Feeling that his father was abandoning him, he became extremely angry. His anger practically succeeded in convincing Bill that he could not marry. In one session in my office, Matt spilled out much anger, saying that he knew that now that his father wanted to marry Sylvia he would stop caring for him. In fact, he said, his father was already taking her out without Matt. Matt further complained that his father was spending money on Sylvia, which would mean that he and his father wouldn't have money to take some of the trips they had planned together. He also knew that if the three of them were to go canoeing together and the boat tipped, his father would go to her rescue first. This child could perceive the relationship only as a displacement of him. He felt caught in a triangular love affair that complicated Bill's early marriage years. No one really had understood the inappropriate nature of the near-peer relationship that Bill had developed with his son, and Sylvia had a great deal of difficulty in contending with her own resentment of Matt because of his attitude toward her. They both got caught up in competing for Bill, his time, attention, and love.

In another sole father household, a situation evolved that was not dissimilar to Bill and Matt's. Henry loved his ten-year-old daughter, whose mother had left home, and wanted to be all things to her. Tender and attentive, he treated her as though she were a fragile doll. He read to her every evening and tucked her into bed. He was a loving mother and father rolled into one. When Henry decided to remarry, he assured his beloved daughter that she had nothing to worry about, that she would have two people to love and care for her. He conveyed that she would remain the pivotol figure in the home. This turned out to be a major problem for the remarriage. The child tested her father's undying devotion in many ways. She acted in a demanding manner and was resentful toward the separate relationship between her father and his wife. Thus the single-parent pattern between father and daughter brought conflicts to the new marital relationship.

There is little doubt that fathers can be as loving and nurturing as mothers can be. As sole custodial parents, they can also fall into the same overinvolved patterns that mothers can. Either parent can develop an enmeshment that restricts both parent and child from getting on with their own stages of interests and growth. The ways in which families reorganize after separation can then have a great impact on the entry of a new partner into the new family at a later date. The ability to parent and consider the best interests of the child are not determined by gender. They are rather determined by legal craftsmanship. Parenting can be loving by either the mother or the father. There is no evidence to bear out the recommendation that continuity of one primary parent is better than shared parenting by both parents, whereby both remain actively and vitally present in the children's lives. Even though the legal-marital union is dissolved, there will still be a parenting bond. Parents know who their children are and children know who their natural parents are. As difficult as divorce and family disorganization is, it is nevertheless a positive experience for a child to know that both parents love him or her enough to plan for him or her in their new family life. As one child said, "I'm happy neither of them will lose us."

There is no doubt that despite the numbers of couples of the 1980s who have divorced and the 75%–80% who are remarried, there is not yet enough history to know how shared parenting will work for children, for the parents, or for a future marriage. It is a new concept for fathers to begin to share primary care of their children on a part-time basis rather than be host to visiting children. This may require a reshifting of priorities for men. For the most part, cooperative fathers have been in the role of "helping" their wives with the children in the intact family, not in that of primary caretaker. Sharing parenting out of the marriage usually takes time and some experimentation and flexibility to evolve into a comfortable arrangement. The process of how each parent uses the time with the children and cooperates with the other is an important foundation. If the parents compete or tear each other down, or try to enlist the loyalty of a child, the consequences can be too burdensome for everyone.

Each parent must come to grips with the rights of the former partner to be living in a different life-style. Certainly influences in each of the homes, as well as childrearing attitudes and rules, may be different. The financial standards, particularly after remarriage, are frequently not the same; one parent may be living in cramped quarters with minimal income while the other parent is living comfortably on a grander scale. This could be either the mother or the father, and unless there is respectful acceptance of different standards, values and rules, children can become confused and may feel they must choose loyalty to one parent over the other. Although children may identify more with one parental model, they should be able to arrive at this by themselves without feeling they have been influenced to reject one parent. Children tend to relate to the quality of the parental love rather than differences in life-style.

One divorced father described his experience of joint custody. He said that it would never have worked for either him or his former wife to be "weekend parents, because that would have caused an unnatural situation for their daughter Mary, who would have felt like a guest in one parent's house." This father, who has been separated for a couple of years, is now ready to file for divorce, and he admits "One quiet nightmare I have is that when we file for divorce, we hit a judge who disregards the success of our arrangement and insists that one parent take custody." Their schedule is that the child stays with each parent on alternating months, and during the month she spends Friday night and Saturday with the other parent. He admits that he is aware of the fact that this may be "bouncing the child back and forth."

According to this father, his daughter appears to have adapted to this living arrangement but it had taken time for her to accept it. At the beginning, on one occasion, she refused to go with him and he took her kicking and screaming. Once with him, she quieted down and seemed calm and happy. He added that he is never quite certain how she feels despite the fact that he encourages her to express her feelings about the separation and about dividing her time between her two loving parents. After a period with this arrangement, on one occasion the child said to her mother, "You have your turn, Mom, and Daddy has his." The father said, "It is an astoundingly amicable agreement. We seem so relieved to be released of each other that we are all cooperating, and we feel awful that we hurt Mary, and want to do everything to stop hurting her." This couple agreed by contract to commit themselves to a biannual meeting to assess how the arrangement was working for them and for their daughter. At these meetings they talk about finances and the custody arrangement. Mary is a preschool child who will start school in a year. The father expressed his concern about how this will affect the arrangements. He believes that he might have to consider moving into his ex-spouse's neighborhood, where the school system, he feels, is superior to the one near his home.

There is also the question of Mary's friends, who are in her mother's neighborhood. The father expressed much apprehension that Mary will not want to live part-time with him after she starts school. Not wanting to lose his child, he worries about the future, since Mary's needs will change. This custody arrangement leaves unanswered questions because it is so recent and at the preschool stage of the child's life. however, it does convey strongly the mystique of biological parental love. How the joint custody arrangements will work as the child reaches different stages of her life and as each parent moves into different phases of his or her life remains to be seen. The message conveyed is that the parents' love for their child will be the priority in future plans.

Wallerstein and Kelly[14] report the interesting finding that adults who disagreed strongly with each other on a great many issues were still able to cooperate in the care of their children. Childrearing issues were not a source of disagreement for over one-third of the parents studied in their survey. Their report says, "Parents who related extremely poorly to each other were still able to share the parenting and caring function and to maintain the other partner at his or her best as a parent" (p. 15). Their work with children of divorce revealed that "regardless of the legal allocation of responsibility and custody, the emotional significance of the relationship with each of the two parents did not diminish" during the course of their five-year period of study. Another interesting observation of the study was that many parents who lacked legal rights tended to withdraw from children's lives in grief and frustration.

The next chapter will describe the experiences that remarried couples had in the educational group seminars that I led at the Clarke Institute of Psychiatry.

REFERENCES

[1]Nizer, L. *My Life in Court*. New York: Doubleday & Co., 1961, p. 153.
[2]Elken, M. *Joint Custody: A Handbook*. Portland, Oregon: Association of Family Conciliation Courts, 1980.
[3]Goldstein, J. Freud, A., and Solnit, A. J.: *Beyond the Best Interests of the Child*. New York: The Free Press, 1973.
[4]Roman, M., and Haddad, W. *The Disposable Parent*. New York: Holt, Rinehart, & Winston, 1978.
[5]Grief, G. L. "Single Fathers Finding Family Success." In *Sarasota Suncoast Today*, reporting on Philadelphia news release, January 20, 1983.
[6]Statistics Canada. Vital Statistics, Vol. 11: Marriages and Divorces, 1975. Ottawa: Ministry of Industry, Trade and Commerce, 1977.
[7]Noble, J., and Noble, W. *The Custody Trap*. New York: Hawthorn, 1975.
[8]*Time*. February 8, 1982.
[9]Burger, W. E. Editorial. *Family Mediation*, March/April, 1982, p. 2.
[10]Berger, S. J. Letters to the Editor. *Family Mediation*, March/April, 1982, p. 2.
[11]"Divorce American Style" *Newsweek*, January 10, 1983, pp. 42-48.
[12]*Globe and Mail*. Toronto, Ontario, Canada, May 12, 1983.
[13]Erikson, E. *Childhood and Society*. New York: Norton, 1950.
[14]Wallerstein, J., and Kelly, J. B. *Surviving the Break Up*. New York: Basic Books, 1980.

CHAPTER 5

THE GROUP EXPERIENCE
GLAD TO MEET YOU

"Glad to meet you" was the greeting that people extended to one another when they met in the group seminars for remarrieds at the Clarke Institute of Psychiatry. They conveyed to each other the relief of travelers in a foreign country who met other speakers of their native tongue. Understanding one another, they quickly identified with the emotions, confusions, and conflicts that were being expressed. In the group setting they felt the right to risk voicing some of their personal concerns. It was like opening Pandora's box in a group experience with people whom they had never met before. They talked about feelings they had never dared to discuss with people whom they had known much better and for a long period of time.

This phase of our study explored whether group seminars could serve as an effective medium for preparing couples for some of the stresses unique to second marriages with children from a previous marriage. Since couples had conveyed that there had been many surprises and unanticipated disappointments, our goal was to get people together who had lived through family disruption and reorganization after separation and divorce and were now trying to establish a new family with a different membership. The people, with whom we had had contact through our questionnaires and interviews, reported that they had no guidelines to help them. Since there were no precedents in establishing guidelines for stepfamilies, many of the people going into a second marriage had felt like lonely pioneers in search of norms. The problems that people discussed in the seminars had common themes that began to define remarriage and the features unique to it. There was little doubt that the stepparent–stepchild roles were poorly defined and poorly understood and were thus causing the major stress in remarriages.

The parent, his or her nonparent spouse, and the children from the previous marriage were overwhelmed with confusion, guilt, and ambivalence about who they were supposed to be in one another's lives. The socially accepted and expected bonds between members of a family were not present among all the members of the reconstituted family. A marriage, which is a choice made by the adults and designed to meet their needs, is not necessarily the choice of the children, although they all may live together in the same household.

In the groups, the remarried couples discussed their ambivalence about how actively they wanted their partners to participate in the children's lives. As one mother put it, "I love my husband, but I consider his discipline of my children intrusive." The parents also expressed concern about how well the children would accept the new adult's right to be an authority figure in their lives. The nonparent felt ambivalence regarding the nature of the relationship that he or she really wanted to achieve with someone else's children. Children, who do not perceive their parents as sexual persons, expressed puzzlement over why a parent should want to remarry. The children felt the new member was intrusive to the family group, after the single-parent household had stabilized its reorganized life-style.

Conflicts that had not been put to rest at the time of separation spilled over into the remarriage, influencing the attitudes of the children, the ex-spouse and the new partner. Ex-spouses frequently found it difficult to accept that the former partner had remarried. Power struggles between the ex-partner and present partner would then erupt over the children. When children visited in both parents' homes, they would often be used as message carriers for hostile feelings. The ex-spouse might try to influence the children's attitudes towards the stepparent, or the stepparent might compete for the parent's role by acting like a "super-parent" with the children. The battles that raged between ex-spouses and between ex-spouse and present spouse were as divisive to the remarriage as the conflicts between steprelations.

As for the children, they would often play one parent off against another. For example, if a child did not get his way with his mother, he might respond by threatening to call his father. The absent father, who wanted to be "the good parent," might respond quickly with sympathy and might even offer to take the child into his home, thus undermining the mother's authority over the children. Many fathers who live apart from their children harbor painful feelings of guilt at having complicated their children's lives by the divorce. In an attempt to compensate, they will tell their children that they are available to them any time. Although being available can be thoughtful, it is often influenced by a desire to punish the ex-spouse.

Many of the group discussions reflected how ex-spouses knew each others' sensitive buttons and were quick to push them and quick to react. They would deliberately push these buttons over differences regarding the children, finances, the ways in which child support money was being spent, or complaints about the inadequacy of care the children received in either mother's or father's home and by the stepparent.

The many ways in which various members of the new family group perceived preferential treatment between "his, hers, and ours" was a volatile issue. Angry exchanges tumbled out among members in the group on the various aspects of these concepts in questions concerning how custody arrangements and finances were sources of conflict in the new family. These exchanges spewed forth as though they had been bottled up to a point of explosiveness. Aside from cathartically releasing rage, the participants felt a great sense of relief in learning that as upsetting as their problems were, they were not unique to them as a couple or due to their peculiar inability to cope. Rather, they were within the normal range of conflicts experienced in a remarriage.

Having lived through divorce, some group participants who had taken up residence together talked about the apprehension of legalizing the relationship. They were fearful of risking themselves in another marriage commitment. It had taken time to stabilize themselves and their families after separation and divorce. At long last, they felt that they had come out of the divorce by drawing on individual resources and strengths they had not known they had. However, they were very uncertain as to whether they were ready to give up their independence and whether another marriage would mean they could no longer continue to function with their newly found sense of self. They recalled the panic they had first felt in not having a partner to share in making decisions and talked about how much more confident they were now in decision-making. Many of them feared that another marriage would mean loss of this newly gained independence. Many felt uncertainty about whether they were ready to be once more accountable to someone else about personal and family affairs. As Evelyn said, "I love Frank, but I'm not sure I want to give up my present life style. It means once more disrupting family life for me and the girls."

During these discussions, Paula talked about her fear about legalizing her relationship with Michael. Paula said she really liked having Michael live with her, since he made her feel good about herself. But to marry Michael rather than just living with him might be quite a different thing. Having been burnt once, she wasn't sure to what extent she wanted to commit herself to another marriage and to impose a new husband and surrogate father on the children. Paula felt the children had been put through so many changes in their young lives that she hesitated to disturb them again. When she and Michael had first become friends and Michael had begun visiting her, the children had been friendly with him; but once he moved in, they had a wholly different reaction to him. He was no longer a visitor, but an intruder between them and their mother. The children were no longer friendly and did not respond to Michael's friendliness. Some of the same behavior they had shown when Jack, their father, had left home was once more in evidence. They clung to Paula and wanted all her attention; Michael became a threat to them. They feared he would take their mother away and did everything they could to keep Michael away from her. Paula reported that at night one of the children was sure to climb into bed between her and Michael; or when they went for a drive, she could be sure that Gwen, the six-year-old, would already be in the car, parked between Michael, the driver, and herself.

Some other members of the group identified immediately with this kind of behavior, and many recounted stories of how their own children did all kinds of things to sabotage a new relationship and another marriage. In these exchanges, the parents become aware of how frightening it was for the children, who now felt dependent on only one parent, to think that a new partner might take all that parent's time, attention, and love, and perhaps even take the parent away as well. After all, had not one loving parent already left them? What guarantee did they have that the other parent wouldn't do the same? And then, if their mother remarried, that would burst the fantasy which so many children hold that their parents will be reunited. Many children display their worst behavior to a potential new partner to discourage a remarriage to anyone but the ex-spouse.

During one of the sessions, Paula said she had found herself saying to Michael, "I don't understand what got into Gwen; she never acts like that." Once she had said it, she felt angry with herself for essentially apologizing for her daughter's behavior. She told the group, "It's peculiar that Jack was sometimes rough with the children, and I sure didn't like the fact that he would occasionally push or smack them, but I knew, and the children knew, it was just that he was in a bad mood. We all know he loves his children. But, if Michael were ever to lay a hand on one of my children, I would leave him immediately. They are not his children and I don't even know what rights I want him to have with them."

Michael's response to this was, "I am not their father. We all know that they have their father. I have to learn what I want to be to them, and they have to learn what they want me to be in their lives. It will take time for them to trust me and to begin a relationship with me. I can't honestly say I feel the same toward them as I do toward my son, Gary. They are nice kids, but I don't really know them yet and they certainly don't know or trust me. They have been far from friendly since I've moved in and I know they resent my living in their home."

The response of Kate's new husband, Tom, to Michael was, "Scott, Kate's son, not only resents me, he rejects me totally. He has made it clear that he doesn't want any relationship with me. Last week on his birthday, I gave him a gift which he simply returned unopened. That really bothered me. I've never had children, but I'm usually good with them. I don't know how to reach Scott and I've just about decided that since he doesn't like me, I'll just steer clear of him. Kate has handled him by herself for the last couple of years, so she can continue to do that. I'll stay out of his way and just enjoy my marriage with Kate." Other members of the group protested that this was not a way in which Kate and Tom could ever have a family life. It would be too divisive. It would be like two family units living under one roof. There would be Kate and Scott, and Kate and Tom, with Kate caught in the middle. When she was with Scott, Tom would feel left out, and when she was with Tom, Scott would feel left out.

Caution and apprehension about making a legal commitment after having one marriage terminate was a serious and almost universal concern among the group members. A number of conflicts revolved around disrupting the newly achieved stability of being a single parent. For many of those present in the groups, this was an immediate concern, since many of them were in the process of considering remarriage, with the desire for a marital relationship. Though they had a partner who was important to them, they had anxiety over how much of a commitment they really wanted to make to that other person. Even when they had taken up residence together, the question remained whether they really wanted to incorporate the partner into the life of the family, or whether they wanted the relationship to remain only between them as a couple on a voluntary basis rather than a legal one.

Many of the couples, who were living together without legal sanction, said that signing a marriage certificate did not mean anything to them. They loved each other and wanted to live together. Nonetheless, they admitted that there were personal and social inconveniences that often created uncomfortable situations. One of the mothers said that her twelve-year-old daughter faced her squarely one day and said defiantly, "How would you like me to take a boy into my bedroom to sleep with me?" This filled the mother with guilt. Here was her child, standing in moral judgment of her mother's behavior. The woman was concerned that she was setting a poor example for her daughter by living in a style she would not want her daughter to copy. She felt she was losing her right to offer guidance when her daughter said, "Sure, you're good at do as I say, but not as I do."

Despite the increase in common-law unions, they continue to lack an institutional form with public acceptance and religious sanction. The absence of any formal recognition of this kind of a relationship is stressful to some people. There are no rituals as there are for traditional weddings, nor is there even language to define or describe this kind of coupling. It becomes awkward for some people to introduce a partner. As one man said, he didn't want to introduce his partner as "my friend or my mistress. She's more than a friend, and mistress denotes only sexual relationships and she's more than a sexual partner."

Children also are troubled with a parent's having an unmarried mate living in the home as part of the family. There is confusion about who this adult who lives in the home is supposed to be to the child, and there is ambiguity about what role the adult can assume with the children. As one man in the group declared, "I can only bite my tongue so long, and then I explode with rage at her children's rudeness to her and to me too. If we are carrying on a conversation and her son turns the radio on so loud that I can't even hear myself talk, am I supposed to shut up? Laura says it's her business to discipline her children, not mine. I don't even want to but I want to have some rights if I'm going to live there and if her home is my home too."

Step roles are ambiguous enough after a remarriage in terms of the rights of a stepparent to be an authority figure to the partner's children. However, they are even less clearly defined if the new partner is the mother's live-in mate, without legal sanction. Studies have reported that daughters of a divorced parent who is involved with a live-in partner display more acting-out, precocious sexual behavior. Mavis Hetherington reported that adolescent girls of divorced parents displayed seductive and inappropriate sexual behavior.[1]

One mother reported an experience she had with her fifteen-year-old daughter, Mary, who brought a boyfriend up to her bedroom and closed the door. The woman said she rushed up and banged on the door shouting: "What do you think you're doing?" Her daughter's reply was: "Nothing that you don't do when Doug is in your bedroom."

Children tend to consider that a parent's function is to be a parent. They do not want to perceive their parent as a sexual person. Another mother reported that Hilda, her ten-year-old daughter, was pleased that her mother had a male friend. The daughter was happy that her mother had someone to date and keep her company in the evening. But when her mother said her friend was going to move in, Hilda was aghast. The child said,

"But you're not even married. Why does he have to move in and spoil everything? He's not even related to us."

Dating and sexual activity for divorced people was one of the topics which the groups discussed. The general agreement was that divorced persons who choose to have sexual relations should not have casual partners stay overnight. As one woman said, "I think having a parade of uncles sleeping over is quite different from developing a relationship that has become important enough to consider whether you both want marriage." The "parade of uncles" brought laughter from the group. Many of the parents related episodes of neighbors or friends who had short-term relationsips with men who were introduced to the children as "uncle." There was consensus that these casual relationships belonged outside the home, not in the home where there are children. It can set an example that most parents would not want their children to follow.

It was interesting to learn how significant the legality of the marriage vows are in people's lives, especially as they relate to family life. Even those who described themselves as nontraditionalists felt this way. Partners who had spent several years living together without matrimonial sanction described a sense of social discomfort in their personal relationship, for their children, parents, and extended family. In the past couple of decades, parents of adult children who are living in common law are readier to accept the living arrangement than children are for their parents. They do wish, however, that there were a language and ritual to acknowledge the son or daughter "out-of-law." The nature of the voluntary live-in relationship has commonly been perceived as easier to separate from than those of a formal marriage. However, when couples who are not legally married separate they feel the same attachment loss and grief that people do for any significant relationship that they lose. The introduction of "palimony" is evidence of the trend toward institutionalizing common-law unions as relationships that have commitment and obligations. The English vocabulary has not kept up with contemporary life, either in the usage of *stepparent*, or in the names referring to remarriage family and its members, or in regard to common-law alliances.

Time quoted from an advertisement referring to live-together relationships as "P.O.S.S.L.Q.," which was an abbreviation for "Persons of the Opposite Sex Sharing Living Quarters."[2]

There is more social acceptance and therefore more comfort with institutionalized modes of life. Some couples who have lived together, even for long periods, and then were legally married described the extent to which they felt more comfortable with their newly acquired marital status and the ways it affected their position in the family. One man said, "I've lived in Ellie's home for five years, but I never felt there was a place in the house I could call my own. I thought that maybe it was because I had moved into her former marriage home. But after we got married, it was like going from being a boarder to being accepted as part of the family."

Another man who had recently become a husband after four years of being a boyfriend declared himself in the more comfortable position now of being introduced by his wife's parents as "my son-in-law." Still another partner, a young woman, declared that although the legal document meant nothing to her, she had vowed she would not become pregnant unless they were married. When members questioned her logic, she said she felt it would be awkward for the child to be raised by unmarried parents and uncomfortable for her parents and family to accept a pregnancy and a baby born out-of-wedlock. She said her parents had been tolerant of her relationship, but she felt that they viewed it as a temporary one. She admitted that she had kept hoping her partner would also feel that legalizing the relationship would bring more public credibility to it. Still another woman said she felt that since she and her husband had married she had lost a good friend. She said she found that now there were different expectations put on her. There were different rules for being a wife than for being just an unmarried partner. Now there was accountability to her husband's family with daily telephone calls and family responsibilities. Much of what she had done voluntarily for the family before marriage was now expected and taken for granted. She added that she liked the security of being admitted into the family fold but had mixed feelings about how her wife role was now being stereotyped both by the family and, she added, by her husband too.

Couples compared notes on the kinds of weddings they had had and how these differed from their first weddings. In every case the weddings were smaller and less formal. In most cases their children were present along with the parents, immediate family, and sometimes intimate friends. The majority of the participants had been married by clergy or in a Marriage License Bureau. Vows were usually exchanged in the home, not in a church. Couples showed much interest in comparing notes on how other couples had told their children about their plans to be married. The exchanges of experiences in dealing with this issue indicated that parents had found it difficult to tell their children about their plans to be married. Moreover, it was evident that people handled the situation in a variety of ways. A few couples admitted that they had not told their children until after they were married, which, they added, had had unfortunate repercussions. One woman said that she and her husband were married while the children were at camp. The couple's rationale was that this would give them honeymoon time. However, they had not anticipated the hurt and upset the children would feel when they were told at camp; the children cried, feeling deceived and abandoned. Their homecoming became a very stressful experience. They felt that a man had moved into their home and was sleeping in their father's place—this despite the fact that the children had been quite friendly to him before the marriage. Treating him like a stranger who had invaded their home, they protested his right to walk around in his bathrobe as though this were his home. He exclaimed: "They treated me like a nonperson. I often wondered whether they would have felt I had more rights if they had attended our wedding." As it was, at the dinner table the children could be seated right beside him, but if they wanted something passed, they would reach across him. His feeling was that "they did their darndest to sabotage our marriage." Other couples identified quickly with his story and related many similar stories.

This confirmed for me and for the group members that a remarriage is not between two people only; it is a family affair. The children must be included in some way during the period of courtship. Relationships must be developed between the children and the husband or wife to be. Plans for marriage must also be discussed with the children. It is not up to the children to accept or reject the idea of the marriage, but after the adults have made the decision and moved on to the planning stage, the children should be informed and involved. Remarriage is a major life event not only for the adults but also for the children. The more preparation and involvement there is for everyone, the more possibility there is of reducing the stress of the marriage and legitimizing its reality.

The discomfort of having a new partner move into the life of the family can be eased with premarital planning. Rituals usually dictate guidelines for behavior. When there is a first wedding, it marks a fresh beginning of a new stage in life for a couple. It is the absence of a different model for the second marriage that makes it stressful. With no traditional honeymoon period for the couple to establish a couple relationship, compounded by cultural expectations that the marriage will create a new, "instant family" life, instant family tensions frequently develop. Children cannot play an incidental role in the process of forming a new family; they will require a good deal of emotional interaction before they feel part of it. Certainly, the couple relationship is vital, but the couple relationship must leave room for the children to adapt to the new life so they will not feel that the marriage will push them aside. If the children feel confident that they are included in the new family group, they are more likely to feel less threatened; and if they feel less threatened, they can then be more accepting of the marriage.

Group members reported the different hopes and dreams with which they had approached their new marriages. Some hoped that a new marriage would make up for the hurts and disappointments of the first marriage. Others said they felt they were depriving the children of a family life without both a mother and father. Still others expressed concern about the absence of a male or female role model with whom the children could identify. And some others felt it would be wonderful to have a dependable partner to share the home and family responsibilities. Yet when they moved in with the spouse and children, life did not go exactly as planned. Some men have a predefined notion of man as head of the family. Once they moved into the family home, to secure a status for themselves, they took on the role of authority. Though many had not yet really become acquainted with the children—their temperaments, their habits and customary behavior, or their mother's way of dealing with them—they imposed themselves as instant heads of household. The result was "culture shock" for all concerned: The mother was not accustomed to her husband's approach to her children; the children were suddenly confronted with different rules and attitudes from a nonparent; and the new spouse felt he had the right to reconstruct the children, whose behavior was alien to him. Frequently men have said they wanted to protect their wives from the difficult behavior of children. What many of the men did not recognize was that a parent might react with anger to a child's behavior, but the love remained firm. Where there is not yet a relationship or affectionate base, discipline can come across like disapproval and rejection of the child himself, not just of the behavior. One mother in the group was having difficulty with her new partner, who she claimed was "generous with his criticism and stingy with his praise." She said, "he can't see anything nice about my children, only all their faults."

There is little doubt that the term *blended family* used for a family constructed through remarriage is a misnomer. The process of blending is the most difficult experience for a family to attain after acquiring a new membership. It takes time and patience to achieve the sense of family integration that comes with blending. This quality of feeling like a "real family" is perhaps the most complex part of remarriage.

The seminars had a mix of couples who came together from different marriage backgrounds and different stages of their life cycle. When both partners had a previous marriage and divorce and both had custody of their children, they discussed a variety of ways of dealing with setting up family life with two sets of children. Children who had lived through parental divorce and through the disorganization of the family were now brought together to live in the intimacy of one family household with other children whose life-styles were often quite different from theirs. The age and sex of the children and their ordinal position in the family were all significant factors in the merging of the families. The baby was no longer the baby, the eldest no longer the eldest. Personalities, interests, academic achievements, and so forth could all change when children of different backgrounds and stages of life are thrown together.

Some children were orderly, some untidy, some noisy, some loners, some intellectual, some sports-minded. Certainly different personalities can be part of any intact family. The big difference is that in the intact family the children have grown up together, know each other's idiosyncracies, and have learned to live with them. This is different from children who suddenly are forced to move in together and share the intimacies of bathrooms and sometimes bedrooms. There are so many daily routines, habits, customs, and rituals taken for granted in our family life that become self-conscious and inhibited acts when exposed to other people within a family situation. Wandering around the house skimpily dressed and keeping the bathroom door unlocked are no longer freedoms. Home loses the comfort of home.

Couples reported that while they were dating they frequently included all the children in outings, even for overnight camping trips, but that there was a big difference between visiting and having recreational activities together on the one hand and moving into one home together on the other. Parents tend to be primitive in their protective responses to their own children. They are proud to display their children's skills and strengths but want to cover up or defend any weaknesses. At the same time, they may feel critical and quickly aware of any misbehavior on the part of their partner's children.

There were a variety of ways in which couples in the groups had made plans for their joint living arrangements. Some plans were made for economic reasons or other practical reasons such as size of the home. Other couples established their priority for planning around what would make for the easiest transition for their children.

Anne and Charlie, a couple in one of the groups, talked about their housing situation. They had three children between them; Anne's son and daughter were eight and ten, and Charlie's son was four. In describing their housing plans to the group, they explained that they had decided it would make sense for them to move into Anne's three-bedroom home because it was the larger of the two. Charlie's son Jimmie was to share a bedroom with Anne's eight-year-old son, Tim. The plan seemed practical, but Tim had always had his own bedroom, and he was a collector. Jimmie, the four-year-old, was a curious little boy who poked around into Tim's possessions. Because of the boys' differences, Anne and Charlie had little time for each other. Anne, particularly, found herself constantly restricting Jimmie, the stepchild, and scolding her son Tim for being rough with the younger child. Moreover, she later complained that she found herself tied down during the day with Jimmie while the other

children were at school. Having finished the preschool stage
with her own children, Anne began to feel exploited at this
point in her life. She was now questioning whether Charlie had
made his decision to get married in order to have someone to
take care of his child. She said, "I began to wonder, what did I
get myself into? They've made more work for me. I don't have
time for my children. I don't have time for the marriage. Jimmie
is wild, noisy, and rebellious and Charlie doesn't seem to do anything to discipline him." At the same time, she felt very troubled,
and Charlie felt puzzled and frustrated. Before their marriage
Anne had told him how much she enjoyed being a homemaker
and a mother. She had said that since her children were born,
taking care of them had been a rewarding full-time job. Charlie
had thus felt that his son would fit easily into this child-centered
home. Once they were married, Charlie couldn't understand
how Anne could help but love this cute little boy. Anne's
response was, "It's easy for you to say that, you're not home with
him all day. I have no freedom or respite now. I can't let him out
of my sight or he'll be into some kind of trouble."

The group was sympathetic to Anne. The discussion dealt
with Charlie's expecting Anne to love his son immediately in the
way that he, Charlie, loved him. He also took for granted that he
could turn all the parenting responsibilities over to her. After all,
she was a mother and she had said she loved taking care of children. When Jimmie would act up, Charlie's view of Jimmie's
pranks was to pamper and laugh at them, explaining them away
to Anne and her children. This gave Jimmie his father's approval
without Charlie's assuming his rightful position in being the primary parent to guide his child.

The group members acknowledged that a parent and a stepparent can have very different perspectives of the same child's
behavior depending on whose child it is. To Charlie, Jimmie was
cute and endearing. He may have been those things, but to Anne
he was someone else's child whose responsibility had been
turned over to her as part of her marriage. She became especially

resentful since it was spoiling her feelings toward Charlie. Thus Anne had been put in the posiition of being an authority figure and sole disciplinarian in Jimmie's life. The child had been handed over to her, and Charlie was conveying, "We're married, I'm your husband, and Jimmie is our child now."

The discussion about the effect of Jimmie's behavior on Anne and Charlie's marriage helped the members to recognize that when two sets of children are brought into a marriage each parent has a particular responsibility in relation to his or her own children. Agreement should be reached about family tasks, children's bedtimes, and other daily routines. They cannot be taken for granted. The marriage in itself does not produce stable family life. There must be rules and roles negotiated and established. Each parent must assume responsibility for ensuring that their own children respect the house rules, at least until steprelations are formed with trust. Certainly, a period of disequilibrium must be expected before the household can stabilize and family life can take on a pattern.

The group discussions once more reinforced the idea that remarriage does not create an instant family. The fact of being married does not turn a nonparent into a parent. Each parent continues the responsibility to his or her own child and must reassure him or her that the marriage will not mean abandonment by dumping the child on the other partner. On the other hand, the stepparent should be encouraged to become involved with the partner's child by exchanging views on child rearing, interests, and background with the parent. And if a child complains about the stepparent, the parent should encourage him or her to bring the complaints directly to the partner. The middleman role of the parent tends to inhibit a sense of trust and comfort with the family by preventing the stepparent from dealing directly with the child's feelings. When a parent acts as the middleman, it prolongs the life of two families with two family systems living under one roof.

In one of the groups, a father described how he and his wife (who obviously had an excellent relationship) had dealt with beginning their married life as two custodial parents to their four children. Grace had two daughters, aged five and seven years; Tony had two boys, six and eight. Their children were close enough in age for the parents to be able to establish a home routine that could accommodate all of them. The couple and the children were in the same life stages. This was an important factor in terms of immediate tasks, responsibilities, and goals. Because the couple felt that a new house would symbolize the beginning of a new family life for everyone, and everyone would be making adjustments anyway, the couple agreed on buying a larger house for the four children. If, instead, they had moved into either of their former homes, one family might have felt that they were being invaded while the other might have felt that they were intruders. In a new home everyone would be adapting to new surroundings, a different neighborhood, and a new school. For Grace and Tony this became a unifying factor that consolidated them into a family group. The children all supported one another in meeting their new situations.

When possible, it is wise for a couple with children to begin their married life in a different home, rather than in either of the former matrimonial homes. In Grace and Tony's case, they purchased their home, then took the children to the house, assigned bedrooms for them, and told them to decide where they wanted to place their furniture and which colors they wanted the walls painted. They all explored the area together. Together they went to the neighborhood school and introduced themselves to the principal. They told the principal that they were planning to be married and that many new things were happening in the children's lives. They further explained to the principal that both sets of children had a parent with whom they were not living but who loved them and would want to be kept informed of the children's progress and notified of parent meetings. This was a significant way to help the school recognize the rights of both parents to remain actively involved with the children's school life, despite the fact that the parents were divorced and were being remarried. In addition, it conveyed to the children that there was no need for them to feel ashamed about their parent's divorce or embarrassed about having different surnames. It became more matter of fact. There was an openness about the reality of the family situation. It left the children feeling free to know that the remarriage did not mean that their other parent would lose contact with them because they had moved and were not living with both parents. The children, part of the new family plans, became caught up in the anticipation of the new life ahead.

Tony told the group that he had not moved into Grace's children's lives with any expectation of an immediate relationship. Instead, he waited for them to come to him. He said he felt that his job as the adult was to hold himself available until they reached out to him. He wanted them to know that he was there for them, but he did not come on strong in order to try to establish an unrealistic picture of who he was in their lives. Both Grace and Tony talked to the children about the children's other parents, reassuring them that they weren't going to take their absent parents' place. They both told the children that they loved each other and that they hoped the children would also learn to love them. In the group Tony said he felt that it was essential for these children, who had all lived with poor models of marriage and adult relationships, to have now the opportunity of experiencing a loving adult relationship between their parent and stepparent.

One group member said that he and his wife had felt the same but that the first time they had a disagreement her children were frightened and asked if she was going to have another divorce. The group discussed the importance of demonstrating to the children that people are bound to have differences but that they can discuss them and either come to some agreement or accept each other's right not to agree. Divorce does not happen when two people love each other. Though they may disagree about something, it does not mean they will reject the person any more than if a parent and child disagree. The group members found this a productive way of viewing fighting; every fight or disagreement does not have to end with mutual agreement. The recognition that there is not one absolute way of perceiving anything demonstrated the need for flexibility and openmindedness. When this message is conveyed or demonstrated to the children, they will not feel so threatened that the new marriage will also fall apart just because the adults disagree. This discussion was significant for the divorced people who knew that the previous patterns for resolving conflict had not worked for them and had been a poor model for their children. It had left both the adults and the children apprehensive about disagreeing with one another. There was the threat that having differences or being angry could lead to another divorce, or to rejection, which created hesitation about feeling free to express differences.

Tony said that despite all the planning to ease the transition into a new family for the children, Grace's five-year-old daughter, Marie, was frightened of him and kept a room's length distance between them. Tony said he made no effort to transgress the boundaries the child set up. Though extending his friendliness, he did not react to her lack of response to him. This estrangement went on for close to a year. Even though Marie kept aloof, she was very aware of him. When he came into a room, she moved away without looking in his direction. One day, he came home and Marie was watching the Muppets on television. He sat down on the sofa and Marie didn't move. Tony described how good that made him feel. Maybe she was beginning to trust him. He didn't take advantage of the moment by trying to move closer. The next day, this closeness was again permitted to him. After a few days, Marie came over to him and said, "Tony, I have a knot in my shoelace, can you undo it?" Tony said his heart pounded. He wanted to hug the child. He was making friends with her. Struggling over the knot, he finally undid it, at which point Marie kicked him in the shins, saying, "My daddy could have done that in half the time." Tony related this story with tears in his eyes.

This demonstrates the profound conflict which children experience. Marie wanted to be close to Tony; she had begun to care for him and to trust him. But she felt that this would be unfaithful to her own father. Tony was wise enough to understand and not feel this was personal rejection of him, but rather the child's fear that if she began to care for him she would be unfaithful to her father, who would be jealous. Children must be assured that there is enough love for everyone and that there are different kinds of love. Marie found that her mother's love for Tony did not take away from her mother's love for her. In the same way, if she loved Tony, it did not mean her love for her father would be any less. This loyalty conflict is strong for children and is frequently misconstrued by a stepparent as personal rejection rather than fear of how this closeness can affect the feeling between the absent parent and child. It is equally important for the noncustodial parent to understand that if the child cares about the same-sex stepparent, it is not a threat to the child's love for his nonresident parent. When the absent parent undermines the stepparent and any rights the stepparent has with the child, this can only confuse the child, intensify loyalty conflicts, and inhibit the child's right to feel affection for the stepparent. Children frequently fight against good feelings by being rebellious, disobedient, or withdrawn.

The groups also discussed how careful custodial parents must be not to show preferential treatment to their own child. The counterpart might be that parents, in order to establish a friendly, parental-type relationship with the partner's child, would bend over backwards with their stepchild, thus creating resentment and jealousy from their natural child. Children have complained, "Why do you let him do that when you don't let me do it?" or "You always take his side, not mine." Such an approach can intensify sibling rivalry between stepsibs. There are natural emotions that parents have a right to express to their own children. The love and protection that parents feel for their natural children of course have priority. It takes time to develop a relationship with and affection for a partner's children. Pretenses of instant love are too obvious and contrived. However, fairness to all the children with no preferential treatment can avoid antagonism and resentment. Logical, flexible house rules that can adapt to the different ages and stages of the children will go a long way toward giving stability and serenity to family life.

One parent expressed surprise that there should be any problem in making the new family into a "real family." She went on to say that at every meal time, she, her husband, and their five children all sat down together and every meal was like a party. She added that a friend who visited asked which children belonged to whom. "I really forget, because they are all my children," was her reply. Moreover, she went on to say that a different friend had even commented on the resemblance between one of her husband's children and one of hers.

The group members were skeptical. It sounded to them like some kind of game, that everyone was playing at being one big happy, "real" family. The inference was that the family was denying the reality that there had been a first marriage and that there was an absent parent, as well as other kin. Interestingly enough, this kind of game playing does tend to lead to a pseudofamily, blocking the possibility of its becoming a real family. Such a cover-up is comparable to the case of an adopted child who is not told about the facts of his adoption and thus feels that discussion of it must be taboo. A family relationship based on denial can leave all members of the family alone with a sense of loss for the missing people of their lives. "Parent-finders" groups for adopted children have brought public recognition to the need and right of adopted children to know about their biological ties. Identifying these ties does not lessen the love adopted children carry for the parents who have reared and cared for them. Nor, in the same way, do ties between children of divorce and both parents preclude the love that can develop between children and stepparents.

Our group discussions left no doubt that families during second marriages have to deal with special concerns that are not present in the intact nuclear family and for which there are few guidelines to help them. Certainly bringing two sets of children together from previous marriages requires time and understanding before the children will feel comfortable living together. Parents who do not acknowledge the discomforts involved are fooling themselves. Denial is no answer. Expecting or acting as if everyone were part of an instantly homogeneous family will not accomplish the end.

There are numerous variables which affect the new family including different backgrounds and ages among the children. When both sets of children are young and within the same age range, there is more possibility for comfort. It is easier for them to accept their parents' marriage when they share family life with children of similar ages who are also undergoing this experience. It helps put divorce and remarriage into a more normal perspective. It hasn't just happened to them. There is then less need for the children to feel ashamed or wish to conceal the fact that they live with a stepparent. The more comfortable they feel about the family, the more easily they can contend with inquisitive people who ask, Why are your surnames different from your brother? How does it feel to have a stepparent? What do you call your stepparent? Do you feel like Cinderella? These questions continue to this day to plague the stepchild. The more openly the remarriage is acknowledged, the less pretense and ambiguity there is in the step relationship. Wide differences in age between the two sets of children require different and more flexible ground rules for living together.

Another problem which surfaced through group discussions dealt with two sets of adolescents dating each other. Parents in the groups expressed their apprehension about this, even though they recognized that such attraction was outside the boundaries of the biological incest taboo. When a teenage boy and girl live in the same home it is not unusual for them to become sexually aware of each other. There is no single answer to this perplexing situation, since sexual awareness is a normal, healthy response in teenagers. In sharing family life, the young male and female are exposed to each other within the close daily intimacy of the home, and sexual curiosity may well be aroused. Some parents reported that their teenagers tended to protect themselves from sexual arousal by avoiding each other or displaying antagonistic, quarrelsome attitudes toward each other. Parents cannot pretend or expect that an adolescent boy and girl are going to accept each other as natural brother and sister as though they had grown up together. Thus tension and attraction may well arise from these feelings, which cause great concern to the couple relationship. Parental control, through restrictive or punitive devices, can promote sexual acting-out in rebellion against such disciplinary measures. Probably, as with any other concern, the more the family is ready to discuss the tensions and potential consequences of such problems in an open and honest way, the more personal responsibility the young adults are likely to assume for the protection and stability of all the members of the remarriage family.

Yet another potential source of tension which was brought up for discussion in some of the groups occurred in remarriages in which men marry women who have preteen or teenage daughters. Ralph, one of the participants, discussed some confusing emotions he had experienced when he first went into his marriage with a woman who had a fifteen-year-old daughter. His comments brought forth expressions of gratitude from some of the other members, who said they felt relieved that they were not alone in experiencing such upsetting feelings. Evidently sexual attraction between stepparent and stepchild was not an unusual phenomenon. In fact, this issue came up for discussion in most of the seminars.

Ralph talked about his stepdaughter's seductive behavior with him, describing how she would snuggle up to him, preening herself, and ask him if she looked attractive. She would ask him to pick her up at school, and when he did, she would introduce him to her friends and show him off in a way that made him feel uncomfortable. A sexual tension had become apparent to him. In being honest with himself about his confused emotions, he knew he had to clear the air by describing what he was aware was happening. Finally he said to her, "Claire, I think that you're an attractive kid. As your mother's husband, I'm glad we like each other and that we get along okay, but I am not your boyfriend." When he was able to get this off his chest in an adult, matter-of-fact way, he felt better, for he was the adult talking to the child. Once he had dealt with this discomfort, he was then able to tell Claire when she looked nice and also when she was play-acting in an inappropriate way. This also gave him the right to be an authority figure as an adult within the family and in Claire's life.

Another group member, the father of two sons, expressed a sense of relief when he heard about Ralph's experience with Claire and his management of it. He said he was accustomed to "horsing around" with his ten- and twelve-year-old boys. When he married Elsa, who had a fifteen-year-old daughter, he thought he could use the same kind of camaraderie to establish a friendly relationship with the girl. However, he sensed both his own discomfort and her sexual overtones. His response was to back away from her, not knowing how to clear the air between them. He had not known how to develop a role as an adult or authority figure in her life. Elsa, who interpreted his withdrawal from her daughter as rejection, was offended. Both Elsa and her husband had to redefine the roles and tasks they should have in the lives of both sets of children.

David, who had married Susan, a younger woman, told of coming into the remarriage family with a seventeen-year-old son. During the school year, Cliff, his son, was away at school.

However, when holiday time arrived, Susan was intolerably tense. She said she just couldn't be left in a room alone with Cliff and described a "tension you could cut with a knife." She said she really had not understood what it all meant until the discussions had touched upon libidinous feelings that can emerge when new members join together in a remarriage family.

When people keep uncomfortable emotions to themselves, they feel isolated and wonder about the normality of their feelings. Clearing the air about perplexing topics brought relief to those people who were concerned that something awful was the matter with them or their children. It was therapeutic to find that others experienced the same kinds of thoughts and feelings. Ralph's description of Claire's behavior and his way of coping with it demonstrated clearly how important it is to convey to the children that the couple bond of husband and wife is secure and loving. This helps to clarify the boundaries in the family between the marital team and the stepparent-to-child parameters. Essential as boundaries are within the intact family, they have additional significance in remarriage families in order to bring more clarity to steprelations. The issue was forcefully driven home that the ambiguity of the step roles was one of the most burdensome problems in remarriage and every effort must be made to clarify who a parent's new partner is in the family. The boundaries between stepparents and children, and between stepchildren, including sexual boundaries, are essentially different. No rose-colored glasses or pretense can cover the fact that unless or until the parent, the stepparent, and the children are all able to accept one another in their appropriate roles and tasks relationships can have problems growing.

Some of the parents talked about their sense of guilt that the divorce had disrupted their children's lives. The parents were now driven to compensate for the children's loss by making the relationship with the children supersede all other relationships. Because of this, if a choice had to be made between the child and partner, many present partners complained that they would be the loser. Children are wise enough to test this power and thereby get into a power struggle with the stepparent.

In each of our groups, the composition was a mix of different ages and stages of life for the couple and for the children. The cases cited above describe remarriages in which both parents are custodial parents and brought children from their previous marriages into the new family. Divorced fathers with custody have increased over the past two decades. *Statistics Canada* reports that the increase is on an upward trend and that by the end of the twentieth century there will be a 73% increase of custodial fathers.[3] However, to date, the post-divorce remarriage family that has both sets of children remains in the minority.

The largest number of our participants were couples with custodial mothers and noncustodial fathers whose children were in the custody of their former wife. This arrangement presented its own conflicts. Stepfathers talked about their feelings regarding their daily responsibility for someone else's children living in the home, while they were only seeing their own children by appointment. They talked about their dual roles as full-time stepfathers and part-time "visitors" in their own children's lives and the guilt and resentment this created for them.

One father said, "I feel guilty when I don't like her children and guilty when I do. I feel guilty when we are all having a good time together and my kids aren't with us. I feel guilty when my kids are with me and I want to spend all my time alone with them, to make up for the time we aren't together. The more time we are apart, the harder it gets for us to keep close to one another. Sometimes I feel that I would be doing them a favor if I stepped out of their lives and cut off all visits. They're hard on all of us, my wife and her children, my children and me." Another father admitted, "I feel guilty that I am enjoying a nice family life and my ex-wife isn't married. I am embarrassed letting my children see me enjoying myself when they see their mother miserable." Another father said, "I feel that the only function I really have in my children's lives is paying for their maintenance. We are really becoming strangers to one another."

Still another father commented, "Surely there must be a better way of handling child custody than having them 'visit' with me every other weekend. We never get into a comfortable father–child feeling when we're together. I feel as though my week is spent waiting for them, and when they are with me I spend time worrying about how soon they will have to leave. I take them out for dinner on Wednesday evenings. It is all so awkward, it gets embarrassing. I don't want to discipline them on the few times we're together, which the kids seem to know since they sure test my patience. They can be impossible in a restaurant, jumping up and down, talking too loud, and being downright rude. I don't know how to be a real father on weekend visits and I don't know whether I have to accept the fact that maybe because I am divorced I have lost my right to be a real father."

Another man responded to this by reporting that his wife is remarried and he has to acknowledge that her husband is in the real father's seat. "He is with the children every day, so he has the right to bring them up and to discipline and direct them. He's good to them and I'm glad, but sad that he may mean more to them than I do." The response to this from another father was to say he is in the same situation with his children who have a stepfather. A conflict wells up in him when he thinks about someone else bringing up his children, and he wonders whether, for their sakes, he should not just step aside. He asked the children what they called their stepfather and was very relieved when they said they called him by his first name. Knowing he was putting them on the spot, he asked his children whether the man was good to them and whether they liked him. When the children reassured him that they didn't like their stepfather and that they wished that their own father would come home again, he said he knew he had no right to be inviting his children to try to please him with their answers. He knew that the children would see that he was not giving them permission to like their stepfather, a man with whom they were living on a daily basis and who was taking responsibility for them; and he knew that this was unfair.

It is so much easier to see that someone else is doing something unproductive than to recognize it in oneself. But during these discussions it became apparent to most of the noncustodial fathers that they too had been guilty of quizzing the children about their stepparents. They realized that they had no right to add to the children's difficulties in adapting to a stepparent by conveying jealousy and making the children feel guilty if they liked their stepparents. Many of the fathers knew that it was up to them to keep the father–child ties strong and consistent and that they could do this without competing with the stepparent or undermining him. The caring that a child can have for a stepparent does not have to detract from the father–child love. Some fathers who were indignant that they had had their guardianship rights taken from them realized that they were using their children to criticize their ex-spouses and the stepparents.

All participants mentioned ways in which ex-spouses would undermine each other. For example, when his children would visit with one father, he admitted complaining about how the children were dressed. He would say, "You'd imagine that with all the money I give your mother, she could buy better clothes for you." Or a custodial mother would put the children on the spot by asking their father in front of them for something she said that she couldn't afford to buy them. One father was very upset when his daughter complained in front of his present wife and her children, "Gabby has it, why can't I? Did you buy it for her, Daddy?" This child was evidently carrying her mother's resentments about the financial differences between the two homes. Her father explained to his daughter that his wife worked and paid for her own children's clothes. This may have brought the child some comfort, but the fact remained that her father was taking care of Gabby and not of her; from her point of view, her father had another daughter, a stepdaughter, for whom he was doing things, and this made this child angry. Her mother was angry too and often said, "Why don't you ask your Dad? He seems to be living in grand style." This also demonstrated clearly to the group that children undoubtedly feel compelled to choose loyalty to one parent over the other and that they experience conflict about their right to love both parents, as though to be loyal love must be exclusive. This would indicate that once parents divorce the children may feel they are expected to divorce their affection from one of the parents.

What is a parent, and in a stepfamily what is a stepparent? The answer to this question was a major source of confusion for some parents and stepparents. The stepfathers who were responsible for the children on a daily basis protested that they were just like a father, whereas the actual father did little for the children other than being a "Sunday father." These stepfathers frequently wanted to have full authoritative rights over the children, whether or not the affectional ties were strong. There seemed to be a great deal of discomfort about the question of authority, which often was made to sound synonymous with parenting.

In my clinical experience, some full-time stepmothers reported even more resentment than stepfathers. When children lived with a custodial father and a stepmother, she usually had many functional responsibilities for the children, depending on their age. One stepmother, Donna, expressed a great deal of conflict about her feelings for her six-year-old stepdaughter, Debby. She was resentful that Debby's mother had turned this child over to her father to bring up shortly after he and Donna had married. Donna said she felt "dumped on." Debby's mother had visitation access and she and Debby enjoyed their free weekend time together, whereas Donna had the difficult daily responsibility. She was very concerned about allowing herself to love this little girl. She kept saying that no matter how much she did for her,

Debby would never be her child, and there was always the fear that at some point Debby would leave her to live with her mother.

In view of the large numbers of remarriages, with the confusion over roles and the competition for parental roles between the absent parent and stepparent, we discussed the wisdom of bringing together ex-spouses who were the biological parents of the children and the stepparents who lived with the children. The suggestion was somewhat of a shock to the group, evoking the spontaneous response that it could not possibly work and could only generate hostile feelings. The strident response this question produced made evident the unresolved conflicts that can continue between ex-spouses as well as between biological parents and same sex stepparents and new partners. It should not be forgotten that the children are moving between the homes of both the parents who carry these highly charged emotions.

One father said his children had told him that their stepfather was great. They said, "You'd like him, Dad. He likes the same kinds of things you do." The father wondered whether he could really feel comfortable being friends with his former wife's husband. An interesting question!

Holiday times like Christmas, Thanksgiving, birthdays, graduations, and weddings could be observed by both biological parents and the stepfamilies. These are traditional family occasions that both parents want to share with their children. There is no proven way for remarried families to observe such events. Couples in the seminars reported a wide range of different practices. One couple suggested that perhaps for the children's sake both parents and their partners could celebrate Christmas together. A woman responded that this would be complicated since in her case both parents had remarried, so that both former families would have to get together with the present families, including relatives, which would be too complex for them. Another parent asked, "Why not just have Christmas with the two sets of biological parents and their children, so that it could

be the real family together?" The ideas put forth reflected that
for the most part, for special occasions, both parents wanted to
celebrate with the children, since they accepted that biological
ties have permanent significance in children's lives. The group
members confirmed for one another that even though the marriage ties no longer exist the ex-partners remain parents to their
children and retain certain bonds which do not negate or undermine the loving bond between the remarried couple.

Another volatile topic that came up for discussion was child
support, and the different ways of managing the finances for
families that had one set of children living in the home and the
other set visiting the home. Usually there was money coming in
for child support and money going out for child support. Such
arrangements proved to touch on very sensitive feelings among
the group members. Though couples were reluctant to get
involved in this aspect of discussion, once it was opened it
turned into a highly charged debate.

Some women felt their present partners were paying too
much to the former mate, and stepfathers complained that absent
fathers were not contributing enough for childcare. The financial arrangements between the ex-spouses kept former marital
conflicts alive and spilled over into their present marriages. One
woman said she had never asked her new husband what his
income or assets were, since she did not want him to feel she had
married him to support her children. Therefore, they never
talked about finances or future protection. The silence between
the couple on this topic seemed to indicate to the group an air of
marital insecurity.

Another woman voiced a similar belief that her present husband should not have to have any financial responsibility for her
children from the former marriage. Yet if the child support coming in did not take care of the children, there was often tension
and sometimes resentment between husband and wife. Another
opinion on this matter was that the husband's expenditures
within the remarriage added to guilt feelings for the stepfather,
who might well resent not only spending daily time with his

partner's children but frequently a large part of his income toward supporting someone else's children. And then there were some remarried men who said their concern could only be with supporting the present family and who resented obligations to former family expenditures, particularly when the ex-wife had remarried.

The second largest group of remarriages were between a divorced parent with either custodial or noncustodial care to a partner who had never been married before. In either case, the new, previously single partner was not only a new bride or groom but also an instant stepparent with no previous parenting experience. Some of the first-time brides found this a difficult role and felt cheated. They complained that they felt they were competing with their husbands' children for his attention. Arlene, a young woman, had married a noncustodial parent who had two children whom he loved dearly. During the week she would feel like a loved wife with an affectionate, attentive husband; but on weekends with her husband's two children, aged ten and seven, she would feel like neither wife nor mother. The home would become busy with the activities of two young children. Since her husband loved having the children with him, he planned that he and the children would share all their activities together.

Arlene said she had never seen a father so devoted to his children, particularly his daughter. She wondered whether fathers and daughters usually had so close a relationship. But never having been a parent, she attributed her surprise to her own inexperience. She went on to say, however, that his daughter followed him around "like a puppy dog, from room to room, and all her questions were directed only to him. Her conversations were exclusively with her dad." This made Arlene feel like an outsider whenever father and daughter were together. "This ten-year-old child has the ability to make me feel nonexistent, and my husband doesn't see that at all." She added, "I think he's flattered that he means so much to her."

Allan, Arlene's husband, suggested that Arlene just refused

to understand how he felt about the fact that his children missed him; weekends were their only time together, whereas he and Arlene were together all week. The group responded to Arlene's pain. The general feeling was that she had withdrawn from trying to get into the weekend family by reacting to the child's possessiveness with a feeling of rejection. On the other hand, members were critical of Allan for not including Arlene and for not giving Arlene a role in the children's lives. He accepted the weekend activity pattern that the children created and turned his back on Arlene to the extent that she was excluded by both her husband and the children. They were setting the pace. With no leadership in this family, whatever family life there was between Allan and his children had been reorganized in a way that did not include Arlene. Arlene's voice was plaintive when she said, "I want to be liked and loved; instead, I feel rejected and like a nonentity." Arlene turned to Allan and said, "I love you, but I'm furious with you. No matter how much I do, it's never right or enough. And even when your children are not complaining, they treat me like a second-class citizen." We suggested that this couple seek counseling together for further help in handling this two-family-system remarriage. The group response to this couple indicated the importance of reorgnizing part-time parent–child time and activities in ways that would include a new partner in the remarriage family.

The opportunity to share feelings and experiences with other divorced and remarried couples proved very productive for the seminar members. The seminars created a sense of normality for many of the bewildering emotions and experiences that people have in a marriage that inherits children from a previous marriage.

Other groups for remarried people are springing up all over the United States and Canada. Among these are the Stepfamily Foundation, an association with branches in many cities which issues bulletins to which remarried people contribute. Information is also available from their California headquarters. In New

York City there is the Remarriage Consultation Service, which deals with remarried couples and their families. Family service associations, which are found in most communities, are probably the most effective sources to direct interested couples to other seminar locations.

There was never enough time for full discussion of all problems, feelings, and experiences in the short hours of the group sessions. Many group members formed ongoing friendships and continued their discussions over coffee long after the meetings were finished. Kinship bonds were formed between couples who confirmed for one another that their problems were not unique and did not arise from personal inadequacy. It was a relief to learn that the guilt stepparents feel when they cannot love their partners' children as they love their partners was widely shared. Guilt feelings of noncustodial parents for disrupting their children's lives and over having to take care of someone else's children were shared by other noncustodial parents. Resentment of custodial or noncustodial parents over the knowledge that their partners, stepparents to their children, did not love the children was a feeling shared by many parents. The reality emerged clearly in the seminars that second marriages with children form a different kind of family. They have different kinds of roles and relationships unique to this family structure that is increasing so rapidly in the 1980s.

The next chapter will deal with remarriage, based on much that was learned from the group experience and the many remarried couples in therapy.

REFERENCES

[1]Hetherington, M. "Effects of Father's Absence on Personality Development in Adolescent Daughters." *Developmental Psychology*, 1972, 313–326.
[2]Time, February 8, 1982.
[3]Statistics Canada. *Divorce: Law and the Family in Canada*. Ottawa Ministry of Supply and Services, 1983, p. 260.

CHAPTER 6

REMARRIAGE

A FAMILY AFFAIR

Stepfamilies must be built with more than good intentions, dreams and hopes. Awareness, skills and realistic expectations can provide a stable structure.[1]

We tend always to be somewhat behind actual events in our knowledge about our social world. Much of our thinking about divorce is, therefore, out of date relating to the way things used to be rather than to the way they are.[2]

We are having a hard time readjusting our picture of marriage and divorce to the reality of what they are, actually, now, today.[3]

The divorce and remarriage rates in the past decade have introduced contradictions to which contemporary society has not been able to adjust. The late Margaret Mead said that this breakdown in marriage represents

> any failure to observe the whole sequence of behaviors that are regarded as appropriate in Judaeo-Christian forms of marriage and parenthood. We are a society in which the union of a male and female institutes a new social unit, and the identity and care of the children depend upon the maintenance of the social unit. The large extended family, or

149

clan, which takes responsibility for all the descendants of
both male and female members, and thus provides for every
child, does not exist in law, and is seldom found in fact. (p.
113)[4]

Mead continues:

Each American child learns early and in terror, that his
whole security depends on that single set of parents who,
more often than not, are arguing furiously in the next room
over some detail in their lives. A desperate demand upon
the permanence and all-satisfyingness of monogamous marriage is set up in the cradle. (p. 113)[4]

Our children are not prepared to trust anyone but their own
parents, and as adults are not prepared to establish close and
trusting ties with anyone except their own children. (p.
114)[4]

Social scientists today appear to agree that certain child-rearing practices inhere in the traditional nuclear family which in
the event of divorce contribute to stress in remarriage. The thesis
is that our society fosters in children an overdependence on the
nuclear family which leads to their making an investment for
security in their parents alone. This is a consequence of the fact
that historically the nuclear family—the marital couple and their
children—has been the sole support unit, internally interdependent and exclusive. This interdependency within the nuclear
family is poor preparation for children of divorce and actually
inhibits their ability to establish primary ties beyond their close
blood kin. We find ourselves with a traditional family system
that does not work in our contemporary society with its large
range of alternate family systems. In addition, myths persist that
plague steprelations in remarriage. Margaret Mead writes that
fairy tales learned at the parent's knee "are permeated with the
terrible fear of cruel stepparents, that children have suffered and
were expected to suffer within a system that decreed exclusive
relationships between parents and children that admitted no
substitutes" (p. 114).[4]

The large numbers of remarried families of the 1980s have an enormous stigma to overcome because of the prevailing conventional notions of what marriages and families should be. Despite the prophetic doom and gloom for children of divorce, they are surviving, and families are surviving with models different from that of the intact, nuclear family, many within a reorganized remarriage family.

Studies are rapidly emerging to report that life goes on. People are resilient. An article in the Canadian magazine *Chatelaine* (December, 1977) on second marriages told of a woman who reported, "A couple of years ago, I had one of those conversations that help clarify part of the buzzing confusion of everyday life. 'Hello,' said an unfamiliar voice at the other end of the telephone line. 'I'm your ex-husband's wife's ex-husband's wife, and I'm calling to tell you that your ex-husband's wife phoned from the Caribbean to say your children will be home on Saturday.' I thanked her, hung up, took a few deep yoga breaths and laughed. 'That,' I said to a friend who was watching me in fascinated horror, 'is the language of the seventies'" (p. 45).[5]

In November, 1980, the *New York Times Magazine* featured a story entitled "The New Extended Family: Divorce Reshapes the American Household."[6] It noted, "The instant expansion of families caused by remarriage after divorce, has altered the meaning of *family*." The article stressed that divorce and remarriage cut across the broad spectrum of race, color, creed, and economic status and have created a new extended family which challenges some of the basic notions of family life, "about the relationships between men and women, between parents, children, step-children, step-parents, grandparents and step-grandparents." Family life goes on, but with different membership. Members of one family are extended over several households. In the same article, sociologist Paul Bohannan comments: "My ex-wife will always be my son's mother and my ex-wife's mother will always be his grandmother."

Remarriages invite the questions: What is a family and what

connection is there between biological parents, stepparents, and children? Who are all the people to one another who now constitute families that are developing a chain of links through divorces and remarriages and through a variety of attachments and mutual responsibilities? Some sociologists have stated that the increase in divorce heralds the demise of the family. Psychiatrist and author Clifford J. Sager more optimistically suggests that "the American family, whatever its design, will outlive those who prophesy its death" (p. 3).[7]

We shall now focus on remarriages, the unique family system that evolves with its ties which extend far beyond the nuclear family. Families in remarriage have emerged in such numbers that they can no longer remain unnoticed and unrecognized. The transitional stages of the first marriage are more or less anticipated phases for which people are prepared. But for people who enter post-divorce marriages no transitional stages of adjustment have yet been accepted or anticipated to guide people on how to adapt to this different family structure. Sociologist Frank F. Furstenberg points out that "there are no rules, no stereotypes for these people to draw on in this new social arrangement."[8] The tendency consequently, has been to use the same traditional model of the ideal nuclear family. There is as yet no accepted public image with clearly defined roles that appropriately fits the stepfamily. The new stepfamilies, therefore, find themselves confused by unaccustomed experiences and feelings and have no way of assessing to what extent their experiences fall within a range of normal responses.

Stepfamilies are erected on complex foundations. They are connected by ties to the past and to the present. Clifford Sager and the other authors of *Treating the Remarried Family* define the remarriage family system as:

> a network of people and relationships created through the prior divorce and the formalization of the remarriage. These include the former spouses of one or both of the Remarriage

adults, the families of origin of all adults, the Remarriage couple and their former spouses and the children of each of the adults. (pp. 50–54)[7]

Grandparents, aunts, uncles, cousins, and stepgrandparents belong here as well. The authors refer to these systems and subsystems, which run simultaneously, as "multiple life-cycle tracks which the family is on at all times" (pp. 6–7).[7] They describe the members of the remarriage family as living on "multiple tracks, individual, marital and family systems life cycles" (p. 45).[7] "Multiple tracks" refers to the concept that individual members of a family have a developmental life cycle, as do the couples in a marriage, as a marital pair, and then as parents to their children. Whatever age and stage this cycle is in at the time of divorce, each of the members then begins a different life cycle which must be restructured to add still another life cycle track for the remarriage life cycle. The former family cycle continues while the new remarriage cycle evolves.

I am impressed by the number of couples in second marriages who report that they began the marriage with high hopes for happiness and were soon devastated to find themselves unprepared for coping with the difficulties of a stepparent role. They had not anticipated what their responses would be when a stepchild would share memories of the absent parent and background history that the stepparent would never know. When this did occur, it brought home forcefully the realization that the stepparent would always be excluded from the history that parents and their children have shared together, memories like: "Daddy, do you remember when Mommy and you and I went up to Aunt Helen's cottage and Fluffy was drowned?" The unexpressed reaction would often be: "What cottage, who is Aunt Helen, or Fluffy? I don't want to hear about your Mommy's and Daddy's activities." The past is full of memories, good and bad, but it is an unfamiliar chapter for the new stepparent. This is only one of the realities of a marriage preceded by a former mar-

riage, a family that lives beyond the divorce and into the remarriage—and they must be accepted.

In addition to the complex family structure in post-divorce
remarriage and the difficulty that children experience in adapting to the new family life, stepparents have intense problems in
accepting that their partners have had a former marriage with a
former love and children by that marriage. Clinically, a large
proportion of persons in remarriage who seek help discuss their
difficulty in coping with their feelings about the children and
the ex-spouse. At a cognitive level they recognize the reality of
the situation; however, at an emotional level they have difficulty
accepting that the children and the ties to the ex-spouse, the children's parent, will always be part of the remarriage.

Couples remarry with love and hope for a shared life
together. But statistics show that 44% of remarriages end in
divorce. This is reported to be 6% higher than in first marriages.[6]
Can the stress of remarriage be reduced so that this large group
of remarrieds will not have to disrupt their lives a second time
through divorce?

The many couples whom I have counseled emphasized the
problems children have with the new partner and the problems
partners have with someone else's children. Added to this, many
couples report that the new partner and the ex-spouse frequently
get caught in a triangular power struggle. The new partner may
want to extend warmth and guidance in a parental way to the
child, in which case the biological ex-spouse may feel threatened. Only a small percentage of ex-spouses are, as yet, able to
accept that in the interests of the child the divorced parent's new
spouse must have a role in the child's life. This role of stepparent
is an important key to the success of the new union and to the
formation of the new family life. One woman confided her hope
that problems related to the first marriage would "just go away."
She said she did not want to think negatively nor talk about the
past because she was afraid that would just be "opening a can of
worms." And yet there was a past that had to be recognized.

There had been a former family life with shared experiences to which members were bound to refer. These experiences simply cannot be cut out of life. In one remarriage the wife became hysterical whenever her husband made any reference to his ex-spouse or any of his friends, activities, or interests from the past. This marriage could not continue because the wife's demand that her husband be "reborn" was completely unrealistic and unfair.

In another situation, Elise, who was planning to marry Norman, a divorced man with two sons, eight- and ten-years old, wisely felt cautious about marrying him without giving consideration to his family situation. Norman and his ex-wife had been sharing the parenting of their sons since their divorce and their arrangements were working well for them. Norman lived close to his former home and was always available to his children, who dropped by his home several times a week after school. They often had dinner together without advance planning. Norman was pleased that his children chose to spend time with him. It was much more satisfying to him and less contrived than court-ordered visitation arrangements. Moreover, Norman frequently accommodated his ex-wife when it was convenient for her to have the children stay at his house. Norman and his sons loved one another and the boys loved their mother.

The informal arrangement among the members of the family worked until Elise came into Norman's life. Elise and Norman clearly loved each other, but Elise, a custodial parent of her own two children, felt that it would be impossible for her to establish a stable life with the loose visiting arrangements Norman had with his two sons. This couple became deeply concerned over this conflict. They wanted to get married and they wanted to live together, but Norman did not want to discourage his children's spontaneity in being with him. His wish was that the remarriage household would be a second home for his boys. Elise was concerned that the friendliness that the boys had extended to her in their casual encounters would change once their father married and became part of a new family with Elise and her two children.

Thus the couple reached an impasse. To compromise, Norman suggested that he would impose a structure of regular visiting days for his boys. Elise then worried that if his sons were told when they could and could not visit they would feel resentful toward her, the marriage, and her children and might even feel rejected by having restrictions placed upon their time with their father.

This situation is not uncommon after an amicable divorce with the ex-spouses sharing parenting. A remarriage requires reassessment of the former parenting arrangements to accommodate the structure of the new family. Since a new system is formed through remarriage, the former parenting arrangements may not be appropriate for the new spouse. The new partner may be left outside the existing system, preventing the remarriage unit from becoming a true family. Elise and Norman were well advised to recognize prior to their marriage that they must work out plans that would fit into their new married life. Ideally, Norman's ex-wife would have to be included in these plans as well, since both parental homes were families to the children. There is not a long enough post-divorce history of shared parenting arrangements to know how this will work for the remarried team. However, to date, clinical evidence indicates that meetings between ex-spouse and current spouse in the interest of the children are not easily accepted. There is more likelihood that joint sessions can be planned when the ex-spousal conflicts have been laid to rest and also usually when both ex-partners are remarried with a stable current marriage.

The goal for a second marriage is toward making the family work in an integrated and harmonious way. This reality can only grow out of the recognition and acceptance that the remarriage family structure and family membership include parts of two previous families. To deny the existence of children from a previous marriage is asking for trouble between the new partners. Of course this is not simple. The children from a previous marriage are a constant reminder to both the new partner and to the spouse that there was a previous love with a marriage that bore children who are the products of that love and marriage. The divorce does not terminate the former marriage ties. In marriage, most people look for exclusivity of love and loyalty invested in each other. In remarriage, there can be exclusivity in the marital love of the couple, but the family life cannot be exclusive. It is necessarily linked through the children to the former marriage and family. Many new partners feel threatened by these ties. They feel that the former marriage is not finished, and they frequently want proof that the new marriage is a fresh beginning. The proof cannot be given through denying former family bonds.

A parenting arrangement between ex-spouses that worked during the separate parenting period may not work when a new partner is introduced. Another woman, Phyllis, did what Elise did not do; she rushed into remarriage without giving prior consideration to the unique aspects of remarriage with children from the previous marriage. She complained bitterly that her husband's former wife had drawn up visitation rules that were now affecting her life in the present marriage. She complained that her husband was still letting his former wife control and organize his life and that he had agreed to a schedule with the ex-spouse prior to his second marriage that was not working for their present life. To continue the former pattern, Phyllis would have been expected to fit into the previous schedule without her having any say as to whether it could accommodate itself to her life. The danger in expecting Phyllis to adapt to a schedule drawn up by the former partners could be that she would be left feeling that she was a peripheral part of the former established system. If this marriage was to feel real to her, she would have to be involved with her husband in reconstructing plans for their new life, including plans for his children. When last seen, Phyllis was intensely antagonistic to her husband's former wife. She was projecting some of this hostility onto the children and criticizing her husband for not asserting himself with his ex-spouse. She felt like the outsider. If she was to be his real wife, she said, she had to create a place for herself in his life. A family system changes with a remarriage, and to create a real sense of family requires the inclusion and participation of all the new members.

In another remarriage, the new wife felt intensely antagonistic over the time the children spent with their father and posed an ultimatum: "It is either them or me." Her husband did not want another marriage breakup, and he considered the wisdom of withdrawing from his children's lives entirely. He wondered whether their lives and his would seem less complicated if he gave his children over for adoption to his ex-spouse's new partner, who was a good man; the children liked him and he liked them. This would make for a cleaner, more complete break from his former life. He was supported in this idea by his lawyer.

A clean break. Is it possible? This is not an unusual legal recommendation. In the past, a large number of adoptions were indeed the result of divorced noncustodial fathers' giving up their parental rights to a stepparent. Divorce lawyers have recommended this action as a clean break from the first marriage. This would allow the father to start another marriage with a fresh slate, the rationale being that both parents would be able to terminate all contact. There would be no visiting ties, and monetary obligations could be arranged by a one-time financial settlement. The past could be relegated to the past. From a management point of view, this would appear to relieve some of the complexities and ambiguities of stepparent roles. Adoption by the stepparent would make him the parent with legal guardianship rights and responsibilities for the child. The remarriage family would then have the appearance of being a self-contained unit. The children could take on the surname of the adoptive parent. The family would be like a nuclear family with all the members having the same name; no one would need to know this was a merged family. The act of adoption by a new spouse could also be evidence of his commitment and permanent intentions toward the marriage. To all appearances, this could be a neat way of wrapping up a divorce and disposing of controversial issues regarding the custodial, visitation, and financial arrangements. However, there is too much evidence that when both biological parents are alive the emotional needs do not terminate with the legality of either the divorce or adoption; many natural parents and children seek each other out long after a divorce. Cultural influences of biological relationships may be a strong determinant, but people appear to be impelled by an emotion that supersedes legal judgments to retain biological family ties.

In a recent situation, I received a phone call from a twenty-four-year-old married woman, mother of two children, which reaffirmed my convictions on this point. She had just had an experience that confused and excited her, which she felt she had to relate to someone. She said she certainly could not discuss it with her mother, since her mother had been deserted and left with two children twenty years before. The caller had then been four years old when the father left, at which time her mother moved with her and her brother into the maternal grandparents' home. Cara, the daughter, had learned to believe that her father was a wicked man who had run away, leaving all his responsibilities behind. Cara had told her friends and later her husband and in-laws that her father had died, though she had been left plagued by many questions with no answers. Was he alive or was he really dead? What kind of person was he? What did he look like? Was he tall or short, dark-haired or fair-haired? How was he spending his life? Did she have other grandparents and other aunts, uncles, and cousins? Though wanting to know the answers to these questions, she could not approach her mother, who still carried only bitter feelings. The morning Cara called me, she had received a telephone call from a man who told her he was her father. He said he knew he had no right to call her or to expect that she would want to talk to him. In a voice filled with emotion, he told Cara that he was now married and had two children but that there was an unfinished part of his life that hounded him. There was a highly charged exchange between these two people, strangers to each other, but with a yearning for each other. He pleaded for at least one meeting.

This sense of a missing link is not uncommon. The bond, like the one between Cara and her father, can continue for years to hound parents and children. It is a drive that closely resembles the need of adopted children who join Parent Finders groups. Parents who have given a child up for adoption at birth have been known to respond years later to establish a connection. The significance of parent–child bonding has become recognized only in recent years to the point of formalizing services for locating and helping to connect birth parent with child. With this advance in recognizing the significance of emotional bonds that tie biological parents and their children, there is an increasing desire not to allow marital divorce to cause parent and child to lose each other.

The rapid escalation of divorce and remarriage has been too recent for any follow-up studies to learn how divorced parents who later remarry can most effectively continue to remain actively involved in their children's lives without damaging the second marriage for the remarried parent, for the new partner, or for the children, no matter which household they live in. For this to work successfully for all concerned, a new definition of *family* must be created for the remarried household. There must be a new awareness of how a family created by remarriage can be a strong, loving, real family, different from the former nuclear family, without denying that it arose from the ashes of other marriages.

We know much about what remarriage is *not*. Next we want to describe a model of what remarriage *is* and can be, in order to confer on remarriage the legitimacy of its own identity based on its own reality as a different family system. Remarriage is a system created out of a parent's marriage which creates a new family group, with a new adult who takes on family responsibilities and comes with his or her own family connections. These relations have their rights and desire to be related to the new family group just as members of the former family with its biological ties have their rights and desire to continue to be in the family. The relationships of the new family develop from day one of the marriage, with each partner bringing his and her family members together. All relationships necessarily alter as the children pass through their various stages of development.

Each nuclear family group achieves a daily life style that is built on a common history with shared experiences, customs, and traditions. From a cultural perspective, this first marriage and family are well defined. People know who they are expected to be to one another; as a married couple, as mother to child, as father to child and as brothers and sisters to one another. Bound together with protection, affection and loyalty, parental authority and guidance are expected and necessary. It is within this family group that both the personal and family identities are formed and merged.

Stress and discomfort are bound to arise in a family that comes together in remarriage with no taken-for-granted life style, with no common history, customs, and traditions. Instead, when the new family members find themselves within the intimacy of the new home, there is a self-consciousness in everyone's efforts to achieve some sense of comfort. The discomfort has been described by therapist Virginia Goldner as "Having to think about how to walk while trying to walk, or to think about how to make love while trying to make love" (p. 194).[9] In other words, the members are living as a family while trying to learn how to *become* a family.

Children frequently complain, "We're not a family—we're a bunch of people living together. We live in a house, not a home." The home can have a pseudoclose and familial appearance, but the feelings between the members can remain distant, tense, and even hostile.

Our experience as well as that of other therapists shows that it takes a minimum of two to five years for remarried families to begin to stabilize and develop their own customs, rituals, and history.

People in a remarriage family can feel optimistic about a real sense of family evolving if they are a caring group with a sense of loyalty and responsibility to one another. But it takes time and patience. People cannot be forced into a pseudosense of family nor can they be expected to cut off their ties with the first family. And of course the process will happen more effectively if it is not hampered by a continued feud between ex-partners. The feud can extend beyond the ex-partners to in-laws who may have been an important part of the family. Frequently, in the first marriage both partners merge their personal lives and lose the sense of "my family" and "your family." Families become "our families." There are certainly no social or legal rules that state that divorce between a couple means divorce from in-laws to turn them into ex-laws. However, to date, the legal adversarial system betwen divorcing couples appears to form adversarial camps within the whole family system. Children and grandparents can be deprived of their relationship, even forbidden to see one another. Ex-ing the family members out of the lives of the ex-spouses only adds to the loss and discontinuity for all concerned.

Culturally, it is essential that we undergo a metamorphosis in our attitudes to make it possible for divorced persons who remarry to accept the reality that only the partners are divorced, not the children, not the parent nor the grandparents. In addition, we must adjust our lens to expand our vision beyond the view that the only real family is the biological family. Remarried partners come to each other with their own families. For the new group to restructure into a family, the extended kin, past and present, must have their place in the remarriage family as an extension of the extended family. Couples deal differently with this integration into a family. When children move between their maternal and paternal homes, their relatives remain part of their lives. In remarriage, the new partners have their extended families. The family network then is expanded to add stepkin, in addition to the biological kin. The post-divorce family of the 1980s increasingly includes four parent figures, eight grandparents, and other extended-family members, both biological and step. Remarried couples and their families deal differently with these ties. Some families do not acknowledge each other or can be competitive and divisive, whereas other families can open up an enriching network of family support. This was well demonstrated in one case when a child was hospitalized following an accident. Only family was permitted to visit the child. Because of the remarriage, there were several role duplications among the visiting family members: two mothers, two fathers, four grandmothers, and a large number of siblings. In this case, the recognition and acceptance of the wider family boundaries produced by the remarriage appeared to give the child an extended world of love and support.

There have been many different kinds of family systems over the years that have sustained strong loyalty, support, affection, and responsibility. L. S. Kubie says, "The essence of normality is flexibility, in contrast to the freezing of behavior into patterns of unalterability" (p. 182).[10] Anthropological and sociological studies of the family confirm that numerous modes and patterns of family life have existed in our history and exist across societies today, each normal by the standards of that society. Normality in remarriage is different from normality in the intact family. In this day and age, in this culture, remarriage must have its own range of normality in order to reduce the stress of unrealistic expectations which develop goals that are appropriate for life in a post-divorce marriage.

Too frequently we tend to group all second marriages together as though they represented one kind of family. But unlike the intact family with its single structure, remarriages have a minimum of twelve different family structures, each with its own dynamics. To understand the remarriage household, it is important to know in what stage of life the partners and the children are, the ages of both the partners, in addition to their previous marital experiences, and the ages of the children. Then

there are different subsystems within each different family structure that affect the ways the family functions. For example, if
only one of the divorced partners has remarried and the other
has not, there can be a different set of obligations and ties. If
there is a wide diversity in the socioeconomic conditions of the
second marriage from the first family life, this requires still different kinds of adjustments. Another factor that has a major
impact on the remarriage family is the gender of the custodial
parent. There are different sets of expectations for the husband
who takes responsibility for his new wife's children and for the
new wife marrying a man who has custody of his children. Studies and clinical experience confirm that women are still viewed
as the nurturing figures whereas men are viewed in terms of
functional roles. The stepmother–child relationship has been
proven to be more stressful than the stepfather–child relationship. But even the most affectionate woman does not become a
mother instantly, nor will even the most amenable child
instantly accept his new stepmother. In *Step Families* Emily and
John Visher describe the unrealistic expectations that stepmothers often struggle with. According to the Vishers, they tend to
try to:

1. Make up to the children for the upset caused by divorce
   or death in the original family.
2. Create a close-knit happy family in an attempt to return
   to square one (the nuclear family).
3. Keep all members of the family happy and contented.
4. Be living examples that the wicked step-mother myth is
   untrue.
5. Love their step-children instantly and equally to their
   natural children and receive love from their step-children instantly. (p. 50)[11]

This however, is not the pattern that emerges instantly in
steprelations.

    If the differences in remarriage systems have been described
as complex, it is because they are so complex, and must be antic-

ipated, understood, and acknowledged by couples contemplating remarriage and by clinicians and educators who deal with remarrieds and their families.

The following descriptions of some remarried couples and their families have been selected to demonstrate common problems that often plague the reconstituted family. Since the largest number of remarriages are formed by divorced persons who marry other divorced persons, we shall begin with them.

To review Paula's divorce from Jack, who left Paula five years ago: Paula was very apprehensive about making another commitment to a man. Her friendship with Michael, however, restored her confidence in men to the point at which she eventually accepted him into her home. This required another adjustment on the part of everyone in the home after a sense of stability had already been achieved in Paula's single-parent household. When Michael moved in with Paula, family life was once more disrupted, but Michael handled the situation well. He understood the children's fear that they would lose their mother to him and that he would try to take Jack's place in their lives. Michael moved gently into their daily life, not taking away any of Paula's responsibilities for the children. He neither invaded their life pattern nor remained on the outside. Being friendly and available, he found that the children began to trust him.

Two years ago, Michael married Paula. At that time, he was a noncustodial parent to his eight-year-old son, Gary, who visited Paula's home frequently. Since Michael's life was now within a stable family situation, his ex-wife agreed with him that instead of Gary's having occasional visits to a home with children around his age, he would be better off living with his father in his remarried home and visiting his mother, who was unmarried and had a busy working schedule. (The changing of the custodial arrangements in such circumstances are, by the way, not unusual.)

Paula's family now consisted of her two children, who usually spent every other weekend with their father, Jack, and Michael, Paula's new husband, and his son, Gary, who spent every other weekend with his mother. The weekend visits were usually arranged to permit Paula and Michael every other weekend to themselves. Thus far this arrangement has been working well. Each is a parent to his or her own children and a stepparent to the other's child or children. While both have agreed on the shared responsibilities for all children to create a sense of family unity, they also recognize the need to spend some separate time with their own children.

This couple has spent a great deal of time discussing and planning how to help the children feel good about their new family life. The partners' relationship is strengthened by their arriving at mutual plans about goals for the children and the family. Moreover, another plus contributing to a good family situation is that Paula is a "giver." She loves to do things for others and is enjoying her role of working with Gary to help him fit into the family life. Furthermore, Michael feels more comfortable now about his stepparent role because while he is offering a relationship to Paula's children, he is also a full-time parent to his son. Hence, the care and responsibility for the children are even and cooperatively managed between Paula and Michael. Michael did not have to carry the guilt which frequently burdens a noncustodial parent living with someone else's children.

Another remarriage in which two custodial parents joined forces did not sail so smoothly as that of Paula and Michael. Both Patty and Eric had custody of the children from their previous marriages. Patty, thirty-seven, had three children, aged ten, eight and five; and Eric, forty had custody of his ten-year-old son, Benjie. In this case, as in Paula's, the ages of the parents and of the children were close enough for a family routine to be established. This couple met and were drawn to each other and within six months of their meeting were married. Eric's former wife had been a psychiatric patient, in and out of the hospital, who when depressed would neglect and abuse Benjie and when manic would overwhelm the child with her affection. Consequently, Benjie was a timid child, fearful of trusting people. To make up for Benjie's unfortunate experiences with his mother, Eric had been both mother and father to his son, bending over backwards whenever possible.

Patty, Eric's new wife, had spent fourteen years in a marriage which became too bleak and lonely for her. Her former husband, a salesman, had been away from home more than he was home. When he was at home, he had little to give in relationships either as a husband or a father. Patty had virtually been a single parent to her three children throughout their lives. The children's emotional investment had thus been in their mother.

When Patty and Eric told their children that they were going to be married, the children all felt frightened and threatened. They feared that the marriage would take their only available parent away from them. Both sets of children were hostile to the new partner, and Patty's children said they hated Benjie, which of course, made Benjie even more withdrawn. Patty, who wanted this marriage, assured herself and her children that they would all get used to the idea of marriage and would learn to live together. Patty was certain her girls would learn to love Eric. She told them what a gentle and thoughtful person and what a wonderful father he was. Having seen how kind and loving he was with Benjie, Patty assured her children that they would now know what it was like to have a loving stepfather, when they had never really known what it was like to have an attentive father. What Patty did not anticipate, however, was that although Eric was a good father, his concern and care for his son had created an interdependence between the two of them that tied them closely together, making it difficult for anyone else to gain a foothold in their affections. This closeness also inhibited Eric from dividing his parental attentions.

These partners, in their marriage with four children, had difficulty knowing how to unhook themselves from the interdependence of their separate parent–child relationships. Neither Eric nor Patty wanted the new marriage nor their children to suffer. They did not know how to begin to reorganize from the former separate family life into a combined new family group. For the first year of the marriage, Eric and his son, and Patty and her daughters, lived together under one roof as two separate families. And the demands and behavior of the children left little private time for the couple. Benjie, accustomed to having his father available to him at all times, continued to crawl into bed with Eric in the middle of the night. Patty's children would make a scapegoat of Benjie, calling him a "weirdo." Both Patty and Eric were confused about their children's behavior and put their marriage on the back burner, hoping the tensions would ease and everyone would get used to living together like a family. They finally decided that they needed help.

In counseling sessions it became apparent that Eric had established a primary loyalty to his child and did not know how to disentangle himself from that role. Patty's children had also become increasingly clingy and demanding. Eric and Patty began to understand how threatened their children felt that they would lose their parent through the marriage. They understood that this left the children feeling antagonistic to the partner who they believed was taking their parent away. It was not a personal rejection of the partner, but rather a rejection of remarriage. Both parents had believed that they were protecting their respective children, but they in fact were doing them a disservice in nurturing their dependence. As long as the children could feel they could own the parent exclusively, they would never let anyone into the marriage, and the marriage would never get off the ground.

Each parent was advised to become disengaged from the inappropriate subsystems which were divisive to the family unity. Patty and Eric had to believe that they had a right to the couple relationship and their own time as a couple. Up to this point, they had concealed their affection, which they were then advised to demonstrate toward each other. This had to be accompanied by reassurance that the love between the couple would not take away any of the parental love. The children needed to be persuaded that there are different kinds of love for different relationships and different persons. Loving a marital partner does not mean loving children less.

They were assisted in recognizing that to begin to become a family, they had to develop relationships with each other's children, as well as encourage all the children to develop relationships, interests, and activities with one another. Both parents were alerted to the fact that they would probably meet with resistance. It would not be easy for either Patty's children or for Benjie to see their parent taking responsibility for someone else's children. The children would surely test their parent's patience and understanding; hence consistency would be required. This was a difficult process, but one that in varying degrees reflects many similar situations when custodial parents marry and bring two sets of children into one household.

There is an added complexity, however, when children at different life stages are brought together and are expected to become a family unit. Such was the case with Paul and Connie. Paul was a parent to his two sons, fifteen and seventeen years of age. When Paul's wife had died eight years before, he had taken full responsibility for his children and the home. Paul, of British stock, was schooled in discipline and control, to which his children responded well. Paul's obedient sons modeled themselves after their quiet and reserved father. Order in their home was maintained through organization, logic, and family cooperation.

Paul enjoyed his home, children, and responsibilities. He had a good sense of satisfaction for having independently reared his children so well. With the full cooperation of his sons, he did the marketing, prepared the meals, did the washing, and accomplished all the household chores that were needed to maintain the smooth running of the family. Together, they made a good team. Though cleanliness was never a top priority, the family was satisfied with the state of tidiness. In addition, since Paul was something of a health buff, meals were prepared accordingly: no sugar cereals, little salt, a minium of meat, and a maximum of vegetables was their steady diet.

Then Paul met Connie. Connie had qualities that came from a different culture and a different life-style. She was outspoken, vivacious, friendly, and "up front"—a new experience for Paul. She not only awakened in him a sexual response but showed him a different world. Since he was socially restrained, Connie became the aggressor in the relationship, which intrigued Paul even further. He found himself quite overwhelmed by her advances.

Connie, who had been divorced from an alcoholic husband, had custody of her eight-year-old son, Derek. After three years of divorce, she was now ready for marriage. Paul's stability and soundness attracted her. In the meantime, Derek continued to spend weekends with his father and his grandparents, who lived together.

During their dating period, Paul never really got to know Derek, since their dates were on weekends. Connie was pleased to have her weekends free for dating because she worked all week. Moreover, since Derek was in school a full day, Connie and Derek spent little time together. Usually, after a weekend with his father and grandparents, Derek would come home to Connie in a demanding and petulant mood. He had been pampered and showered with gifts and had few restrictions placed on him by his parent and grandparents. The child soon learned to get his own way. Rather than be subjected to a noisy hassle, Connie preferred to look the other way.

It was only when Paul and Connie were married and Connie moved into Paul's home that they fully realized that theirs could not be a couple affair, but rather a family affair with three children involved: two independent teenagers with temperaments and discipline quite different from the demanding, noisy eight-year-old. Derek's behavior was completely foreign to Paul and his sons. When Derek demanded, shouted, and screamed, they all looked at him as though he was some peculiar character from outer space. Connie became sensitive about Derek's behavior and began punishing him, more for Paul and his sons' sake than because his behavior bothered her. She was ashamed of him and didn't know how to deal with him other than countering his shouting with more shouting. Her behavior was also alien to the other members. The home soon became divided. Paul and his boys acted aloof and superior to both Connie and to Derek. The boys felt that their home had been invaded and their family life disrupted.

Connie thought she could win them all over by mapping out a homemaker's role for herself. She began reorganizing the home, shifting kitchen utensils to make everything more functional for her management. She went shopping for her favorite recipes, all for gourmet dishes. In short, she displaced Paul and his sons from their household routines. No negotiations were held about the division of family and household responsibilities. Neither Paul nor Connie had wanted to stir up controversy. Connie set out to try to please the family by making home life easier for Paul and attractive for everyone, on her terms. It did not work that way, however. Paul began to feel that his home was no longer his, that Connie was taking it away. Things were no longer in their accustomed places; meals defied his nutritional bias. Derek had sugared cereals for breakfast; Paul's sons continued their unsweetened oatmeal cereal. When Paul attempted to influence Derek's eating habits, the child would just not eat and Connie ended up giving him what he liked. With the house divided, the relationship of the couple was in real trouble. In therapy, Paul stated quietly that he felt he was confronted with one of three choices—Derek could leave; Connie and Derek could leave; or the family could strive to clarify what was happening and to relieve some of the tensions. It appeared wise to try the third route first and work with the family toward helping them understand the problems with which they were living.

The family treatment program worked on several levels. The initial focus was to remove Derek from the scapegoat position in the family by recognizing how the family had ganged up on the child. The little boy had his problems, but the ways in which he was being perceived and defined as the "bad boy" added to the poor self-image which he already had. He felt rejected and unloved, and thus became more aggressive and demanding for his own survival. Another difficulty was that Paul's sons had never accepted their father's marriage. They felt thay had been getting along so comfortably and did not understand why Paul had complicated their home life by getting married. Paul was also beginning to feel that there were too many negative factors for him and his family in this marriage. Yet he did care for Connie and wished she could just fit into his family life. Paul admitted that he did not like Derek and had not developed a relationship with him or even managed to establish a role with him. He also recognized that he and his sons had been united in exchanging exasperated expressions whenever Derek acted up. At the same time, Connie was well aware of the fact that they were ridiculing her son. If there was to be a merger between these two family groups, they all had to get to know one another and learn about their past history and their feelings.

The discussion in these sessions dealt with Paul's and the boys' memories of their mother's illness, her death, and the reorganization of their life afterward, forming a new pattern of life without her. Connie and Derek talked about life in their first family, relating Derek's love for his father and fear of his father's unpredictable behavior when he was drunk. They all opened their feelings to themselves and to one another, and the sharing of these feelings began to create a bond.

Derek's comings and goings on weekends made him party to two different life-styles and subject to two different sets of expectations. In his life with his mother, Paul, and the boys, he was expected to conform to a set of standards and rules in terms of the group; with his father and grandparents, he was the center of attention, with the family conforming to his behavior. With this in mind, we deemed it necessary to include the paternal side of Derek's family in these counseling sessions. Because Derek was important to his father and grandparents, they recognized that it was not productive for them to cater to Derek or give him gifts that were out of line with the standards of the remarriage family. For example, his father had given him his own television set without consulting Connie, which he had told the child to keep in his bedroom so he could watch whenever and whatever programs he chose. When Paul, Connie, and the boys were ready for dinner or had some family acitivty, Derek's response would frequently be, "My daddy says I don't have to—I can watch TV." A helpful task was for Derek's father and his grandparents to understand how difficult it had become for Derek to be continually influenced by his father's family in ways that were not compatible with his mother's new family. Derek's father and grandparents responded positively to the family sessions with Connie and Derek and Paul and his sons.

Professional intervention in family counseling is frequently productive, preferably before remarriage, if couples with children from previous marriages meet with former partners as well as grandparents, who are significant people in the children's lives. Different life-styles, behavior patterns, and child-rearing practises, as well as a wide diversity in ages, can complicate the marriage relationship. To some extent, this is inevitable when families join together with different past histories in different life stages. Couples are well advised to understand these differences and help the children in both families to acknowledge them, share their previous histories, talk about their previous family routines, customs and traditions, and work toward some changes that would modify former practices in order to meet everybody's needs as comfortably as possible.

People in a remarriage family must build a foundation for their family identity that includes their past, present, and plans for their future. There must be a bridge between the old and the new. Remarriages, particularly when there are two sets of children from the previous marriages, need a good deal of family participation in plans for integrating previous life styles into the present. When children spend part time with each parent and possibly with two sets of grandparents, it can be helpful to have the two separated parts of the family come together in sessions that focus on the child. The goal will be to recognize that it complicates the life of the child to live in two different worlds, particularly when one set of parents is defying or undermining the influences of the other.

I have cited this particular case because it has many components that frequently complicate second marriages. To begin with, Connie and Paul had started their relationship as a couple and the children had not been included, so neither partner really knew each other's children before they married. Moreover, the couple never exchanged their ideas on their individual attitudes toward and practice of child-rearing. There were, in addition, cultural differences between Paul's formal British child-rearing practices and Connie's permissive attitudes that they had not discussed. Connie had run a single-parent household for several years, and now she looked forward to creating an attractive family life for Paul. Her concept of being a good wife was to relieve Paul of household duties which he had carried out efficiently (and had enjoyed). This couple, each of whom had headed a household, did not negotiate about how marriage would change their responsibilities. The result was that Paul felt displaced in his home. Neither had foreseen that they would have to have a role toward and responsibility for each other's children and that the children had to have the opportunity to get to know one another.

Couples who will be joining two family lives must recognize that advance consideration must be given to their functions as stepparents, their attitudes to child-rearing, and their plans for home and money management. Such discussions are a minimal base for ground rules.

Still another dynamic enters into the life of the family system when a custodial father with teenage children marries a considerably younger woman who is a parent to young children. The very fact that the man and the woman are at different stages in life complicates the process of establishing a stable household pattern. The young children require one kind of care and responsibility, and the adolescents may want to have the comforts of home with the freedom to come and go without accountability to adults. In adolescence, this is a normal stage of separation from parental influence.

Teenagers may accept the idea of a parent's marriage but choose not to include themselves in the family group, or they may develop family relationships with the new partner and the partner's young children. Many fights and conflicts have grown out of situations in which the young adults take advantage of the comforts of home by dealing with the new partner as a convenient housekeeper. The children's parent must deal with this situation directly by laying out ground rules with his own children, rather than expect the stepparent, as a new adult in the home, to become a disciplinarian before a relationship has developed. The couple relationship must be strong enough to convey the caring between the spouses to the children. Much hinges on the loving relationship that is expressed by the couple if the children are to respect the status of a parent's partner in the home.

We have been discussing some of the complexities involved in a remarriage between two divorced partners each of whom has custody of his or her children and the different family structures which develop relative to the ages of the partners and those of the children. People usually remarry with the hope that together they can once more have a family life, with companionship, as well as someone to share and care for their children. Unfortunately, the unrealistic expectation that a new partner will be able to care instantly for the children may affect the sense of companionship between the couple. When the stepparent–stepchild relationship is in trouble, the happy family life that was a desired goal can instead become a dysfunctioning tangle of tensions. People who plan to remarry are well advised to do so for the right reasons, that is, for love, rather than "for the sake of the children" or to simply have a family life again. These are pitfalls to be aware of that have created unhappiness for many families. The strength and love of the couple relationship can be confirmed by their ability to anticipate and negotiate the complexities of steprelations.

Still another remarriage arrangement that is fraught with potential tensions can occur when parents bring two sets of adolescents into one household, particularly when they are of different sexes. Bringing a fourteen- or a fifteen-year-old girl to live in the intimacy of a family with a sixteen- or seventeen-year-old boy can trigger sexual stirrings. A number of the participants in our group discussions expressed their concern about potential or actual sexual involvement between their teenage children. This is a worrisome issue with no easy answers. Young people at this stage of healthy sexual development who find themselves living in close proximity to each other can respond precociously. Legally, stepsib relations are not incestuous, since there are no blood ties. However, the situation can be threatening to the family and create guilt in the parents for exposing the children to a highly charged atmosphere. Studies of children of divorce have reported a disproportionate rate of pregnancies and illegitimate births to girls of divorce and remarriage. The close spatial relations and family-type ties are fertile ground for erotic attachments to grow. Children do not tend to view their parents as sexual people; however, when a parent is going to bed with a new partner, the parent is now perceived as a sexual person. This intensifies the sexual climate in the home. It is certainly within the range of healthy development for young people to experience sexual attraction toward one another. But whereas this is not frowned upon when adolescents meet through school or other activities and date, there is a different feeling about the naturalness of it when the boy and girl who are dating are part of a remarriage family system.

Within a family setting, sexual activity between stepsibs takes on incestuous overtones. Biological brothers and sisters who grow up together learn to deal with their sexual drives within socially defined norms. However, sexual relations between stepsibs can create anxiety and tensions. In the way that incestuous relations between members of families are of persistent social concern, sexual relations between nonbiological members who live within a remarriage family frequently create problems for which there are no definitive answers. Esther Wald writes in *The Remarried Family:*

> The remarried family are related to the often highly erotic climate in the home as the new couple express their positive sexual feelings to each other. The heightened sexuality in the remarried household stimulates children's curiosity, sexuality and feelings about their parent's sexual involvement with a new partner. If, in addition, these children are adolescent and have only recently met each other, their own sexual drives are exacerbated and sexual acting out between them may occur. (p. 109)[12]

There is still another family structure which evolves when a custodial parent marries a noncustodial parent. The children of one marriage live in the remarriage household, while the noncustodial parent's children live with the ex-spouse and visit in the remarriage household. Different roles and different tasks emerge for everyone. In each case, each parent is both a biological parent and a stepparent, and the rules for each role are different. A parent may know how to be a good loving parent and yet have difficulty with the stepparent role. The same is true for children in relation to their love and loyalty to their biological parent and uncertainty about what they want the stepparent to be in their lives.

Emily and John Visher note "that the relationship in this remarriage must be considered as a structurally different type of child-rearing unit" (p. 15).[11] The authors pose the question, "What is the role of a visiting stepchild in the stepfamily?" (p. 30).[11] Their response is:

Visiting children are caught in a double-bind situation with
no way to win. If the visiting children are considered to be
full members of the family, this doesn't work because they
aren't, and if the visiting children are considered to be visitors in the family, this doesn't work because they aren't. (p.
31)

The Vishers quote Irene Fast and Albert Cain who describe the
difficulties of stepparents who "do not know whether to act as a
parent, stepparent or even a nonparent." They add, "However
strong the stepparent's determination to be a substitute parent,
however skillful his efforts, he cannot succeed totally. Stepfamily
relationships cannot be patterned after those of the traditional
nuclear family."

More frequently, the father is the noncustodial parent and
he has been awarded visitation access with his children. The typical situation is that the noncustodial man will move in with his
new wife and her children and his children will visit him in the
remarriage household every weekend or every second weekend
as well as spend some holiday time with him. Here we see a different set of dynamics. Frequently, the home with the mother
and her children feels like the primary home; hence, the new
partner and his visiting children can feel like intruders or board-
ers trying to fit into the existing family life style.

Evelyn demonstrates this family system in her remarriage.
Two and one half years after her divorce from Ted, Evelyn married Frank. Frank, who had been divorced for six years, was a
noncustodial parent with visitation access to his ten-year-old
son, George. Evelyn's life after separation had not moved so easily as she had anticipated. Looking back at the first six months,
she recalled them as bleak and empty. She had found it difficult
to mobilize her life. Feeling that she had lost her bearings, she
experienced a sense of drifting and loneliness that confused her.
Though she did not think she was lonely for Ted, she missed
marriage and the safety of the couple relationship. Soon she had
begun to wonder whether she was, in fact, as dependent as Ted

had perceived and treated her. She thus had had to fight against succumbing to her parents' enticing protective kindness, knowing that she must not lose her resolve for divorce and independence. It was a painful, lonely route which she knew that she must find alone. Many of her friends were generous with advice, but Evelyn realized that she alone must make decisions, even though she lacked self-confidence.

There was a big gap between what her logic dictated and what her emotions told her. Gradually, after these first few devastating months, Evelyn began to feel as though she were coming out of a long illness and was now on the way to recovery. As her energy returned, she began to think about bringing some structure to her day. She wanted to get away from the "separation environment" that had enveloped her, which would mean getting away from home, children, parents, and friends. They were all wonderful, but when they were with her, and she with them, the marriage breakup was uppermost in everyone's thoughts. A job would be the answer, she felt, but she didn't know where to begin. She really had never worked. Skilled in advertising and art, she had never used them commercially. She began by reading the want ads in the employment section of the paper, but it took time for her to get up the courage to reply to them. Everybody she called wanted to know what experience she had had. She then telephoned a number of employment agencies. That was different; they made promises of job placement. Finally she told one agency that she would be happy to get some experience as an apprentice. They referred her to an advertising agency where she was accepted on a trial basis. She was excited and frightened. Getting into a work environment with people whose sole relationship with her was to her work on a professional level—not one treating her as a recently separated woman—was a big step out of the world of a disrupted family life. She now had to get up early each morning to be at the office on schedule. This was a big step toward her recovery!

On the job, she learned quickly and her work concentration

blocked out the ruminations about the directions for her life that had paralyzed her. She liked what she was doing. As she guarded against allowing herself to become a handmaid to the men in the office because they were men, she began to realize the extent to which she had grown up socialized to accept the stereotypic gender roles. She then learned to work with people as people, rather than as male and female. This lesson struck home forcefully one day when she dared to be critical of the approach a male employee took for his project. She actually voiced her disagreement and then felt a knot in her stomach. She waited. Was he going to laugh at her or demean her for being presumptuous enough to think her judgment better than his? Instead, he listened. He gave her ideas serious consideration and suggested that they meet and discuss the layout of a particular job further; maybe together they could come up with a better proposal. Her contribution was respected! She felt valued—and gratified! In looking back, Evelyn felt that this was the real beginning of applying her skills and energy to her work, rather than dissipating her energies emotionally on how she was being perceived. Her performance on the job improved as her self-image improved. She was able to view herself as a competent employee with a skill to offer.

Family life reorganized around Evelyn as a working mother. Her daughters were cooperative. Now that Evelyn was confident that she could handle her life situation, she was able to accept her parents' help and her friends' support. She was no longer afraid that using their help would undermine her newly gained independence. She knew who she was and she liked who she was. She was emotionally and financially independent now, and her life felt more challenging and exciting. It had taken a year for her to reach this stage, but she now felt that the year had been productive since she had certainly matured.

Feeling confident with Ted was a somewhat slower process. She found she tended to be argumentive with him, overreacting to any suggestions that he might make to her or the girls. Immediately, she would think "There he goes again, telling us what to do; treating us as if we couldn't make decisions without his advice." She would bristle in anticipation before he said anything. She was still fighting the old battles. Even when she knew that his judgment was sound, she had trouble acknowledging it. She also had trouble accepting his rights to "her" two daughters. Her logic told her that she must not deprive the children of their father or Ted of his daughters, but her emotions and her logic frequently did not work well together.

All through this period, Evelyn was finding out a good deal about herself and her emotions. She now realized that the strong, protective man she had fallen in love with had wanted to continue to protect her when she no longer wanted to be the protected little girl. What she had seen as his strength had turned into dominance over her and she had kept her discontent and anger bottled up inside. She knew she must use this insight with Jan and Lisa and encourage them to express their feelings even when they disagreed or were angry with her. They had to recognize that the divorce was not Ted's fault or hers but rather that each adult's needs had grown differently and that they had grown too far apart to be able to remain married. Two years later, by the time the divorce was final, Evelyn felt she understood herself better and had matured as a person. She had achieved an emotional divorce from Ted as well as a legal one. She had, after all, reorganized her life, doing well on the job and reestablishing a social life and a comfortable family life. Dating, too, had helped her to take the transitional steps back to life as a single woman. By the time she met Frank, she was ready for an emotional commitment. Frank and Evelyn were attracted to each other first as friends, then as lovers. They achieved an easy, comfortable friendship as adults before having a love affair.

Frank's first marriage had lasted ten years. However, Frank divorced six years before he and Evelyn met. He was a noncustodial father whose ten-year-old son, George, lived with his mother, Frank's former wife. Frank saw his child every second weekend. The more time Frank spent in Evelyn's home and with her children, the more Frank realized what he and his son were missing together. Lacking the easy, comfortable exchange that Evelyn and the girls had, Frank thought about his time spent with George, which was restrained and contrived. They really had little to say to each other, and this made him feel guilty. He was spending his evenings with Evelyn and developing a more relaxed relationship with Jan and Lisa than he had with his own child.

Once Frank and Evelyn had begun to talk about marriage, Frank wondered what kind of relationship he wanted to have with Evelyn's girls when they became a family. Like many non-custodial parents, he felt he would have trouble taking a parental role with them; yet he could not stay out of their lives if he were to marry Evelyn. He felt friendly, but he did not want to take on a father's role with them. They had a father and he didn't want to even appear to be a father to someone else's children when he wasn't being much of a father to his own son. He talked about these conflicts with Evelyn. Her suggestion was that before they consider marriage, she wanted to get to know George and have George and the girls get to know one another. They both rec-ognized that a marriage between them was not going to be a cou-ple affair. It would include three children who had to participate in some of the planning for the merging of the families. Evelyn said that her hope was that George could begin to feel that he had a second family in the home that would be his father's.

Frank was concerned that George's mother would find this threatening to her. She might feel that Evelyn was competing with her, trying to be a "super mom" to George. Evelyn reas-sured Frank, and later George, that she would be happy to be George's friend, having no desire to try to take George away from his mother or to compete as to who was a better mother in George's life. Evelyn wisely added that before they were married she thought it would be a good idea for her to meet Frank's ex-wife and to talk about George, to learn more about the child, so that when he spent time with his father in the new home Evelyn would be in a better position to understand George and any special needs he might have.

Frank was not the only one with apprehension. Evelyn had her own set of questions about getting married, which she discussed with Frank. While assuring him that she loved him and wanted to marry him, she admitted that the idea of committing herself to marriage was still frightening to her. After reorganizing her personal and her family life following separation, she finally felt good about herself and the way everything was running smoothly in the home. This made her very apprehensive that the marriage could disrupt her family life again.

Another concern was the idea of being a wife again. She knew she didn't want to go back to being the good little housewife, devoting her life to taking care of everybody's needs but her own. After having fought for her separate identity, she did not want to lose it now by becoming just "Frank's wife." She said the idea of having a husband to do things for pleased the traditional side of her personality, but she dreaded the thought of once more taking on the dependently accountable childlike role. Frank assured Evelyn that he was attracted to her independence and that he too wanted companionship, not a little girl to take care of. He wanted them to have a home that would be a cooperative venture for the two of them. Moreover, it would also be a second home for George. Evelyn said she wanted to be a friend to George and would encourage the girls to include him in a family atmosphere. She added that she wanted her parents to meet George, too, because as grandparents, they were an important part of Jan and Lisa's life.

Evelyn had not counted on Jan and Lisa's finding it difficult to accept the idea of her marriage or the friendliness with both Frank and George that her marriage would require. The girls had always been so cooperative with Evelyn that she had not fully appreciated that the cooperation was exclusively between her and them. Frank intruded on this threesome who had settled into a comfortable way of life. Now, instead, it became Evelyn and Frank, talking and laughing together. It made them feel as if something were being taken away from them.

When Evelyn told her daughters that she and Frank were planning to get married, she began to realize that she had been naive in thinking that only her life was going to change. She became aware that she had to be more sensitive to their feelings of loss. Evelyn alone would be the pivotal figure in both relationships: Evelyn and her daughters, and Evelyn and Frank. Thus, she had to continue to demonstrate to her children the love they shared together and to Frank the love she felt for him. As the link between the girls and Frank, she alone carried the emotions for both the girls and her new husband. She knew she had to work toward bringing them together while not abandoning her children for Frank nor Frank for her children. This awareness helped her realize that it would take time and increased sensitivity to everyone's feelings. She and Frank would have the dual role of learning how to live together as a married couple, while at the same time learning how to be a family with each other's children. The warmth and acceptance could not be forced on any of them, it had to be nurtured and encouraged. They could become a family, but a new kind of family different from the first intact family. The test lay in whether they could accept the differences.

The discussions for preparing Frank and Evelyn for marriage went well. Trusting each other, they were able to discuss their fears and doubts. They were wise enough to discuss money management, an area which many couples hesitate to touch. Evelyn discussed the childcare maintenance money from Ted for the girls and Frank discussed his payments to his former wife for George. The wisdom of Evelyn's selling her home, which she had shared with Ted, was another topic of discussion. Similarly, Frank discussed giving up his apartment so that together they would have a fresh start in a home that would belong to this marriage.

Discussions such as these are very important in preparing a couple for a remarriage. They can prevent the surprises and disappointments that too frequently follow the marriage. Unfortunately, many couples do not risk examining the practical issues involved in the management of uniting parts of two former households into one family. There is not much romance in discussing the practical arrangements of daily life. But when both partners trust each other enough to plan ahead, there is less likelihood that the romance will be damaged later. If a relationship is too fragile for couples planning remarriage to discuss essential practical matters before marriage, it may not be strong enough to withstand such matters after marriage.

One of the important aspects that Evelyn and Frank discussed was that Frank would be living with Evelyn's children, while his son would not be living with him. This is frequently very distressing to a noncustodial parent who marries a partner who has custody of the children. There is often a feeling of guilt that can make it difficult for the new spouse to extend warmth and caring toward the partner's children. This, in turn, can lead to resentment between the couple, since the new spouse may interpret the partner's aloofness to the children as outright rejection of them.

When both partners have children, whether both sets or only one live in the remarriage household, the parents must extend reciprocal friendliness and take some responsibilities for all the children. When possible, each partner should strive to develop a separate relationship with the other's children and help to create involvement between the children, whether they live full time or part-time in the home. In order for the new partner to become part of the family, he should be included in family discussions and activities and brought up to date on the preceding background. This will begin to bring the partner into the inner life of the family. On the other hand, it must not be forgotten that the child's own parent will continue to be special to the child and a parent must not expect that the new partner can move immediately into taking over parental responsibilities. One man complained about his new wife, "She's a woman and I expected her to be just like a mother to my children." It does not work that way. A woman cannot suddenly become a mother, nor can a man suddenly become a father to someone else's child because there has been a remarriage. It takes time for affection and a sense of family to grow.

When a parental relationship is forced on children, either a pseudofamily will emerge that will not feel like a real family, or there will be rebellion and rejection between the new partner and the children. As one adult reported, his father had remarried when he was ten-years-old. Now, at thirty, he still has trouble calling his father's wife "Mother" as he had been instructed from the time she moved into the home. He said "It still sticks in my craw to call her mother, even though she has been very good to us." Inducting the new partner into the life and interests of the family is the route that can create a comfortable atmosphere for the family.

When a parent who has custody of the children marries a parent whose children live with a former partner, it is not hard to recognize that guilt can develop when he or she is taking over the daily parenting and responsibilities for someone else's children while his or her own children are visitors in his or her life. This dual parenting adds complexity to the already complex and ambiguous position of a nonparent in trying to map out who he or she can be in the life of someone else's children. Most often, there has been no history with the partner's children and their developmental growth stages from infancy. It is not easy to move into a child's life and feel affection and the instant love which is often expected, particularly when the child is having trouble accepting the idea of a new adult taking the absent parent's place in the home, at the table, and in the parent's bed.

In developing family life in a remarriage with children, the new partner who comes into the home has the right to his comfort and convenience. He cannot be expected to slip into the lifestyle of the family as it was. He has his own life-style, habits, and customs. A partner who comes into an established family system frequently can feel like a boarder in the home. The whole family system has to modify to make room for the new adult. To add to this a daily pattern may be established that works on week days, but when the noncustodial parent's children spend weekends, further accommodations must be made. Furthermore, the custodial parent's children may spend weekends with their nonresident parent, which means that the family undergoes frequent changes in structure. The household must thus be elastic enough to have all the children, some of the children, or no children at any one time in the life of the family. This kind of movement in and out of the family requires flexibility of everyone, even more so when there are children coming and going between different parental homes.

In addition to the question of who the new partner can be in the children's lives, there is the question of the responsibilities that each partner carries for the other's children. One husband was concerned about burdening his wife with the additional chores involved when his children came for weekends. He shopped for them, cooked their meals, and tried to ease any burden that they might present. This meant that during the week he was part of one family group and on weekends he was part of another family group. Remarried partners with children who visit must negotiate how they can both help the children feel part of the remarriage family group. If this duty is neglected, the marriage will suffer the strains of a house divided. The incorporation into a merged group requires sensitive planning and then the patience to allow all members to begin to accept different patterns into their lives.

Gladys, another woman who has her children living with

her in the remarriage household, was eager for her husband,
Leo, to know that she would welcome his children on weekends
to feel part of the family. When Leo's children, a boy of ten and
a girl of twelve, visited, Gladys took them shopping, made a
point of preparing special desserts to please them, and outdid
herself in trying to be a perfect stepmother. Though her own
children were jealous, she was grateful to Leo for being thoughtful to her children and wanted to repay him in kind. She consequently tried to create one big happy family with his and her
children, hoping this would relieve her husband's guilt about
disrupting his family's life through divorce, getting remarried,
and then living with someone else's children.

But Gladys found herself rebuffed. All her attempts at affection were met with rejection. When she tried to delight them
with her baked goodies, they refused them and even said they
didn't like them. Gladys responded to their rejection by withdrawing from them. Hurt and angered, she felt his children were
impossible. She could only conclude that they were ungrateful
and selfish and wondered why she had complicated her life.
Hurt as she was, Gladys did not realize how difficult it was for
Leo's children to see him in another home with another family
with children and another wife. In her desire to accept them,
Gladys had not given them time to grow accustomed to seeing
their father in the different setting. Her desire to please and
incorporate Leo's children into the life of the family was really
her desire to please Leo. She did not understand that she first
had to develop a relationship with Leo's children that would
make them comfortable in their father's new home. Moreover,
she expected a grateful response. There are seldom thanks from
stepchildren for trying to be a substitute parent. Most parents do
not expect gratitude from their own children, and yet stepparents can feel resentful if the stepchildren are not grateful.

In all remarriages when the wife has custody of her children
and marries a man with custody, the responsibilities each parent
assumes for each other's children must be negotiated. When a

woman with custody marries a man whose children visit with him, his present partner has different kinds of responsibilities for his children than she would if they were all living together on a full-time basis. The couple must agree on how much responsibility or disciplinary authority she has a right to have and how much is expected of her from her husband or accepted from his children as well as from the children's mother. Does she assume responsibilities of a stepmother to children who spend occasional weekends by virtue of being the wife of the children's parent? If not, what role and adult supervision and care is she expected to have? As their father's wife, is her role to aim to be a parent, or a caring, interested friend? What is her goal and what is her husband's goal for her relationship with the children?

There is ambiguity about what constitutes the full-time stepmother role and even less clarity when the children visit weekends only. The stepfather's responsibility for his wife's children is equally difficult to establish, particularly when he does not have custody of his own children. A parent's marriage makes the new spouse a husband or a wife. The couple's status is legitimate, but this does not create a legal status for the stepparent vis-à-vis the stepchild. There is no doubt that the function of the steprelation is very ambiguous, particularly when there are unrealistic expectations for how the family should work. The couple does not want to experience another divorce; yet the stepchild complicates the marriage. In order for the remarriage to overcome the stress involved in expecting instant-family feelings, the clearer the steprelations role can be delineated and negotiated, the less ambiguity there is likely to be.

The goal of integration into the new household is one aspect of successfully building a remarriage. Another is the recognition that most divorced partners and children have intergenerational ties. In Evelyn's case, her parents were important to her and to the children. Frank and his parents, and his brother and sister were important to him and to George. No one wanted to lose the members of their family. Everyone wanted this new marriage and the new family to work, not only for the sake of the marriage, but also for the sake of each of the grandchildren and the grandparents. Evelyn had a dinner party to which she invited her parents and Frank's parents, brother, and sister. Though it started out awkwardly, the awkwardness was reduced as they talked frankly about the common bond that they now shared and agreed that it would serve everyone's interests to cooperate and help Frank, Evelyn, Lisa, Jan, and George to feel like a family without losing their blood relatives.

As I look back at Evelyn's marriage, now five years old, my conviction is that to create a blended family in remarriage is an uphill struggle but that it can work and be enriching and challenging for everyone. The family system and the structure of the family for Evelyn and her girls are different now than they were in the first marriage and in the single-parent period. They are also now different for Frank and his son George. With all the wisdom that Evelyn and Frank displayed, it still took about three years for the family to feel comfortable as a family. They have now begun to develop their own history and to settle into their own casual daily rhythms. A sense of family kinship was encouraged by the inclusion of all four grandparents on birthdays and other festive occasions, and having gifts exchanged by everyone for everyone. Moreover, such occasions were celebrated not only in Evelyn's remarriage household, but in their father's home and at times in the homes of each of the sets of grandparents. The children began to feel that they had the best of two worlds, since the divorce did not have to mean losing one part of their family. Each parental home and each parent's family was different, but the important factor was that the children did not have to choose their loyalty between parents or between sets of grandparents.

When both partners have children from previous marriages, each partner in the remarriage household is both a parent and a stepparent. It is a dual role, to which people most frequently attempt to give equal attention, responsibility, and privileges.

Despite the trend toward more equality between the sexes, the father–stepfather role remains different from that of the mother–stepmother role. Women frequently strive to create a family life that will evoke social responses such as "They are just one big happy family." To all appearances, they strive for a house that will mirror the ideal concept of a nuclear family. It is interesting how closely they feel watched by family and friends, who quickly pick up any discrimination between his children and hers. "She's like a real mother to his children" can be the greatest triubute to pay to a stepmother. Ruth Roosevelt and Jeannette Lofas, themselves stepmothers, say in *Living in Step,* "The love may be there: it will never be the same. . . . The children are not yours, and they never will be." They add, "The partner with prior children is not totally yours—and never will be" (p. 1).[13] Couples who marry find it difficult to accept that the past remains, but it is a reality. The history of the past will always be part of the present. Frequently, in efforts to please the new husband, wives may move too quickly into trying to create the sense of family by trying to be super parents, and by being excessive in declarations of love, particularly to the stepchildren. This does not work with children. They cannot become instant children. It is a relationship that has to grow and outgrow many odds against it. One of the odds is the history of the reputation of the "wicked stepmother," which stepmothers try to overcome by trying to act as though there were instant love. Unfortunately, *stepchild* continues to carry negative connotations. As Anne W. Simon points out in *Stepchild in the Family,* "If you want to indicate neglect, say 'stepchild' and everyone will know what you mean" (p. 17).[14]

The ambiguity of steprelations is without doubt the greatest source of stress in remarriage. There are no guidelines. Married adults are expected to assume parenting roles with affection, and children are expected to respond to a parent's spouse with filial affection. In circumstances other than steprelations, in which adults assume specific responsibility, by choice, for children, the functions are defined: a teacher teaches, a babysitter babysits, a foster parent takes charge of children for a fee, adoptive parents make the choice to bring up a child as their own. But a stepparent is thrust into parental roles with parental sorts of tasks and responsibilities as part of "the package deal" in marrying the child's parent. Marriage is the choice, not stepparenting.

Beyond the uncertainty of stepparent roles and responsibilities, the relationship between the remarried couple is handicapped by the fact that there were ex-partners who shared past events. The love relationship of the new couple may be solid, but I am frequently confronted by a new partner who has difficulty living with the reality that there is a former partner who may continue contact with the ex-spouse in relation to the child they share. The attitudes and values of the ex-spouse are important influences in the child's life. The child is the carrier of any parental attitudes from one home to the other. In turn, he then becomes the target of the stepparent's animosity or criticism. Frequently, in order to confirm to the present spouse that he or she is more desirable than the former mate, the ex-spouse is described with disdain and an emphasis placed on his or her shortcomings. From reports describing former mates, they all appear to have been neurotic, unstable, and unbalanced.

The characteristics of a marriage between a custodial parent and a noncustodial parent are in some respects general to all remarriages and in others particular to this combination of partners.

There are no generalizations that can cover the infinite variety of remarriage situations with their different combinations of past experiences, number of children, ages and gender of the children, and relationships between parents and children. Added to these variations are the custody arrangements and the degree of satisfaction each parent feels with the custody and with the financial arrangements.

There is a different set of dynamics in remarriages that take place between a partner with custody of children and a partner who, never married before, comes into a marriage unaccustomed to life with children. This family structure has still another set of complexities and obstacles to surmount. Such was Kate's experience in her remarriage to Tom. Kate, the reader will remember, had married a previously unmarried man two years after her divorce from Jim. In group discussions, Kate's review of her separation from Jim revealed that she still had much to learn about herself as a person as well as about her previous marriage. Her marriage to Tom, an attractive, sought-after bachelor, was in certain respects made for the wrong reasons—reasons tied to her unresolved feelings about her first marriage. Kate's story is yet another confirmation about how unresolved problems from the first marriage can affect the second.

In group discussions, Kate said that she had never expected that she would have found separation from Jim so "horrendous." Having complained to so many people about how irresponsible he was, she had really thought she would feel nothing but relief after getting him out of her life. Instead, she felt emptiness and a sense of uncertainity about how she would fare as a divorced woman. She was amazed at how hard she found it to pull herself together after Jim had left. Kate had described Jim as "a taker," having accused him so often of giving her nothing. Why then was she so devastated? She had complained to everyone about how she carried the full burden of their child and their home. If this had been the case, why, then, was she feeling lost and alone? Kate had warned Jim's mother that he probably would go running home to mama to be taken care of. She accused his mother of having spoilt him, leaving him dependent on her and leaving Kate with the responsibility of taking care of all his needs. Whereas Evelyn was tired of the child role, Kate complained that she was tired of being mother to her husband.

Jim, however, had not run home to mother. Nor did he run back to Kate. Kate realized that she was experiencing some disappointment. She had rehearsed how she would deal with Jim if he came crawling back to her begging to be taken back. But that did not happen. On the contrary, Jim seemed to be adapting to the separation better than Kate. Away from her, Jim seemed more the man. He was doing well in his business and meeting his financial obligations to her conscientiously. He was getting on with his life as though it had been Kate who had been the burden rather than the other way round. Kate began to wonder whether she had in fact been the one who had held Jim back. Thinking back to some of their quarrels, she realized that the quarrels had really been her fighting with him, rather than the reverse. One of her ways of belittling him was to say that she had married beneath her status and that she could have had a much better marriage.

Kate had really felt she would be in great demand as soon as she freed herself from Jim. But after their separation, no one was beating down her door. On the other hand, her friends told her that Jim was taking out bright, attractive women. He was a sought-after, available bachelor. Thus, the single-parent period was an eye-opener for Kate. Her social life changed. Her married friends no longer included her as they had done before the separation, and her separated friends seemed distrustful and competitive. She related one call from someone she had called a friend. This was shortly after her separation, before all her friends knew about her marital breakup. This woman told Kate she was having a dinner party and wanted Kate and Jim to come. When Kate told her they had separated, the woman expressed shock and surprise, conveyed her regrets, and hung up. Kate, as a single woman, no longer part of a couple, was uninvited. She was now caught up in a subculture of formerly marrieds and didn't like her new status.

After the divorce became final, Jim told Kate he had plans for marriage. Kate found it hard to believe that she was really jealous. She had discarded this handsome, active man from her life and another had seen his worth. Moreover, Kate had expected that Jim would be unpredictable and unreliable about his visits with their son, Scott, but instead he kept in touch with Scott, took him on outings, and gave him tennis lessons; a closer relationship developed between Jim and his son than they had had when Jim was in the marriage. One day when Jim came to get his son, before the divorce was final, he and Kate talked more frankly than they had for many years. The discussion was quite sobering for Kate. She had said to Jim: "Who's taking care of you now? You look so good." Jim replied, "You know, Kate, you had a way of making me feel I was helpless. I've had to learn that I really am not. I was always so sure that you would only criticize and tear down anything I told you, that I stopped telling you anything and when I was in trouble I would lie and cheat. That seemed easier than facing the music with you. I'm not excusing myself; I really was a rotten husband, but you sure are one critical dame. Separation was the best thing that happened for both of us. We were bad for each other."

Kate listened and knew that he was right. They had been bad for one another. They had been stuck in a bad script and neither of them had known how to change it. Jim went on, "You told so many people your version of our marriage that I couldn't face anyone, your parents, my parents, our friends. Everybody believed you when you told them that I was weak, and I was weak—too weak to tell you that on my income we couldn't afford to carry the house your parents picked out for you and made the grand gesture of putting a down payment on. I nearly went broke trying to carry the mortgage. I had no right to forge your signature to a mortgage payment check, but I was afraid we would lose our home. My business began to go down the drain, I nearly went broke. I went through a terrible time and I had no one to turn to—certainly not you." Kate listened with a mixture of feelings. Part of her was thinking, "he's right," the other part was angry. The resentment was all there, the lies, her view of his lack of responsibility, the bounced checks. The anger mounted as she dwelt on the years when she felt she had been left to carry the brunt and Jim had escaped into tennis instead of facing the music with her.

Had she been that tough on him and had she really made

him weak? Why hadn't they known how to talk to each other? It was easier for her to deal with her angry feelings than with self-recriminations. Turning to Jim, she said, "You're a good talker and you must make a great date, but you will never be a good husband. You didn't know how to be a husband or a father, and you'll never learn." Jim said nothing. The withdrawal response he had used throughout the marriage was once more evoked. He had not learned how to deal with Kate's attacks. It was when Jim announced his plans to marry that Kate became desperately anxious to get involved in a serious relationship. She wanted to preempt his marriage by being the one to get married first. It felt humiliating to her that Jim might marry before she did. It was as though he had rejected her, not she him. Though Kate had been dating, she now looked at her dating friend differently.

She found Tom, her dating partner, attractive and they had fun together. Kate was flattered by the fact that Tom, three years her junior, could have had his pick of any of the younger women, but he was attentive to her. In many ways, he represented the days when Kate and Jim had first dated and were first married. She wanted to recapture those days. This time she vowed she would do it differently. She wouldn't let herself become the housewife while her husband was having all the fun. They would do everything together.

Kate was focused so entirely on herself and her need to show the world that she could attract a desirable young man in marriage that she gave little thought to Scott or to the fact that he was becoming a loner. Kate did not know what was going on in him, nor was she aware that there was anything going on, and certainly Tom did not get to know him. Like many single men, Tom had had little contact with children and neither liked nor disliked them. He simply did not know them. When Tom was with Kate, Scott usually isolated himself in his room so that, to Tom, Scott was not a real part of Kate's life. They certainly started as though theirs was only a couple relationship with no thought about who Tom would be or wanted to be in Scott's life.

Many remarriages do have the appearance of being like a first marriage. A marriage like Kate and Tom's, which began without preparation for the reality of a child, starts off with strikes against it. Tom's lack of experience with children might have manifested itself in a variety of ways. In other marriages like this one, with the combination of a custodial parent with a previously single person, the new stepparent might have preferred not to assume any responsibility for or interest in the child. Since Scott tended to be a withdrawn child, Tom might have chosen to ignore him, which would have added to problems that Scott had already developed. Or Tom might, with all good intentions but with a lack of sensitivity to Scott's feelings, might have thrust a superficial camaraderie upon the child, who was already having problems with relationships.

The dynamics of a particular remarriage can sometimes affect the custody arrangements. Kate's lack of commitment to Scott, her inability to understand the child's confusion about his parents' separation, and her feeling of being burdened with Scott since the separation all contributed to her decision that it was now time that Scott's father took his share of the responsibility. She consequently turned custody over to Jim. This was an unexpected turn of events for Jim, who had been the noncustodial father during his courtship period and would now, in his coming marriage, have Scott living with him in his remarriage household. Out of punitive feelings for Jim and his coming marriage, and with little regard for Scott's feeling that his mother was rejecting him to get remarried, the decision thus was made to transfer custody. Hence Jim's marriage took an unexpected turn when he became the custodial parent and Scott changed his primary home with the feeling that he had been rejected. Unfortunately, theirs is not an unusual case; custody arrangements are frequently revised to meet the parents' convenience and not necessarily in the best interests of the child.

There certainly are marriages that do well with "mine" and "yours" or "mine" and "ours," but two people who plan to remarry are strongly advised to discuss what they hope the marriage will have for each of them. When a parent who has custody of a child marries a previously single person, the new partner's expectations of married life will depend on his or her age and stage of life. Some partners want only the couple life as in the case of Kate and Tom, so custody is transferred to the other parent. However, some people who have not been married before want all the firsts of a marriage, including a child by the marriage. If a husband with custody of teenage children marries a young woman who wants to have a baby, the man may not want to return to the responsibilities of the early infancy stage. He has been there and had the joys and tribulations of those earlier days. It is, therefore, important for the couple to come to agreement about their plans for a life together. Otherwise, there can be future discontents and frustrations.

In one such situation, a man with two children married a single woman and concurred with her that she had a right to have a child. After the baby was born, the conflict between the couple brought them to counseling. The husband contended that he had "obliged" his wife by impregnating her; he then acted as though the baby was hers alone. Since the woman felt unsupported as a parent, she began devoting herself to her child and gave little attention to him and to his children by the previous marriage. One difficulty in this situation was that the relationship between the new wife and her husband's children had not had time to stabilize before the woman became pregnant. Moreover, this couple had not really come to grips with the husband's feelings toward fathering another child at his stage in life. The man wanted marriage for the couple relationship; the woman considered a child central to her idea of what marriage and family were all about. They were both losers. The man lost the exclusive couple relationship, whereas the woman's concept of marriage and family life involved shared parenting. They had gone into marriage and parenting without a clear contract of expectations.

Another situation concerned the marriage between Susan, a previously single woman, to Phil, a custodial parent of a three-year-old child. The agreement between them was that together they would be parents to this child. After three years of marriage, the woman experienced growing discontent from the realization that no matter how much she loved this six-year-old boy, she would never be his real mother. After all, she had not conceived, carried, and given birth to him. And Susan wanted this experience too. Never allowing the full sense of dissatisfaction to surface to a conscious level, she became pregnant "by accident." When she told Phil, she fervently hoped that Phil would welcome the news, though not allowing herself to acknowledge her own excitement. But Phil accepted Susan's statement that the pregnancy had been an accident and he asked her what she planned to do. When Susan said she would arrange for an abortion, once more Phil accepted her response at face value, that is, that an abortion was Susan's way of dealing with the accident. Doing nothing to stop her or to give them both the opportunity to be sure that abortion was what both of them wanted, Phil had accepted that they were both satisfied with their marriage and family life. Thus, Susan's pregnancy was aborted. She, however, had told the gynecologist that neither she nor her husband wanted children. The doctor had therefore suggested that she have a tubular ligation to prevent future pregnancy, to which Susan and Phil agreed. Susan had, unfortunately, not expressed her real feelings, so Phil had accepted what Susan was telling him. The end result was the terrible pain and depression that Susan experienced after the abortion. She would never have a child. She had allowed something irreversible to take place, when what she desperately had wanted was for Phil to stop her and he had not done so. The resentment she felt toward him was enormous. Susan had trouble taking responsibility for her own behavior and the way she had outwitted herself in her attempt to manipulate the situation. This anger toward Phil and now toward herself has continued and is presently being projected onto Phil's child. This marriage, that had such potential for happiness, may have a tragic ending.

In other remarriages when the mother is the custodial parent and marries a previously single man, the man may come into the family with a preconceived idea of how children should behave. Oliver's marriage to Joanne illustrates such a situation. Oliver had been raised in a traditional home where there had been little tolerance of differences between parents and children and control of emotion was rewarded. He had adopted this philosophy, whereas Joanne was a loving, permissive mother who believed that children had a right to disagree and a right to get angry and show it. To compensate for the disruption to the children's lives when she separated, Joanne curbed neither their displays of exuberance nor those of frustration. When Oliver moved into this noisy household, he found it difficult to control his impulses in disciplining these children. He would say, "That's no way to talk to your mother"or "Do as your mother tells you to, with no questions." His desire was to protect Joanne. Her raising these children alone, he felt, had been too much for her; now he was there to bring order to this chaos. He surprised himself with the amount of anger that welled up in him, admitting later that he did not know what he might be capable of doing if he let go of his anger. Joanne was caught between her children and her husband; between what she viewed as their right to freedom of expression and Oliver's efforts to create a role with her children, a role based on an authority which was alien to her children. Joanne would not abandon her children, nor did she want to undermine Oliver.

Oliver's attempts to map out a role in the family for himself required first that he and Joanne have some agreement about Joanne's children and second that he try to develop a relationship with them before he could expect to have a role with them. He had to earn their respect; he couldn't order it. Third, Oliver's conviction that Joanne required his protection was based on how he perceived the children's behavior with her. Though unacceptable to him, it was not unacceptable to Joanne. Whatever disagreements there were between her and her two children, it was based on a solid foundation of love. It is that aspect of the parent–child relationship that Oliver found hard to understand. He had not achieved affection with the children, nor would they accept him as an authority figure in their lives.

Another marriage with its own dynamics is that of a previously unmarried woman and a noncustodial father. The couple begins in what appears to be virtually a couple relationship, and the bride, like many young brides, wants all the firsts of a marriage, a wedding, a home, and children. Yet this kind of marital relationship has its own unique features. One such couple, Neal and Dawn, were very much in love. Neal had never kept the fact of his children a secret. When the children visited with their father, Dawn usually had spent the time with her own weekend chores. The children seemed nice enough, she said, but she did not spend much time with them. Neal, loving his son and daughter, looked forward to time with them and was grateful that Dawn was satisfied to have the time for herself. When the couple planned their marriage, they went apartment hunting. Dawn found a one-bedroom apartment she liked. She told Neal that it was like "a doll's house." Neal said it was ridiculous. They needed a three-bedroom duplex or house so that his children would each have a bedroom. Dawn said that would cost more than double what a one- or two-bedroom apartment would cost. However, Neal said there were no choices and insisted that that was what they needed.

The original discussion of financial arrangements before marriage had seemed amicable. Both partners were earning good salaries and their plan was to share the household costs equally with each retaining his or her own bank accounts. That was fine until Dawn realized that Neal's contribution was estimated on what was left after he made his childcare payments, not on his full take-home salary, so that his share in the common pot was only based on his partial income, whereas Dawn's share included her whole salary. Dawn protested that this meant that part of her earnings would be contributing to his first-marriage expenses, which made her very indignant. She felt that she had been generous in accepting a man who had had a previous marriage and had children by that marriage, but she resented the fact that part of her salary would go toward the costs of housing adequate for accommodating children of that first marriage. That seemed beyond the call of duty. But Dawn loved Neal and wanted the marriage. This meant she had to accept the reality that he had been married and was a father to two children whom he loved. Beyond the financial problem, Dawn learned that she had to share Neal with his children. When every weekend was lost for the couple because Neal was with his children, the visitation was changed to every other weekend. But Dawn became increasingly resentful of Neal's full concentration on his children when they were with him, particularly after having to contribute to their expenses. She was an outsider, exluded from the father–children activity and the discussions they had. During the week, she was wife and lover; weekends she became a nonperson. When the children visited, they did not let Neal out of their sight—"Where's Daddy?" was about all they ever said to her. Dawn complained that she had never seen a man so devoted to his children. She also added that there was no question in her mind that if he had to make a choice between her and the children, she would be the loser. Yet she did not want to lose this marriage.

During the week she and Neal enjoyed each other. Dawn felt the marriage was great except for the children, and she consoled herself with the possibility that in a few years the children would be less interested in spending time with their father. But Neal was singing a different tune. He said his daughter told him that she would like to live with him, because she did not like her mother's new partner. Neal was delighted.

The marriage became shaky. In counseling sessions, this couple was strongly advised to include the visiting children as part of the paternal household with Neal and Dawn. This marriage had formed itself into two family groups, the couple unit, and Neal and his children as a separate unit. The children were possessive of their father and gave no recognition that Dawn was a significant part of their father's life, nor did Neal help them to do that. The changes they had to work on were aimed at including the children in their family. As a result of our sessions, this has begun to happen. Dawn has become available to be part of the family, sharing the activities, discussions, and interests with Neal and the children. She no longer absents herself. Neal has made a conscious effort to include Dawn. And Dawn has responded. At last report, when Neal's daughter took Dawn's hand, not Neal's, as they walked on the beach, they knew that the children were beginning to respond as well.

Dawn's acceptance of the children reduced her feeling of being exploited in the matter of the household finances, and Neal was proposing further that they reassess the budget so that he would carry the additional expenses for his children. The resolution of the budget and Dawn's involvement in Neal's family life eased the anxiety and enriched the marriage.

In another situation wherein a noncustodial father married a single woman, this woman had been warned by family and friends that she was taking on a load that could spoil the marriage. As a schoolteacher, she declared that she loved children and had had years of experience with children. However, she learned that being a nine-to-five teacher is different from assuming a stepparenting role. She had only taught children; she had never lived with them. The structure imposed in a classroom is quite different from unstructured family living. She was not in control on the children's weekend visiting days the way she was in her classroom, nor did she even want to be. She had a home and family responsibilities but knew little about cooking and less about the children's eating preferences. She also found that the children's table manners, their use of cutlery, their boarding-house reach, and their insistence on talking with their mouths full all irritated her. When she corrected them, her husband would say, "Here comes your schoolmarm voice." She blamed the three children for her inability to deal with them when she was so proficient in handling thirty. It took time for her to learn the differences. She began to learn that she could not come into children's lives and take over the way she did in a classroom.

Many single people who marry a divorced parent with children meet with new experiences, having not known what to expect or what to accept as normal behavior for particular stages of a child's development. It is very different to know children in a casual way and to live with them in the intimacy of a home.

Another couple who were living together and contemplating legalizing their relationship had another problem. Matt, the custodial father of two daughters of eight and fourteen years, felt his obligation to his children required him to insist that if he married Deana he did not want any more children. Having finished with that stage of his ife, he was direct and honest in his statement. Deana struggled with her decision as to whether she was ready to forego having children. Finally she decided that it was too much of a sacrifice to expect that she should have responsibilities for someone else's children and not be able to have her own, and she left the relationship.

In still other remarriages when a divorced man with children marries a woman who has never been married and who is past the childbearing years, she may be delighted to have the responsibility of children. Since she never had children of her own, she now has the family she always wanted. Della, a fifty-year-old woman who married into this situation was ready to devote herself to becoming her ideal of a wife, a homemaker, and a mother. The custodial care of her husband's children was confined to weekends and a full week once a month, as well as some holiday time. Della, a competent woman who had worked until her marriage, was happy with her new role and her new job. She received the children with warmth, catered to their every need, did their laundry, cleaned their bedrooms—in short, she turned herself into an excellent housekeeper. Later she said no housekeeper would have kept the job with the treatment she received. The children—two girls, fourteen and sixteen years— accepted the comforts and conveniences she offered them, but gave nothing in return. Having an ideal concept of the mother-daughter relationship, Della wanted to be their confidant. She welcomed their friends into the home, served them treats, and waited on them. It was a thankless job. Della had been too anxious to move into their lives and create a home life for them, before they had developed a relationship together. She earned the role of housekeeper, but not the role of father's wife, or that of a second parent or of a friend. Time and patience are essential to learn what everyone needs, wants, and can accept in a remarriage.

Because step roles have few guidelines and are so complex, in order to be strong enough to withstand the stress in ambiguous roles the couple relationship must first be solid. Basic as this is for the first marriage, it is even more important for subsequent marriages, since second marriages with children require more adaptation than first marriages. The couple must trust each other enough to discuss their hopes, dreams, and expectations for the marriage and for the family. If ever negotiations and compatibility are indicated in any contractual agreement, it is highly relevant between two people planning a marriage when there has been a divorce and where there are children. There is nothing black and white about the contract, as there is in a business contract. The relationship must grow and change and will be subject to renegotiation and recontracting as they evolve. Flexibility is essential.

No two stories are the same in second marriages with children. When divorced people marry and neither has sole custody of their children but both share the parenting, this tends to give the remarriage two story lines, one during the time when the children are living in the home, and one during the time the children are living with the other parent. Usually both partners are working and their family life schedule changes radically from one period to another. Careful, considerate planning is essential.

Claudia and Robert have been married for three years. This is Claudia's first marriage. Robert has been divorced for five years and shares custody for his six-year-old son with his former wife. The ex-spouses live close to each other and both homes have been available to their son, Artie, who attends the school in the neighborhood. The structure of the child's time in each parental home has been agreed on for one month in each home, with the midmonth weekend in the other parent's home. Artie seems to be accepting his parents' plan for him comfortably. The ex-spouse agreement seems compatible and they accommodate each other when any change is involved. It is Claudia who is having problems. She says her life hasn't been able to take on a stable rhythm. Artie is either coming or going. When he is in the home, the household is organized to accommodate him, the meals are on time and need a different kind of planning. There is the extra bedroom to clean, the extra shopping, washing, and all the chores that revolve around having a child in the house. Finally, just when the family is beginning to adjust, Artie leaves to go to his mother's home, and the house becomes empty and the rhythm and pattern change.

Entry and reentry of a child into family life is unquestionably complex. In addition to the physical adjustments, Claudia finds that Artie brings with him the atmosphere of the former marriage. He talks about his mother and events in his other home. Claudia says she knows that it is natural, but when she comes home from work she doesn't want to hear stories about the former wife. She is upset with herself for responding to Artie coldly. In discussing what her alternatives are, she acknowledges that she is handling the fact of her husband's former marriage, his ex-wife, and their child poorly, and she knows she will either have to accept the fact that Artie is and always will be there, or she will have to leave the marriage, for her sake as well as for

Robert and Artie's. She is in a conflict that I have witnessed with many women in remarriage. Claudia loves Robert and knows that Artie is part of the package and that Artie's mother and Robert will continue to have ties to each other through their love for this child. This means that Claudia's marriage to Robert will always be linked to Robert's former marriage. Claudia knows those are the facts. What she does not know is whether she can learn to accept them and to define a role for herself with Artie.

The examples I have described are merely a bird's-eye view of the infinite combinations of remarried family life. The above descriptions represent many of the real life situations with their diverse systems, structures, and substructures that may alert couples and therapists to some of the stresses and potential pitfalls. There is a need to understand each particular couple in regard to the ages and stages of the partners, custody and visiting arrangements, and the ages, stages and sex of the children, and the extent to which the previous marital relationships have been satisfactorily terminated. These examples may underscore the importance of negotiations between the couple before they embark on a remarriage.

Additional complexities are apparent in the ambiguous rights for noncustodial parents and for stepparents. Furthermore, as the Vishers confirm, "There are complications in such issues as inheritance wills, family heirlooms, and the like." They add that "blood relations run deep" and "a stepfather often does not feel that his stepchildren are really his own and he is reluctant to have them inherit his assets." Family antiques and heirlooms are sources of dissension, as questions arise such as "Shouldn't grandmother B's things stay in the B family?" (p. 103).[11]

There will be anguish in having to figure out who has the right to be present at a child's graduation, a child's confirmation, a bar mitzvah, or a wedding. What functions does the nonresident parent have with such rituals in the children's lives and what functions does the resident stepparent have? The are both significant to the children and the children to them; therefore, surely, they both have rights.

Because roles tend to be defined in institutionalized, ritualistic ways, the father traditionally walks his daughter down the aisle at her wedding, and gives her away to the groom. There is frequently much anguish about this ritual in divorce–remarriage families. When the ex-spouses have not worked out their feelings toward each other, the old feelings can be revived. "What right does he have?" many mothers ask their daughters, and many daughters reply, "He's my father and I want him to." Christmas, Thanksgiving, Chanukah and other traditional holidays are other times of potential difficulty. Parents want to share with their children and children with their parents at these times, and they have the right to be together. The ways in which traditional celebrations can be divided between two parental homes can only be determined at the convenience of each parent's situation. This means that ex-spouses must be able to arrive at agreement on plans that are also mutually agreeable to the remarriage partners. At Christmas time, children, for example, frequently spend Christmas Eve with one parent and Christmas Day with the other. This is often reversed, as are other holidays when the children take turns in each parent's home. The fairness with which both parents, each with their relatives and their remarried families, can divide the time for family occasions between the children from the nuclear families who live or visit in the remarried families demonstrates the wisdom and maturity achieved by parents who care about the best interests of their children.

I was impressed with one bar mitzvah service (the Jewish coming-of-age ritual for thirteen-year-olds), at which I was a guest, that demonstrated that parents can remain actively involved in sharing their children's lives. Tina and Lorne, the divorced parents of the boy, both remarried new partners, each with a child. Tina and Lorne did not want this special occasion

in their son's life and in the grandparents' lives to be spoiled by
the parental divorce. Hence, the parents collaborated on the
plans, each wanting new partners and families to be included,
and both recognizing the rights of the former families.

Much thought was given to the seating arrangement. Bert,
the son, sat between his parents and each new spouse beside
their partner. The two families were respected as separate units,
with Bert as the link between them. Bert was not subjected to
choosing loyalty to one parent or the other. The rabbi who offi-
ciated at the service made a positive contribution by recognizing
that the child now had two families and that he was important
to both. In accordance with tradition, he called upon the father
and the stepfather and the grandfathers and the stepgrandfa-
thers to join in the service prayers.

This demonstrated the significant role that clergymen, as a
social support system, can have in influencing social attitudes by
accepting the changes in contemporary families and the rightful
roles of all members. They can offer guidelines which are sorely
needed and can help to avoid embarrassment, conflict, and
uncertainty about how to deal with changing traditional
practices.

Unfortunately, and too frequently, the new partner and
family are treated as nonkin, or the new members deal with the
former family as a finished part of the present families' life. This
becomes clearly illustrated on some occasions when the former
family, ex-partner and his or her parents are not invited to a fes-
tivity that revolves around the child of the previous marriage.
Or the former family may invite the children and ex-partner, but
not the new partner, to some celebration. When both remarried
partners bring children into the marriage and only the children
of one of the partners is given Christmas or birthday gifts, it is
deeply destructive to the sense of family integrity. It reflects the
sad reality that the second family is not considered a real family
by the ex-spouse's parents and family.

When a parent withdraws from a child's life, there is a profound loss. One fifteen-year-old girl, Ada, demonstrated the pain she felt when she had to enter the hospital to undergo surgery. Her parents had been divorced and both were remarried. Her father lived in another city and had not kept in touch with his children. Ada reported that she needed to tell her father that she was going to have an operation, thinking "he needs to know, he's my father." She telephoned him. Her hope was that his response would be to come right home to be with her during and after the operation, as her mother and stepfather would be. Instead, he wished her good luck and told her to let him know how things were going. Ada cried as she related this experience, that had taken place over a year before. The pain and rejection had not subsided for her. In another situation, a child had met with a car accident and was rushed to the hospital. His divorced mother and her husband were at the child's bedside constantly. His father learned about the accident and went to the hospital, but he was not permitted to be with the child. The mother had told the nurse that it would upset the child.

In still another situation, when a child was in the hospital, the orders for visiting were that only the family could visit. This child's family consisted of four parents, eight grandparents, two brothers and two stepbrothers, all of whom visited as family members. These situations illustrate the range of flexibility or rigidity of boundaries. Many families are able to arrive at a comfortable middle path where no one has to lose rights. Though the family composition is different for each remarried family, neither family need be lost to the children.

Second marriages and family life can stabilize and be rewardingly compatible. This progress will depend on the realistic attitudes the new partners have from the beginning of their relationship. If the hope is that the marriage will create an instant blended family with instant love for the partners' children, there will doubtless be grave disappointments. The feeling of blending does not usually arise for three to five years, and then only if the adults have been patient and understanding about the inherent difficulties, especially when there are children. It takes time to work out the functions, roles, and relationships among parents, stepparents, and children. A new partner (with best intentions) cannot come into an existing family expecting to make new rules and change old patterns. Such an attempt is far more likely to create antagonism than gratitude, no matter how generous the stepparent may want to be. Compromise and flexibility are the essential ingredients if all family members are to feel they belong.

In intact nuclear families, couples feel responsible for protecting each other and their children in the event of unpredictable exigencies. It is customary for couples to carry life insurance policies and to draw up wills in the event of death. Partners frequently reserve burial plots. However, when there is a divorce, these families' security arrangements are often changed. Children may be left in the insurance policies as the beneficiaries and the ex-spouse withdrawn from benefits.

In remarriage, many partners have reported that they have found that there is reticence on the part of the new partner, particularly the husband, to commit himself to insuring his new wife or in any way protecting her children in the event of his death. Many couples in remarriage have also reported that they have not changed provision for funeral plots, particularly when the first marriage has been a long-term marriage and the plot is beside the plots of other family members. The plan then is that at the death of a remarried partner he or she will return to be buried beside the former spouse. In the obituary notice of a divorced remarried man his wife added to her report of her husband's death that her husband would be sorely missed by his two sons and his former wife. This gave formal recognition to the fact that both families would feel the loss.

Situations such as these illustrate that the past is not erased. Divorce does not end the existence of a former spouse and family, and especially in critical periods, both festivities and deaths, the fact remains that there was a former marriage with attachments and family memories of a shared life. The successful remarriage must accept and acknowledge the reality of the former life. This does not mean that the present life in another marriage is not also a real marriage and the family a real family.

In my studies with remarried couples financial security, insurance, and wills present one of the most sensitive areas for discussion. This appeared to be tied to the lack of precedents. People wanted their present marriage to be good and secure, but they were cautious and in conflict. When they had spent a period of their lives with another partner who had filled many needs, they questioned whether they had the right to abandon them financially in order to protect a new partner, or the new partner's children. It is a difficult and real dilemma. Perhaps in the coming decade we will see progress toward social and legal solutions.

Only recently has the concept of keeping relationships alive between the parental extended family and the former family begun to be perceived as vital in remarriage. Families are testing a variety of different approaches to reducing the loss of attachment to members of the former family. This is only possible when the remarriage family accepts the continued relationships and when the former members accept the present family membership. The case of Blanche and Ken is a good instance. During their marriage Blanche and Ken had had a close and loving relationship with each other's extended families. Their divorce was very upsetting to everyone. Ken's parents loved Blanche and Blanche's parents loved Ken. There had always been harmony and social compatibility between the parents-in-law, who had also, of course, loved their grandchildren. After the divorce, the friendship continued between Blanche's parents and Ken's parents, and all kept close relationships with the children.

Ken remarried three years after the divorce. Elsa, his new wife, was a divorcée with a five-year-old daughter, and had joint custody with her ex-husband. Both Elsa's parents and the paternal grandparents loved the little girl. The question then became how would Ken's ex-wife's family respond to Elsa and her little girl? This marriage between Ken and Elsa and both their families raises many questions with which our present family system is poorly prepared to cope. Our premise has been to support the continuity of relationships from a first into a second marriage. When this second marriage partner is also a product of a former marriage with continuity of kin relations, the remarriage inherits ex-spouses, grandparents, and stepgrandparents. There is now an extended family group of in-laws, aunts, uncles, and cousins from the new marriage. There are potentially eight grandparents (sometimes more), and all the other family members who may retain an emotional investment in the family. Too frequently, the family of a remarried person must make choices in loyalty and affiliation. This conveys to children that divorce means that one part of the family is either lost or secondary and that the other parent and that parent's family are no longer in the in family.

The evidence is good that when divorced people are able to separate the reasons for the divorce from what is in the best interests of the children and the extended families it is possible to arrive at compatible and amicable decisions together. Once there is a divorce, the multifaceted family of a remarriage can add enrichment and offer a network of social supports that may fill social and emotional needs that could not be met if members of the former intact family were lost to the children and to either of the parental families, or if the new family members were not admitted into the life of the remarriage.

REFERENCES

[1]Einstein, E. *The Stepfamily*. New York: Mcmillan, 1982, p. 2.
[2]Bernard J. "No News, But New News." In *Divorce and After*, edited by P. Bohannan. New York: Doubleday, 1968, p. 1.
[3]Bernard, J. Foreword to *Divorce and Separation*, edited by G. Levinger and O. C. Moles. New York: Basic Books, 1979, p. ix.
[4]Mead, M. "Anomalies in American Post-Divorce Relationships." In *Divorce and After*, edited by P. Bohannan. New York: Doubleday, 1968.
[5]Newman, Paris E. "Second Marriages." *Chatelaine*, December, 1977.

[6]Norman, M. "The New Extended Family: Divorce Reshapes the American Household." *The New York Times Magazine*, November 23, 1980.

[7]Sager, C. J., Brown, H. S., Crohn, H., Smith, A. A., Jones, B. B., Doe, C. C., and Jones, E. L. *Treating the Remarried Family*. New York: Brunner/Mazel, 1983.

[8]Furstenberg, F., Jr. "Recycling the Family." *Marriage and Family Review* Vol. 2. New York: Haworth Press, Fall 1973.

[9]Goldner, V. "Remarriage: Structure, System, Future." In *Therapy with Remarriage Families*, edited by L. Messinger. Rockville, Maryland: Aspen Publications, 1982.

[10]Kubic, L. S. "Fundamental Nature of the Distinction between Normality and Neurosis." *Psychoanalytic Quarterly* 1954, 23, 167.

[11]Visher, E. B. and Visher, J. S. *Step Families: A Guide to Working with Stepparents and Stepchildren*. New York: Brunner/Mazel, 1979.

[12]Wald, E. *The Remarried Family*. New York: Family Service Association of America, 1981.

[13]Roosevelt, R., and Lofas, J. *Living in Step*. New York: McGraw-Hill, 1977.

[14]Simon, A. W. *Stepchild in the Family*. New York: Odyssey Press, 1964.

CHAPTER 7

THE SHAPE OF THE NEW FAMILY OF THE 1980s

We are living in a transitional period in which the social organization of family life is changing more quickly than the cultural images and rituals that give it meaning.[1]

There is little doubt that the story of this rapidly increasing multifaceted family structure with its many variations cannot be covered in one book. I have, therefore, turned my attention to the population with which I work to describe common themes of experience that these people share. The purpose has been to bring a perception of what can be considered a normal range of concerns that remarried people encounter. I have referred to remarriages which include both legally married couples and post-divorce couples living together without legal sanction. The latter social marriages are not included in any statistical census. There is, to date, limited knowledge about divorces and remarriages that result from desertion of one of the partners. The population I studied, as well as that of most other reported studies, represents primarily white, middle-class Western society, and unfortunately little is known about the extent to which the complexities described relate in the same ways to remarriages among the poor or among different cultural and ethnic groups.

The objective of the preceding chapters has been to alert the reader to complexities that arise in remarried families with the hope that remarrieds can anticipate and prepare for the fact that they have a different kind of family structure with stepfamily roles which can achieve their own definition of normality, while not trying to duplicate the first-family roles.

Esther Wald in *The Remarried Family* says,

> Divorcing parents are caught in the struggle of achieving a balance between two primary functions of the family—the socialization and needs of their children and their adult needs for companionate marriage, emotional gratification and self-actualization—establishing a balance between the needs of parents and children so that all may have an opportunity for growth and gratification. (p. 51)[2]

There is, therefore, a dual function that second marriages hope to achieve. They want to maintain their parenting while at the same time forming a new marital bond to achieve adult emotional gratification. The complexities for both the couple who marry and for the children arise from unrealistic expectations associated with the myths of "instant family" and "instant love." Since this is not the way it happens for the remarried family, resentment and resistance can erupt and block developing roles that are appropriate to steprelations and which acknowledge continued ties with the biological relations from the disrupted family group. The ensuing conflicts can impact on all aspects of the remarriage.

The problems inherent in bringing parts of two families together through parental marriage are so complex and the major transformations in life-styles have been so revolutionary that social, cultural, and legislative changes have not been able to keep abreast of them. Society is still in the first stage in knowing how best to legitimize post-divorce remarriages and how to frame new ranges of normality for different family structures and household arrangements that are not like those of intact families. Please note that I said "different," which does not necessarily imply better or worse. There is still this lag in acceptance despite the fact that the divorced and remarried population form the largest minority group in our society and the further fact that the number of remarriages will probably exceed the number of first marriages by the end of the century.[3]

An understanding of the growth of the divorced-remarried population can best be achieved by examining statistical data. In 1973 an article in the journal, *Demography*, pointed out that in the United States an estimated 25% to 29% of all women near thirty-years-old had ended or would end their first marriage in divorce.[4] Further, since divorce laws were liberalized to include the marriage breakdown clause, the divorce rate in the United States had been going up close to 10% per year for the five-year period between 1967 and 1972. (In Canada, Ontario Vital Statistics reported that there was a 205% increase in the same period.[5]) The divorce and remarriage rate turned upward around 1960 and increased dramatically during the following decade reaching a higher rate than any previously recorded in the United States. Demographers attribute the rapid change in the stability of marriage not only to the liberalization of divorce laws in 1968, but also to the transitory state of change in all social institutions in the decades of the 1960s and 1970s. There was, as well, the growing acceptance of the principle that divorce is a reasonable alternative to an unhappy marriage and the removal of many previous barriers to divorce with such measures as the introduction of a form of "no fault" divorce.

Following divorce, 75% to 80% legally remarry within three to five years and many others establish social remarriages that are not recorded in statistics. Wald reports an estimate that approximately one in five families are remarried families. The Vishers state that by 1975 there were fifteen million children under eighteen living in stepfamilies and about twenty-five million stepparents with a million more children added each year; further, one-half million adults become members of stepfamilies.[6]

The U.S. Bureau of the Census estimated that by 1978 one out of eight children under eighteen was a stepchild living with one biological parent and a stepparent.[7] Wald estimates that "if no interventions occur to modify existing and identified trends, 45% of children born in 1977 will live for some period of time during their first eighteen years (to 1995) as a child in a single-parent family." If it continues to be true that over three-quarters of divorced persons remarry, one out of four children or 25% of these children will have experienced the stepchild role for some time during their childhood.

Glick reported in 1973 that 44% of post-divorce remarriages in the United States end in divorce, and this number is rapidly approaching 50%. He estimated that by 1985 almost half of all children in the country will be stepchildren.[8]

The average age of the population in my study, as well as in other studies of divorce, was thirty-five years for women and thirty-seven years for men. The significance of this age group is that divorce affects minor children growing up in the 1970s. In the United States it is estimated that over a million children under eighteen years of age annually become children of divorce.

In a recent report, *Divorce: Law and the Family in Canada*, the editors reported that 40% of Canadian marriages end in divorce and nearly half a million children have experienced parental divorce over the last ten years. Of these divorces, about 60% involved minor-age children.[9] The report stated "Canadians seem less sure these days of the institutions and the ideas by which they can mark out their individual place in the world." It continues, "A great many Canadians find it hard to understand and harder still to accept the statistical fact that during their lengthening lifespan, they are increasingly likely to marry more than once." The editors add, "Every society perpetuates its existence mainly through its marriage customs which are vital to the full understanding of that society.... Of all the activities to which human beings devote time and energy, one of the most enduring is the maintenance of orderly family relationships and lines of succession."

However, through divorce and remarriage, the traditional "maintenance of orderly family relationship and lines of succession" is shattered. The confusion arises from the conventional view of the definition of the family, which uses the intact nuclear family as the only model of an "orderly family relationship." However, this no longer represents the current reality, with the rapid escalation of divorce and remarriage since the 1970s and the proliferation of different family patterns. The dilemma remains: how best to preserve the biological "lines of succession."

Canadian divorce and remarriage data follow the American scene closely. A demographic study of 1981 Canadian family trends reported that there were 67,909 Canadians married for the second time, of whom 82% were divorced persons, and that one out of four marriages had at least one partner who had been married for the second time.[10] The recent statistics of remarried families indicate that society is faced with the responsibility of recognizing that a stepfamily culture has emerged and is now full grown in our world, and can no longer be viewed as deviant, but rather as a new stage in a more complex family cycle. Our concept of what constitutes the only kind of normal family life must be revised and broadened. A new institution of family exists, with a form qualitatively different from the intact nuclear family. Theoretically we are beginning to understand this, but socially, legally, and culturally it has not become clear how to legitimize and institutionalize a family formed from parts of two previous families. Remarried families have to learn how to balance ties with the members of the former family and loyalties to members of the present family. The current family inherits an unknown past with its developmental history. It will never achieve the status of the intact biological family, and the boundaries between past and present will always have physical, psychological, and perhaps legal attachments. This is not to say that the remarried family cannot achieve its own identity and develop its own history, so long as it does not try to bury its past.

The present generation of remarrieds are pioneers in paving a route through their trials and errors and their successes to form guidelines for the post-divorce stepfamilies.

Cultural anomalies are inevitable when assumptions continue to exist that marriage is a permanent union, "'til death do us part." In view of the mushrooming of divorces and subsequent remarriage, this different family system must be given its full support and recognition. Frank F. Furstenberg a sociologist, contends, "Family sociologists are disinclined to acknowledge the complexity of our marriage system and continue to treat divorce and remarriage as departures from accepted marriage practise rather than as regularities in a changing system of kinship."[11] Furstenberg goes on to comment on the "conflict between the strong emphasis placed on the integrity of the nuclear family and the relatively amorphous system of kinship obligations outside the conjugal unit" (pp. 11–12).[11] Intact families with kinship ties are accepted as an integral part of the family. However, when a family is disrupted through divorce, the kinship ties tend to become "amorphous." Socially, remarriage restructures the kinship attachments and dramatically alters the traditional extended biological family arrangements. Through parental remarriage, children acquire a surrogate parent and his or her relatives. The new ties inherited by the new marriage must be balanced with the ties of the former marriage. This becomes complex when denial or rejection of the first or second marriage persists with hostile or competitive struggles between former partners and/or between present partner and ex-partner.

Margaret Mead pointed out that there are no provisions for the kin of the ex-spouse to exert their claims to the children in the remarried family. In a growing number of states, the rights of grandparents to visit their grandchildren after divorce are being recognized in some courts. This certainly would reduce the loss of family continuity for children. It points up the importance of educating the public to the firm recognition that divorce need only be between the divorcing couple, not between members of the two families, and the "lines of succession" can be preserved.[12]

People who leave one marriage and go into another do not want to lose the family that was part of that former marriage, but they also, through the remarriage, want to establish another family. There are pressures, however, both from the internal functioning of the family and from external factors (e.g., kin) that add to the stress which works against the remarried family. Acceptance of the reality of the differences is basic to a successful remarriage. Denial of the reality can lead only to dissension and discomfort in a pseudofamily charade.

Virginia Goldner, a family therapist, maintains that in view of the large population living in alternate life-styles, steprelations and step "kinship arrangements lose their status as deviant and emerge as new stages in a more complex family life cycle" (p. 204).[1] Once couples are able to acknowledge that remarriage inherits former alliances which must be built into the texture of the new family life and involve ties to a past marriage, the second family will be off to a more realistic start. To describe realistic expectations for a successful remarriage, I will quote from an article in the journal, *Family Process,* which reported on conclusions of our study:

> The establishment of a remarriage household appears to require an understanding of the influence of first-marriage experiences and expectations while avoiding the attempt to duplicate these experiences in a first-marriage mold. It may be useful to conceptualize the remarriage family as consisting of persons who have dual memberships in two families, the first-marriage nuclear family and the remarriage household. Like countries that permit dual citizenship, the 'successful' remarriage family would be one that fully acknowledges the prior allegiance and affection that may exist between parents and children, whether living together or not, but also expects some sense of membership in the remarriage household. The two memberships overlap and need not conflict if neither 'family' demands exclusive loy-

alty from its members. The members, especially children, may enjoy the benefits of both memberships, which widen their acquaintanceship and kinship network, increase the pleasurable social occasions in which they take part and in a sense provide a new form of the extended family, thus increasing the social supports available to its members. Members of these two 'families' would have to learn to live with two sets of relatively permeable boundaries, rather than the relatively impermeable ones of the nuclear family household in which the physical and psychic boundaries of members tend to coincide—in defining the term *boundary*, as we use it, it 'refers to those factors that contribute to the sense of identity differentiating the members of one group from another.' These include shared experience, space, property, ritual activities and beliefs. Boundaries can be physical, such as the walls of a house and the fences or hedges separating it from its neighbors, or they can be psychological, such as the implicit boundaries defining the degree of intimacy and physical closeness members may share with each other and nonmembers. (pp. 191–192)[13]

Clifford Sager *et al.* refer to the open boundaries of the two families as a "suprasystem."[14] The first marriage family owns its history; the second marriage projects itself into the midstream of the established life of the former group and must begin to build its own history. The beginning of couple life is simultaneous with learning to live as a family. Living together in the intimacy of the remarried family, before the members have reached some emotional intimacy, can be fraught with embarrassment, especially for children, since personal habits now become exposed to everyone. No matter how friendly the individuals may have felt before living together, now in the intimacy of family everyone's daily life changes. People step on each other's toes; they bump into one another; the casualness of dress or undress, of locking or not locking the bathroom door—all the many habitual intimacies suddenly become strangely self-conscious and inhibiting. Remarriage means reorganizing into a new and different lifestyle. It can certainly be done, and may bring more satisfaction than former family life, but people who plan to marry again must be prepared for change. When two families move in together, no one can be expected to give up his or her former mode and be incorporated into a new partner's mode. Both partners and the children must learn how best to blend their former modes in order to live comfortably together. It takes time, insight, patience, honest discussion, and the participation and motivation of everyone in the family to make changes. To be motivated for such changes and to achieve some integration, people must get to know and to like one another.

The goal in blending two families is to achieve a sense of normal living within this social structure rather than have it remain an oddity. Reorganizing family life and adapting to new relationships are important functions of this blending process. Another and more complex aspect is the attitudinal questions of who does everyone become to everyone else in the second family. The ambiguity of steprelationships is probably the most difficult aspect of post-divorce marriage. In addition to ambiguity, there are inconsistencies imposed by society, notably our typical adversarial system of divorce legislation. On the one hand, there is the attempt to deny the differences between the intact family and the remarriage family; on the other hand, steprelations have no acknowledged legitimacy.

As we have reported, mothers are generally awarded sole custody, with fathers in a noncustodial status, usually with court-determined visitation rights. At the same time, the fathers are obliged to continue financial responsibility for alimony and/or child-support payments. The continuity of custodial and financial arrangements is largely dependent on the extent to which the ex-spouses have arrived at a mutual agreement about the divorce settlement. This is a major factor in the emotional comfort for each of the former partners, for their children, and for the future marriage. The resolution of the emotional aspects of the marriage ties and conflicts and the ability to separate the marital feelings from the rights of each parent to remain in the chil-

dren's lives are basic determinants for a successful divorce and
for a successful remarriage. The adversary system frequently
works against parents' achieving mutual agreement. When this
has not been laid to rest, ghosts from the former marriage can
remain to haunt the remarriage.

Contradictions are rampant for noncustodial parents and for
steprelations, in large part because legislation has not kept up
with the realities of today's world. When a sole-custody mother
remarries, the event is frequently celebrated with the hope that
the new partner will share the responsibilities for the children.
The stepfather, despite his parenting designation, has no legal
parental status. He is not a guardian and has, furthermore, no
custodial rights. He is not legally committed or even entitled to
assume legal protection of the children. In the event of a physical
emergency wherein the child requires surgery or other radical
treatment, and the mother is not available to sign her consent for
such treatment, the stepparent has no legal authority to sign his
consent. In the event of the custodial mother's death or inability
to continue to care for her children, the children are left with no
legal guardian. In such an instance, the noncustodial father may
become eligible to take over custody, even if the relationship has
become distant. The biological father's rights to custody may be
contested by grandparents who have remained actively involved
in the children's lives, or the father may feel it best to give his
consent to the stepparent to take over the adoption of the children. But because the divorce has deposed the father from his
custodial rights, the adoption must go through the official guardian's office like any other adoption process.

The services that have authority over the family are archaic.
If, through illness or death of the sole-custody mother, the children have a noncustodial father and a stepfather with no guardianship rights, they are left with no legal guardian. There can be
problems for the child, depending on who is awarded custody,
unless the biological father and the stepfather are able to achieve
a relationship that acknowledges the needs of the children. Too

frequently, there is an overt or covert struggle between these two adults, with the children caught in the middle, as they compete for who has what rights. This lack of legal status for both the noncustodial parent and for the stepparent must certainly affect the nature of commitment each makes to the child. The responsibility a stepparent feels for his partner's children is often reflected in his will. When men draw up a will, they usually protect their wives and natural family in the event of death. If a stepparent dies without leaving a will, the state determines that blood lines are the significant ones for inheritance. There is no mention made of a stepchild as next of kin. This dramatically conveys the point that steprelations are not even recognized to the extent that stepchildren are considered family kin. Goldner states that families in remarriages are "facing a crisis of legitimacy in which their identity as a family is in question. It is this underlying identity crisis that paralyzes them" (p. 192).[1]

There are many unanswered questions about the future direction of remarriage law in order to reduce some of the stresses. These questions will require further study. In the meantime, however, there is need for change in the services that have authority over these families and which end up adding to external pressures. The adversarial system in divorce legislation is beginning to incur increasingly severe disapproval. Some divorce lawyers are acknowledging that the emotional components in divorce can overpower and prejudice divorce judgments so that the child's best interests are not served. Keeping hostile and punitive feelings alive betwen the ex-spouses who are the children's parents cannot be in the best interests of the child.

Whereas further study is required to validate the effectiveness of emerging trends in favor of the presumption of joint custody or shared parenting rather than sole custody to one parent, studies both in the United States and Canada have confirmed that when both parents have the opportunity of arriving at the custody decision through mediation process rather than coercive measures, 75% to 80% reach some mutual agreement.[15]

It is well established through research and clinical experience that for parents to be able to consider their children's best interests they must first learn to separate their marital emotions from their responsibilities in parenting their children. If they are not able to achieve this emotional separation, the marital battle can go on, focused on disagreements regarding the children. When the marital battle continues, it can infect the new partner's attitude to the ex-spouse, which in turn, contaminates attitudes to the children and to the remarriage.

The approach to shared or coparenting or joint custody of children is yet in its initial stage. Since most divorced people enter another marriage, the new partner necessarily becomes involved in the shared parenting arrangements. The remarriage is entitled to a happy and stable marriage with shared parenting. The situation for the newlywed is that he or she is now in the position of having a spouse who is in a collaborative relationship with the former partner, with whom he or she is sharing the most treasured possession of their lives, their children. Though this may seem very threatening to a new marriage, it is a reality of remarriage that must be reckoned with and prepared for by all concerned.

To accept this reality the first essential is a solid, loving, trusting relationship between the remarried couple. With these feelings, both partners in the remarriage will be readier to accept the children as a significant part of their lives, whether on a full-time or part-time basis. Part of every parent belongs with his or her children. The new marriage must build a bridge with the former marriage that will not weaken the new union. Hence, the collaboration regarding the children must be not only between the former spouses, but with the present partners. In order that the present partner(s) may be included in sharing their lives not only with the spouse but with the spouse's children, there must be confidence that the first marriage is finished and that the emotional aspects of the ties concern only the children.

When children have two families, each with a parent, after

the parents remarry, each home will have a stepparent, with both families concerned with the children. Such a prospect can be considered challenging. It requires a redefinition of what constitutes a normal family in remarriage.

Binuclear families can function with two stepfamily homes, each with a parent, only when the new partner accepts and agrees to this open family life, and when the ex-spouses allow the children to move comfortably between the homes without competing or undermining the other parent and/or stepparent. The alternative can be damaging; children can be caught in the middle among competing parents and competing nonresident biological parent and stepparent. The binuclear family has the potential to emerge with a sense of community that can extend the branches of a family tree over the members of both families. This view presents a fundamental philosophical change in attitude to the traditional view of family. The rapid escalation of this post-divorce family has as yet little research or theory, since there is no precedent in the history of Western society from which to learn. The statistics of the preponderance of these families are well documented, but their outcome is highly speculative in terms of stress and their achievement of a sense of normality.

We are in a transitional period; we believe in the continuity of parental primary caretakers for children, and at the same time we are beginning to question the efficacy of the intensely demanding involvment of the small, intact, nuclear family. Sager describes the successful remarriage family as having a great deal to offer adults and children by providing exposure to a variety of life-styles, opinions, feelings, and enriching relationships. He says, "In remarriage, children can learn to appreciate and respect differences in people and ways of living, can receive affection and support from a new step-parent and the new suprasystem and can observe the removed parent in a good and loving marital relationship" (p. 247).[14]

In reviewing what we know about the post-divorce family

that reorganizes in remarriage, we recognize that much of our traditional ideology about the institution of family must now be revised to fit a remarriage model that is becoming increasingly common. The remarriage family is a complex structure; however, some of this complexity could be reduced if we were not inhibited by a nuclear family system model that no longer works for the large population in alternate family life styles. The unrealistic social and cultural expectations for remarriage add to the reorganizational problems and create additional vulnerability for an already vulnerable system.

In order to understand the differences between the intact family and the remarried family, I have described a framework for the intact family, as we know it, and compared the remarriage family to the nuclear family. The differences lie primarily in the boundaries, the roles and the structure of the remarried family as compared to the intact family. The remarriage family is distinct from the first-marriage family in these three main concepts. The boundary that encloses the intact family and gives it its family identity is clearly defined and understood in terms of the couple and their progeny, as well as the couples' parents and families of origin. The intact family begins with the couple, who then bear children and share the parenting from infancy through each successive step of the child's growth. The family unit and the marriage cycle move through each of the stages of growth and development within the natural family life cycle. The family members develop a common history, a family identity with a unique life-style with its own internal structure and subsystems, its own daily rituals and customs for observing special occasions, both festive and sorrowful.

The intact family has physical boundaries wherein parents and children live together. There are psychological boundaries that develop between the couple and the couple as parents and the children as siblings to each other. Their family identity is clear. They know who the members of their family are, and what functions and roles each member fulfills. The parents share in the care and physical and emotional nurturing of their children. They are the executive team in the family and as parents have the full vested authority for the children. The parents are legally and financially responsible for the protection of their minor children. These are given, taken-for-granted responsibilities that parents have and that define the parental role and identity. If we consider our own families of origin, we recognize that most of us have grown up with a strong sense of family loyalty and integration that makes the family a unit.

There is almost a mystique to what biological ties mean for family identity. The intact family shares a common family name. The family genealogy is shared by its members. Families have been described as groups who carry more love and more hate for one another than for anyone outside the family. They are first to criticize and first to protect one another. They carry a strong sense of responsibility one for the other.

Let us now examine how the remarriage family compares to the description of the intact family. To begin with, the remarriage, as we know, does not start with the couple alone, but with the family of children who have preceded the couple relation. The children from the previous marriage may live either full time or part-time with the newly married couple, or they may be visitors, regular or infrequent, in the remarriage home, dependent on the custody arrangements and how these arrangements are handled by the remarried couple. Since the parents live in separate homes, the physical boundaries are different. When a parent is no longer living with the children on a daily basis, the psychological boundaries change, and attitudes, influences, and authority are no longer easily transmitted. When one or both parents remarry, the children then have two parental homes, each with a parent and a stepparent. This creates a complex family life structure for all the members of the disrupted family and a complex system for the steprelations. The functions and the roles of steprelations are poorly defined. It is hard to formulate who the new members are to one another, and the roles have no rules. The remarried couple, unlike the parental couple, do not share parental authority in the care, nurturing and affection of children from a previous marriage. The stepparent has no legal or financial obligation for the partner's children. The remarriage family boundary is open to the ex-spouse's continued financial support and usually some degree of authority, nurturing, and affection. The family loyalty is no longer confined to the one family, but divided or even in conflict between the two parental households. Steprelations have no role prescriptions that assign to stepparents their rights and obligations. Only by developing trust in relationship can they achieve a family status. The obligation that the new spouse should love, support, and protect his or her partner's children is probably incongruous with the actual sentiments of the steprelations, both for the new mate and for the children of the former marriage.

I am describing a group of people whose complex undertaking is to develop a sense of family when a parent remarries and a new partner and his or her family are joined through the parent's marriage. Unlike the intact family, the remarried family must have flexible revolving doors that can accommodate children living in the household and visiting with the nonresident parent, or living part-time in one of the two parental homes, or visiting in the remarriage household and living with the former partner. Whatever the custodial arrangements are, the remarriage family is not a self-contained unit, in terms of its boundaries, nor in terms of who is living full time in the home.

Because remarriage has ties with the first family members, Sager has referred to the two parental homes as "suprasystem," which he defines as "a network between the former and present family and all relations, biological and step" and which is influenced by both family systems. Sager adds that "the suprasystem can be an important positive force, a strongly negative force or a melange of contradictory forces that cannot be ignored" (p. 4).[14]

This is the difficult position couples must anticipate and confront when they remarry into this multidimensional family structure. The family members' names are not the same. Mothers who remarry frequently take on their partners' names; the children and the stepsibs have different surnames. The stepparent has no legal, custodial, or financial obligations to the partner's children.

The developmental history of the parts of the two previous families is different. History for the remarried family starts midstream in their life cycle from the time they move in together. They must now begin to build a new history and to share their former history in the way that all people who develop relationships share their memories and their backgrounds together. It can be done and can be enriching the way other relationships that develop attachment and intimacy become enriching. But it takes time. Members in remarriage families are described as running on "multiple tracks," the former family life cycle and the remarriage family life cycle, each on a different set of tracks and each in a different stage of the cycle (p. 45).[14]

Not only is remarriage confronted with internal problems in achieving a sense of integration and normality, but the social roles are confusing and conflicting. Thomas Szasz, a psychiatrist, says, "A person unclassified is unpredictable and hence a threat to the other members of society" (p. 210).[16] Some of the problems central to remarriage deal with the struggle for definition, a practical vocabulary that easily identifies the remarried family without the negative connotations carried by the term *stepfamily*.

Society has not yet acknowledged the new family system, and situational and environmental difficulties are thus bound to result. There are as yet no historical precedents to guide the pioneers in a second family, nor are there rules for organizing the family system. Time and awareness of the pitfalls in the process of reorganizing a new and different family life are essential for the process integrating into a family system.

We have to look to the future to learn how children will

thrive with two family homes, with one parent and a stepparent in each, with sibs, stepsibs, and maybe halfsibs, as well as a whole set of kinfolk related to both families. Second marriages cannot be an island unto themselves. There must be a bridge between the former marriage and family and the present marriage and family.

This family system is in the process of "becoming." We do not have all the answers for how it can function most effectively. Longitudinal studies are required to follow up the progress of remarried families and their members who have successfully adapted and compare the nature of their adjustments to those of families who have not been able to cope with the stresses of postdivorce remarriages. Educational programs for separating and divorcing couples, as well as courses for preparation for remarriage, will be taking on greater importance to help couples divorce successfully and begin successful remarriages.

REFERENCES

[1]Goldner, V. "Remarriage: Structure, System, Future." In *Therapy with Remarriage Families*, edited by L. Messinger. Rockville, Maryland: Aspen Publications, 1982, p. 205.

[2]Wald, E. *The Remarried Family*. New York: Family Service Association of America, 1981.

[3]Duberman, L. *The Reconstituted Family: A Study of Remarried Couples and Their Children*. Chicago: Nelson-Hall, 1975.

[4]Glick, P. C., and Norton, A. J. "Perspectives on the Recent Upturn in Divorce and Remarriage" *Demography*, 1973, *10*: 301–314.

[5]*Province of Ontario: Vital Statistics for 1972*. Toronto: Queen's Printer,

[6]Visher, E. B., and Visher, J. S. *Step Families: A Guide to Working with Stepparents and Stepchildren*. New York: Brunner/Mazel, 1979.

[7]U. S. Bureau of the Census. *Population Division's American Families and Living Arrangements*. Prepared for the White House Conference on Families. Washington, D. C.: U.S. Government Printing Office, 1980.

[8]Glick, P. C., "The Future of the American Family in Current Population Reports." *Special Studies Series* (Publication No. P–23–78). Washington, D. C.: U. S. Government Printing Office, 1979.

[9] *Divorce: Law and the Family in Canada.* Ottawa: Ministry of Supply and Services, Canada, 1983.

[10] Schlesinger, B. *Families in Canada: Demographic Trends.* Toronto: University of Toronto Faculty of Social Work, 1981.

[11] Furstenberg, F. F., Jr. *Marriage and Family Review.* New York: Haworth Press, 1979.

[12] Mead, M. "Anomalies in American Post-Divorce Relationship." In *Divorce and After,* edited by P. Bohannan. New York: Doubleday, 1968.

[13] Walker, K. N., and Messinger, L. *Remarriage after Divorce: Dissolution and Reconstruction of Family Boundaries.* Family Process, 1979.

[14] Sager, C. J. and associates. *Treating the Remarried Family.* New York, Brunner/Mazel Inc., 1983.

[15] Ontario Association for Family Mediation. *Discussion Paper on Proposed Amendments to the Divorce Act.*

[16] Szasz, Thomas. *Ideology and Insanity.* New York: Doubleday, Anchor, 1973.

EPILOGUE

It was a cold, snowy day, a week before Christmas, and Evelyn, Kate, and Paula were visiting over lunch. These three women had formed a strong bond which had helped them through their rough periods. Having developed trust and intimacy, they shared together like soldiers who had weathered a war on the battlefield.

Many changes had taken place in their lives since they had first met five years ago in seminars preparing them for remarriage. Their experiences in separation, divorce, and remarriage reflect aspects of many post-divorce remarriages. Kate had not fared so well as Evelyn and Paula. Her marriage to Tom had ended in another divorce. She had learned the hard way that she had married Tom for the wrong reason since she had not been in love with him. She married him on impulse, out of jealousy, after learning that Jim, her former husband, was going to be married. His choosing another mate seemed like the ultimate rejection to her. Not really accepting the fact that he was finished with their marriage, she kept reviewing in her mind how she would respond to his returning to her and pleading for a reunion. Instead, he was being married and she heard that his new wife was lovely.

This made Kate take a good look at herself. She had been so busy blaming Jim that she had not really understood what her share had been in the marriage breakdown. When Kate learned that Jim was going to be married, she felt intent on preempting his marriage. She wanted to be the one to leave Jim. That would be consistent with her picture of the separation. To prove to herself and to her world that the divorce had been of her volition and that she was now ready to begin a new life, she married Tom. Her marriage to Tom, flattering as it may have been to have a younger man marry her, was for the wrong reason. She didn't love Tom, certainly not the way she had loved Jim. Kate told her friends that she hoped that by marrying Tom she would be able to recapture the rapture of the carefree days that she and Jim had enjoyed. To her, Tom represented a showcase to display her own desirability to the world. After marriage, however, she found that Tom's attention was self-centered and did not include her, and she felt upstaged and nondescript when they were together. Kate said, "Tom was about as ready for family responsibility as I had been when I was first married." She confessed, "That was one of the reasons I decided to turn full custody of Scott over to Jim. I felt that I had had the responsibility for Scott and now he could have his turn. I didn't want Scott spoiling my marriage, and I didn't care if having Scott would spoil Jim's. I really was full of venom. Fortunately, Scott is doing better with his father than I think he would have done with me. I know I've got a lot to learn and I have to go back to understanding my first marriage before I can understand myself." Kate added, "This is going to be a lonely Christmas for me even though Scott will spend Christmas Day with me and my parents."

Evelyn and Paula were filled with compassion for Kate's unhappiness, and both women urged her to spend Christmas Eve with either of them. Evelyn said that in the four years that she had been married to Frank, this was the first year she was really looking forward to their festivities. "The first three years were strained," she said. "Frank and his family had different ways of celebrating than our family had developed over the years. Not big, nor important differences, but our family has been very traditional, with rituals that I had thought all families had. Ours was more a religious time, while Frank's was more party-time. This year we are going to combine the two practices so that we will have the best of both. Our Christmas dinner had been on Christmas Eve and that was when we exchanged gifts. Frank was in the habit of making Christmas Day the gift-exchanging time. But we have all talked about the differences and laughed over them and it has brought home to all of us how important compromise is when two families get together with a history of different practices and customs. You certainly can't be rigid if you want to make a second marriage and family work. It can't be all one family's ways. This Christmas, my parents and Frank's parents are going to celebrate with us and our three children. The girls will spend Christmas Day with Ted and his parents and George will be with his mother and her family. The children will have the best of both worlds with their two families and, incidentally, a double share of gifts. I have really learned how important it is for the girls to know they haven't lost a parent or grandparents, but rather gained a stepparent and a new family."

Paula told her friends that for her, Christmastime held a mixture of emotions. It stirred up feelings of sadness and nostalgia for cohesive family life with both parents celebrating together with their children. But her children would never have that again. She said, however, that she loved Michael, and life with him was so much easier than life had been with the stresses, strain, and unpredictability of Jack. Though she admitted that she still loved Jack, she conveyed that she was no longer in love with him. Never again would she accept the kind of relationship she had had with Jack.

Life for Paula was more stable now for her and for her children. She and Michael were developing a sense of family blending and beginning to feel like a real family. Paula added that she felt so much more confident, that she liked herself better now. She now could say what she wanted to without being frightened. Though admitting that it had taken time for her to feel motherly toward Michael's son, Gary, his moving in with them had turned out to be a wise move. Originally, she had been apprehensive when Michael and his former wife, Elise, who had been sharing the parenting of Gary, turned over primary living arrangements to Michael. However, Elise was not remarried, and she and Paula and Michael had all agreed that Gary would have more of a family life in his father's home with Paula and the children. They determined that Elise would keep liberal and flexible access to Gary, and she and Paula kept in close touch regarding him. The dual role of parent and stepparent for both Paula and Michael was working well, and, moreover, it was reciprocal. Though parenting the three children, they were very aware of assuring the children that they were not going to displace the nonresident biological parents. Paula's children retained a loving relationship with Jack, learning to accept his unpredictability, and Gary lived in his mother's home a good deal of time. She was always available to him so that he didn't feel she was rejecting him. He was sad that his parents would never live together again but knew that they both loved him and that he had not lost a parent.

There are many aspects of remarried life that Evelyn, Kate, and Paula experienced that are common to all remarried people. A second divorce, as in Kate's case, unfortunately comes to pass for 40% of remarriages. Many second marriages that fail to succeed are for reasons similar to Kate's. Kate had not understood her share in what went wrong in the first marriage, nor did she go through the stages of reviewing the marriage or grieve for the loss. Instead, she hid her feelings even from herself and plunged into another marriage without having grown or changed as a person.

A last-minute change in who will be the custodial parent, as in Scott's case, is also not unusual, but it must be planned with the best interests of the child in mind. Though this could be said for Gary's custody arrangements, it could not be said for those for Scott. Evelyn, unlike Kate, had dealt well with the transitional stages of grieving, denial, and acceptance from her divorce to remarriage. Learning a good deal about herself during her separate-parenting period, she matured considerably. Her "successful divorce" helped her select another partner who could meet her present needs for a "successful remarriage." She claimed that the group discussions had been highly productive for her in helping her learning that marriage itself need not turn her into a dependent person once more. She alone had to take responsibility for herself to define the areas in which she wanted to be independent and adult in making choices and decisions.

Paula's response to these sessions was that she wasn't afraid of her dependence and love of helping others. She knew that she enjoyed being a homemaker, the stability of family life, and the responsibilities of caring for three children. Having always enjoyed caring for others, now she was not only giving, but also receiving from Michael appreciation, love, and respect. No longer intimidated by her present husband, she felt a sense of freedom to be herself. She and Michael had negotiated a way of life and family management that met all their needs. Also, she had learned from her children that in different ways their father was as important a parent to them as she was.

Paula and Evelyn recalled some of the group discussions in which they became aware of the myths with which people enter remarriage. They both knew that they didn't have to feel guilty for wanting to remarry; moreover, remarriage didn't have to mean instant love for their husband's child, feeling toward him just as they felt toward their own children. They also knew that it would take time for all family members to feel like a real family, but not the only family, since the children all had another real family with their other parent whom the childen also loved and who was an essential part of the children's lives. This meant that the two parental homes would have ties through the children. An amiable agreement between the parents would make it easier for the children to accept that their parents were living in different homes.

There is no doubt that in every instance divorce disrupts

family life, and is never easy for anyone. The loss for the marital partner is different from the children's loss. Whereas the partners want to be out of each other's lives, the children want to be part of both parent's lives.

The newly evolved custom whereby both parents continue actively to parent their children after divorce is on the increase. Parents are trying a variety of ways to work out shared parenting from their separate homes and frequently in new marriage homes.

Some partners are more successful than others in coping with their personal conflicts while collaborating as parents. Some parents are successfully organizing a new family group of children and a partner. And some of these new partners work out a modus operandi for a mutually beneficial relationship between the new family group and a former one.

Steprelations are complex and poorly defined; stepmothers have a reputation for carrying out one of the toughest roles in society. Children of divorce whose parents marry need help and permission to begin to love a stepparent without feeling guilty or disloyal to their natural parent. They must be persuaded that there is enough love to go round, with different love for different relationships.

The blending process for remarriage takes time, maturity, compromise, and continuing negotiation between the partners about rules and roles, responsibilities, financial arrangements, and goals. There must be discussion of who the stepparent is to become. This process is continuous and requires cooperation from both maternal and paternal families.

Historically, society has lived through major changes which, in time, have been incorporated into the normal course of life. In the same way, remarriages are now here to stay and must be recognized as a prevailing, permanent, and complex family structure that requires time and acceptance to develop and shape its identity to become a real family in its own right.

INDEX